Adventures in Reading Cormac McCarthy

Pet

THE SCARECROW PRESS, INC.
Lanham • Toronto • Plymouth, UK
2010

Published by Scarecrow Press, Inc.
A wholly owned subsidary of The Rowman & Littlefield Publishing Group, Inc.
4501 Forbes Boulevard, Suite 200, Lanham, Maryland 20706
http://www.scarecrowpress.com

Estover Road, Plymouth PL6 7PY, United Kingdom

Portions of these essays and conversations have appeared in *The Southern Quarterly*; *Southwestern American Literature*; *The Cormac McCarthy Journal*; *Sacred Violence: A Reader's Companion to Cormac McCarthy*; *Myth, Legend, Dust: Critical Responses to Cormac McCarthy*; and in the film *Acting McCarthy: The Making of Billy Bob Thornton's* All the Pretty Horses. Some of the material was given in five talks at conferences of the Cormac McCarthy Society.

British Library Cataloguing in Publication Information Available

Library of Congress Cataloging-in-Publication Data

Josyph, Peter.
   Adventures in reading Cormac McCarthy / Peter Josyph.
     p. cm.
   Includes bibliographical references and index.
   ISBN 978-0-8108-7707-8 (pbk. : alk. paper) — ISBN 978-0-8108-7708-5 (ebook)
   1. McCarthy, Cormac, 1933—Criticism and interpretation. I. Title.
PS3563.C337Z747 2010
813'.54—dc22   2010011085

∞™ The paper used in this publication meets the minimum requirements of American National Standard for Information Sciences—Permanence of Paper for Printed Library Materials, ANSI/NISO Z39.48-1992.

Printed in the United States of America

for Rick

for Ruth and Elijah

and

for Rocco

I like poems by starving men, sick men, pariahs, those who have been poisoned… and the poems of men tortured by language, hemorrhaging as they write…

—Artaud

The critical act must ultimately be the examination of one's own life.

—Vidal

Contents

Acknowledgments

Thanks to Rick Wallach for introducing me to McCarthy's work. Thanks to Raymond Todd for working with me on *Acting McCarthy*. Thanks to Wesley Morgan, Richard Selzer, Wade Hall, Harold Bloom, Ted Tally, Robert Morgan, Billy Bob Thornton, Matt Damon, Henry Thomas, Bruce Dern, Lucas Black, Julio Mechoso, Miriam Colon, Bruce Heller, Bob Salerno, Sally Menke, Barry Markowitz, Béatrice Trotignon, Yu-Ming Shang, Richard Pearce, Brad Dourif, Kevin Conway, Ned Beatty, Jerry Hardin, Anne O'Sullivan, Nan Martin, Fred Murphy, Michael Hausman, Gerry Byrne, Andrew Sarris, Paulo Faria, Jay Ellis, Bill Spencer, David and Sarah Stanke, Jim Welsh, Nick Monk, Tom Cornford, Cormac McCarthy, Donavin and Erika Gratz. Thanks to the Cormac McCarthy Society, especially Marty Priola, Dianne Luce, and Chip Arnold. Thanks to Harlan Fischer, Richard Soden, Butch Purslow, and Arthur Miller. Thanks to Stephen Ryan and all the staff at Scarecrow. Thanks to Barbara Mann for keeping me alive.

I

SUTTREE

Us but not us: the mirror universe is always next to us.

—Vidal

… for there are enough champions of civilization: the minister and the school committee and every one of you will take care of that.

—Thoreau

Suttree's War of the Worlds:
High Noon in Knoxville

A TITLE IS ALL YOU NEED

I was rendering the aftermath of September 11 in Lower Manhattan when Rick Wallach tasked me, for not the first time, to divert the *Suttree* Silver Jubilee in Knoxville with a talk about the novel, which he knew that I rated at the top of my list. I responded, at last, with a strategy of which that old insurance conman is a master: you think no, you say yes, then you do whatever you please. During another call to tease a theme from me, I was cool. A theme is just a title that gives you a license to enter history, to disgrace yourself, or to do something lower, like being dull. I was doing nothing, so a title was all I needed.

When Harrogate says to Suttree: "What if a whole goddamn building was to just up and sink?" and Suttree says: "What about two or three buildings?" and Harrogate says: "What if the whole fuckin city was to cave in?" and Suttree says: "That's the spirit" (259), these are two beerbuds having a croon about shaking up a metropolis that frowns on its improper fractions; a context not of terrorism, or even of vandalism, but of the virtual hijinx that conspire and console among the unchosen everywhere. In Downtown Manhattan a whole goddamn building—three, in fact—*had* up and sank, and a whole fuckin city had, incredibly, caved in. I was using all of my best words, and 225 hours of videotape, to have a look at that. *Suttree* should not subvert my gaze. Besides, I had Cocteau to remind me that when you are in front of a masterpiece, there is not much point in thinking.

Happily that same night, as I reconstructed the floodlit ghostworld in which I had sojourned for two and a half years, there was another catastrophe over my shoulder. The actor Gene Barry, known for playing the natty Bat

Masterson on '50s television, was lurching through ruined streets in a clean bomber jacket defying Martian deathrays. It was California, it was 1953, it was producer George Pal's first pass (before *The Time Machine*) at H. G. Wells: it was *The War of the Worlds* on American Movie Classics, which I sometimes played while working on my film the way Glenn Gould played a pair of radios rehearsing Beethoven.

Now for a subtitle.

Having written, in a previous life, that if you gutted the deathdogs at the conclusion of *Suttree* you would spill out *Blood Meridian*, I pictured the dashing bloatbag hero of that romance, the giant Judge Holden, arriving on a Knoxville train the way Frank Miller inflects Hadleyville toward the end of *High Noon*. Carrying Spencer Tracy's suitcase from *Bad Day at Black Rock*, wearing the simpleton smile of a skilled assassin, a gargoyle stringtie and Hong Kong linens with Romeo y Julietta protruding from his breast pocket, Holden lowers onto the platform at the Southern Depot and contemplates this Celtic town of milkwood Dubliners and a breezy denouement that will hardly call for ammunition, at least no more than he normally takes to bed. Or so he believes. The freefire zones of *Blood Meridian* share strong death-connections with *Suttree*, perhaps inconveniently for critics who, blinded by geography, enflamed by border talk, and unhip to Holden's trickster meta-morphoses to which the barricades of hardcovers mean nothing, delight in the presumption of a Western tetrology. Harold Bloom is missing the boat too, I thought. The great McCarthy showdown isn't the Judge and the Kid, it's the Judge and this riverine, lacrymose, ebriously hypnopompic pukemaster fisherman, after which Suttree, like Gary Cooper, lets his tin star fall to the earth and blows town, closing a masterclass in saying no in the affirmative against near-almighty odds of superior judgment.

After all, wasn't Knoxville named after Washington's War Secretary and wasn't it, according to its Rhode Island Virgil, *like a camp before battle*?

Hadn't kid McCarthy watched the courthouse clocktower tick toward noon?

Hadn't I walked the tracks on which the Judge's train arrived?

Hadn't I painted a canvas in which the getaway car—one of them—was pictured prominently *exactly* the way it looked?

Hadn't a Knoxville barber who had known Sut personally told me all about him?

Down at Ground Zero hadn't I met New Yorkers who had outrun their fate by enacting what, in a summary of everything he has written, McCarthy told them, told Sut, told himself, told all of us to do: *fly them*? In Lower Manhattan it was a pair of hundred and ten story monoliths chasing them down Liberty Street, but wouldn't what goes for Liberty Street, one of the oldest, most storied, and now most tortured in the nation, go for Gay Street as well?

When I asked Donavin Gratz, a daredaveil-carpenter who was one of the principal players in my project, how he could have cheated the black cloud of the South Tower without, literally, *flying* over a rectangular pool on Maiden Lane, he said: "Humans *can* fly in situations like that. It wasn't a good day to die for me." Flying, I've come to see, is always literal. In my own slight way I was doing at Ground Zero what Da Vinci did in his notebooks: capturing the complex motions of flight. It's what McCarthy is doing in *Suttree*, it's what anyone does when they write about this novel that contains and contradicts all of the others. I was *not* writing about it... *and*, you will tell me, a crepuscular handshake with the flaming black streetqueen Trippin Through the Dew is not a remote facsimile of *High Noon*'s celebrated finale... and yet, even a 1955 with barely a scrap of national news is only as politically inert as you want it to be, and we owe it, at least, to Papaw of *The Stonemason* to flag these pages with a few of the headlines in which Suttree wraps up his catfish and carp, remembering Lyndon Johnson's segregationist Senate, a mangled Emmett Till barbwired to an exhaust fan in the Tallahatchie River, and the KKK sprucing itself up as White Citizens Councils. On a lamplit street in an old racist town where the visitor's guide tells you what *to avoid* with the letters *c-o-l* in parentheses, one needn't underestimate the meaning of a handshake: its sentimental *you take care you crazy bastard* atmosphere *can* conceal a smoldering ferocity, a *come get me you sons of bitches* provocation to fathers and other judges everywhere. Besides, the high noon of *High Noon* itself was captured at 3 p.m. with the shadows all wrong, an air-conditioner showing in a second-story window, and the LA skyline serrating the top of its most famous frame... and so my title, I felt, was perfectly defensible—at least in my dreams, or in Rick Wallach's den, which were the only places the issue would ever arise. I sent it off.

EARTHQUAKES

Around midnight I wrote to two people. Perhaps, by then, the faces I'd be looking at in Knoxville were rising up before me.

A fine Portuguese translator, my friend Paulo Faria, had just the day before delivered to his publisher in Lisbon one of the great earthquakes to disrupt that quiet bay since 1755: *Meridiano de Sangue: ou o Crepúsculo Vermelho no Oeste*, a translational Everest about which Maria José Oliveira, in the newspaper *Público*, was to render a just verdict: "Faultless." But Paulo, the most conscientiously driven translator since Jerome, did not agree, for in 2009 he would undertake to translate the novel again—*not* a revision—an entirely fresh attempt, *from scratch*, from *Vede o minino* to *E todos tornam então avançar*—seeking more accurate, elegant solutions to some of the same locutions that had tasked him previously, again taking the little help that I could offer,[1] as well as writing to Knoxville's premiere McCarthyan, Wesley Morgan, and, in dire cases, McCarthy himself. "If McCarthy is the father of this work," Paulo had told me when he sent me his first translation, "I am its stepfather and you must be its uncle." That was too generous, but it was amusing to contemplate being uncle to such a beast. With the prospect of sibling *Meridianos de Sangue*, who would mitigate the rivalry between them? Paulo wasn't worried. "Heaven exists, and I am living in it right now," he wrote to me on the day that he began the novel again. Now, however, taking a breather in the wake of his first entanglement, Paulo had asked me what my reading of the Koran was teaching me about the world of Islamist terror. With lines like *gird yourselves against the fire whose fuel is men and stones, prepared for the unbelievers*, I would save that news, which was not good, for another night.

> Dear Paulo:
> I need you to translate *Suttree*. Can't you get your publisher to let you do it next, after the thriller you were assigned as a punishment for climbing to the summit of *Blood Meridian*?
>   I've been asked for something on *Suttree* for its anniversary blowout. Trouble is, I've been spoiled by rereading McCarthy in disembodied fragments based on your periodic queries to me. How can I return to reading by rote just because that's the way the pages are numbered and the author wants you to read *all the words*? I do recall days when I read them slavishly, cover-to-cover, tracing out the arc of the story, surfeiting myself with accumulations of character, detail, and cosmic signifiers, but that's a custom I can no longer abide. And so I have a scheme. Tell your publisher that the *Suttree* shindig—you can say conference—will be a flop without a song-and-dance man, so the American Peter Josyph needs a steady stream of translational queries from you. If that fails, say that a Portugal without *Suttree* is like a Portugal without *Baywatch* or *Columbo*.

Then I wrote to Bill Spencer, once a master of reading the book with another book, with an idea, and with an actual sense of humor. For over a decade, Bill had understood that for writers of earthly talents who would preserve their sanity, this mindblowing incantation must be reconnoitered from one restricted vantage at a time, without essaying to grasp it as a whole. I had shown a trace of this prudence in wanting to shoot two parallel *Suttree* films that would divide the same chronology into layers. I was wiser now as a writer in not treating the novel at all.

Dear Bill:
How tall is Suttree?

OYSTER MAN

At the beginning of the novel, when he passes the corpse of a suicide, Suttree sees that the dead man's watch is still running—perfect symbolism on which even our protagonist is stirred to ruminate; but coming after half a dozen pages that establish a charming suspension of disbelief—what to make of this lapse, this delicious dubiosity?

If the word *lapse* troubles you, raise an arm at your side, parallel to the ground, positioning your watch so that you see the secondhand, then rotate it to rest, at arm's length, in front of your face, keeping your eye on the second-hand. You can't do it. Now posit twice that distance and a motion as rough as a man walking. You will see that Suttree has done the impossible. Which it isn't impossible to do. In the decade that featured Marlon Brando, James Dean, Jack Parr, Jackie Wilson, Godzilla, Elvis Presley, Les Paul, Paul Newman, Miles Davis, the Drifters, Marcello Mastroianni, Willy Mays, Wyatt Earp, Davy Crockett, the Everly Brothers, Mort Sahl, Jackie Gleason, John Coltrane, Jack Kerouac, John Lee Hooker, Bobby Darin, Alan Freed, Charlie Parker, Jimmy Pearsall, Albert Camus, Dion and the Belmonts, John Cassavetes, Sergeant Bilko, Lenny Bruce, Lord Buckley, Whitey Ford, Jackson Pollack, Stanley Kubrick and other hip cats, a cool character caught in a flash of ophthomologic hype along the banks of the Tennessee ought to go down pretty easy. For me it does—and for me it doesn't.

I mentioned Da Vinci. Due to the unearthly detail with which he caught the motion of birds, it is said of Leonardo that he must have seen tens of times better than the rest of us; but the truth is that artists, for whom seeing is just an atavistic dependency that keeps up appearances, can draw a lot faster than they can see. Delacroix told Baudelaire that we ought to be able to sketch a man falling from the fourth floor. Taking a step further, as he did with everything, the minotauric Picasso, a Spanish prototype for Judge Holden, said that if you want to be a painter you should poke out your eyes. Eyes, he knew, could get in the way. As a painter I have learned the truth of that, and I have felt the force of Delacroix's directive, for in every self-portrait *I* am falling from the fourth floor—or so I narcissistically imagined. In the film I was making, where the lens of the camera did all of the seeing for me, it wasn't narcissism that everything and everyone had fallen, really fallen, from everywhere. A diver-dockbuilder who was making repairs in the waters of the Hudson *under* the World Financial Center when the North Tower was hit, said of the jumpers who were falling overhead: "Some of them were stiff—they were bracing themselves for the impact." A stocky and sturdy chief of security in the World Financial Center was cool and efficient (she led a complete evacuation) until, as she told me, she saw the first body crash through the awning of Tower One and it froze her in place until her husband hustled her away from the first collapse. These were two of many accounts that revised Delacroix for me: an artist, now, has to be able to sketch a man falling from the 104th floor. As for how far a fall reduces a man to a watch, or to the watcher of a watch, Picasso and Holden, two insatiable devourers, would have gotten along well, for they both understood that if you render and therefore see a thing rightly, it might as well vanish, for it is yours now; it is *you* now, whether you want it to be or not. But if Suttree had enough of a pineal eye—that third eye, invisible, the only eye of the artist—to appraise that watch and, presumably, to see himself as he fell, what was he doing in Knoxville getting himself killed?

If he was killing himself to stay alive, as artists of floating worlds and other ethereal wretches are wont to do, and if he was proposing or portraiting a town he could call Suttree, it must, of course, include the watch. A familiar Renoir depicting couples at a *bal musette* is detailed with cigarette butts on the floor. After a year of sleeping on a floor beneath that picture, I appreciated the butts more than the dancers: they were as much a part of the scene as anything else. As with painters, writers too cannot control the motion of the eye within the picture plane. And so you *could* say that *Suttree* is a novel about a dead man's watch—even if you don't see it ticking to high noon—for all of the book, not parts of it, is called *Suttree*; and, by extension, Suttree himself is a dead man's wristwatch—worn, naturally, on the inside of the wrist where a man's pulse is taken, signifying, along with everything else in this novel, not just that one can be dead and alive at the same time, but that one *must* be so—knowingly, cunningly, daringly... which is why William Blake would have loved *Suttree*... and if you said to Blake: "How do you like Suttree passing Harrogate in the jail that time?" Blake would say: "They pass each other in jail on every page," and if you said: "But what's that look between the two that McCarthy won't describe?" Blake would say: "They aren't two, they are one. It's not that Suttree knows he's a lot like Harrogate, it's that Suttree knows that he *is* Harrogate," and if you said to Blake: "The look, though, what about that look that passes between them?" Blake would say: "Enough about the look—the look is a screen for deeper things. McCarthy is subtle, sometimes using his best effects not to discover but to suppress and thus to subvert his own game."

In 1971, when McCarthy told Mark Owen: "It's going to be a city book" (4B), he had not yet written *Child of God* but he was working on, and talking about, *Suttree*. Yes, a city book, one of the greatest of a city, but a city that is more than Knoxville. When McCarthy tells his character, with parental solicitude and affection: "Uneasy sleeper you will live to see the city of your birth pulled down to the last stone" (108), he isn't imitating the voices of the Koran; he isn't sublimating a prophecy to Melville, who was born at the harbor end of Pearl Street and whose bust and whose plaque and whose entire neighborhood were to be smothered under a blizzard of World Trade; he isn't talking about Providence, Rhode Island, *or* Knoxville, Tennessee; he is talking about the cavernous city of Suttree himself. And, of course, the conjunction of Suttree and the suicide's watch is a tipoff—one of several—that *he* will be the secondhand ticking after the corpse is packed away at the end of the story. If one is toasting a masterpiece about a man who does *not* take a job in a shoe store... a man who embodies Joyce's mandate: *As they deny, deny...*[2] a man who quits a town that ceases to have, or be, his hat size... one is raising a glass, too, to a novel about a man who asphyxiates himself with an old trusty stream that sifted the blood of Shiloh and a thousand other battles, a man who doesn't deny but who charges into his darkest destiny head first, the weight of his life having exceeded the posted three-ton limit on the Gay Street Bridge.[3]

The watch that went with him—shouldn't we toast that too?

An ordinary watch is not likely to stop ticking just because its owner does, so that one *could* draw it (as a conclusion) before one really sees it; but this presupposes that a man about to kill himself would properly wind his watch beforehand. Perhaps he did. A man does that in Chekhov. Maybe it was a message to Suttree. Question: Why did the jumper leave his sad shoes on the bridge? Fact: You don't sink slower, you sink faster with shoes on. Answer: Perhaps it was the dead man's feet wanting to live, like his watch, a little more than his heart did; or, maybe it was a gift, or at least a signal to the living, like the wad of chewed gum that Marlon Brando, in Bertolucci's *Last Tango in Paris*, tacks under a rail before dying of a bullet from his fuckstress's revolver. The world has been written in many such gestures, in the tradition of Artaud, for whom theatre meant *burning at the stake, signaling through the flames.* But the world is woven of riddles too and, for all we know, the watch was as temperamental as Suttree himself or the man who died wearing it, and the Tennessee itself started the watch ticking even if, like its wearer, it was not waterproof.

In 1927 a Rolex Oyster swam the English Channel on the wrist of Mercedes Gleitze, a young and aquatically audacious London stenographer, proving that the seal of its double-locked crown was, in fact, hermetic. But even the Rolex Oyster could leak if the winder-button was left up (in the set position), a flaw that was corrected, four years later, with the self-winding Rolex Perpetual. More about the Perpetual later. To this day, all but top-of-the-line submarine watches are only, at best, water-*resistant*, meaning that you might be able to dash through the rain without inviting enough moisture through the casebook, crown, or winder button to ruin them or to cataract the crystal, but you cannot torture them with sudden shifts of pressure and temperature after a 90-foot dive into the Tennessee River. In the comicbooks of Suttree's day, the tickless Tellzall 9-in-1 Sun Watch promised, for the amazing value of $1.98, to tell time, forecast weather, show you the constellations, and give you a glow-in-the-dark compass, the world's smallest pen, Morse Code, an emergency signaling mirror, and a no-risk 10-day money-back guarantee. "Nothing to go out of order," reads the copy. "It may even save your life." Unless, of course, you fall in the water, for waterproofing was one promise, the *only* promise, the Tellzall couldn't make, a promise that the FTC later decreed too extreme for *any* watch to make. As a watch in 1951, you would more or less *need* to be a Rolex to leap off a bridge with even a prayer of survival.

Was it a Rolex man who plunged in yellow socks off the Gay Street Bridge?

With only the vestimentary evidence at hand, nine out of ten McCarthy readers say no. We will posit a Rolex anyway—maybe Lemon Socks pinched the Oyster, or maybe he was murdered and tossed into the river and the shoes and the watch were both planted in their places—and let's say that it was, in fact, a Perpetual, the self-winder introduced in 1931. There is still the question of whether a wrist that was lying under the Tennessee River would move around enough to keep the Perpetual rotor running, or would it likelier announce, like Billy Budd, *I am sleepy and the oozy weeds about me twist?* With this in mind we turn to medical history.

THE ROLEX SIGN

A Portuguese gentleman (not Paulo Faria) who was living in Brazil took a vacation in his native land, where he treated himself to a lifelong ambition: a Rolex. When the watch performed tardily, the man, who was 63, replaced it with an ordinary timepiece powered by a battery. A few months later he submitted to tests for minor health complaints that defeated his physicians—until, about two years along, a neurologist diagnosed Parkinson's disease. As the symptoms of bradykinesia—slowness of motion—are asymmetric, the patient once again strapped on his Rolex, now to his other wrist, where he never had a slow minute again. The problem with the watch had been a problem with his arm: he'd been moving it too little. A Dr. Einstein prone to self-caricature would say that the watch kept perfect time, relative, that is, to the wrist on which it was riding;[4] but Rolex *can* boast a real contribution to the treatment of neuropathology. As early manifestations of Parkinson's disease are difficult to pinpoint, this facilitator of early detection has come to be clinically known as the Rolex Sign.

THE SUTTREE SIGN

Whether the suicide's chronomonaut was Rolex-trusty will never be determined. Perhaps it was just lucky. The fact remains that against an assortment of odds—difficulty of lemon-socked jumper owning Rolex, questions of prewinding, self-winding, annual reconditioning for minimal hydrophilia—the watch was found breathing, and we are left without a forensic explanation as to how, lacking the eyes of a Leonardo, any man in motion could see the secondhand of a wristwatch ticking on the ground.

There is one hypothesis. If Suttree were short, quite short, say midget-sized, wouldn't that lower him close enough to the ground to make his sighting of the secondhand a lot more natural?

I was lying when I wondered this, but it was a way to get Bill Spencer to shed some light for me in case I was forced to drive a thousand miles to Knoxville. If anybody would know Sut's height, Bill would know. In those years I would have trusted Bill's judgment even better than the Knoxville barber's. (I once made the slip of pronouncing Knoxville Knox*bill*.) If Bill Spencer suggested that Suttree is even an inch taller than, say, three feet, I would propose identifying the Suttree Sign. If a character notices something that no one out of a book who is not Leonardo or Picasso could ever see, it is not that they are not credibly written at the time, it's that they are manifesting a hyperneurasthenia that might be symptomatic of profound psychopathology or neurocatastrophe to come. In other words, we don't blame the maker—in this case McCarthy—we blame the user, in this case the suicide Peter Josyph who agrees to give a talk, straps on a novel about the secondhand of a watch, then complains about being able to read it in public.

FANTASIA

The credibility established at the opening of the novel is especially remarkable in light of the highly animistic, almost animational world in which we are placed. The filmmaker Robert Bresson wanted the objects in his art "to look as if they want to be there" (111). McCarthy has turned the trick of making objects that look as if they don't want to be there look as if they do want to be there; want to be there, that is, looking as if they don't. In prodigiously overstuffed pages unparalleled for lexical diversity and charismatic appeal... pages that prove that mankind is smartest in great prose... pages in which alliterations to rival *Beowolf* or *Sir Gawain and the Green Knight*—"his busy freckled fists ferrying folks to sleep" (186)—rest unashamedly within their self-assurance... pages in which a floorbuffer smacks Skull 1 as pure standup—no trace of narrative reality—"When he hit the bouncer with it the bouncer disappeared" (187)—and pummels Skull 2 two paragraphs later so that it hurts as much to read as any passage in *Child of God*... pages in which the hero and his book start as sibilants composed out of an error, an ancient error in alphabetical scholarship, apt antecedence for a man who has mistaken his own character in the academy... pages in which polysyndeton is more than rhetorical armature, it is a glimpse into the demon dreams dictating the measure of McCarthy's paragraphs, where a run-on sentence is truly a deathwalk and the art of the conjunction and its soothing, terrible meter will inscribe and invoke inevitability itself... pages in which Andy Warhol, who spoke of seeing the surface of things by "a kind of mental Braille," and of reading not the meanings but "the textures of words" (87–88), would fall into the black hole of *Suttree*'s logos like the blind man falling into the swamp after the end of *Outer Dark*... pages over which the author of *Ulysses*, whose Bloomsday had its own bash that year, could call McCarthy brother, son, student, thief (sure and Suttree is shacked up with more than one Joyce)... pages over which McCarthy could call himself a thief, for the old horse Captain is lifted, almost entire, from the text of *The Gardener's Son* (or vice versa)... pages that supply for Knoxville what Whitman said the behavior of the commoner—what he called the *unrhymed poetry*—of the United States was waiting for: *the gigantic and generous treatment worthy of it* (Leaves x)... pages that make perfect sense out of the fact that McCarthy has read everything by Henry Miller... pages recommended by Ralph Waldo Emerson, who, after a season of second thoughts, sent *Suttree* to Carlyle, saying: "One book... came out in New York... a nondescript monster which yet has terrible eyes and buffalo strength, & was indisputably American,—which I thought to send to you; but the book throve so badly with the few to whom I showed it, & wanted good morals so much, that I never did" (Norton 1078)... pages that, released in February 1979—*released*, perfect word, as if they were held behind bars—sent the Southern summer of 1951 out of a 40-story tower on 50th and Third in a New York frozen in record subzero temperatures, seething with rhymed couplets in a craze called hiphop, and broiling with disco fever as Rod Stewart released "Do Ya Think I'm Sexy," China released 120,000 troops into Viet Nam, the Ayatolla Khomeini released himself from exile, Jimmy Carter released Patty Hearst, God—the other one, not McCarthy—released three of his children—Jean Renoir, Sid Vicious, and Joseph Mengele—within days of each other, and Pope John Paul II released his Address to the Tribunal of Roman Rota, with *Suttree* persuasively illustrating its counsel to look beyond justice for equity and, *beyond that, for charity*, the salutation "Dear Friend" just right for this encyclical to readers in ecclesiastic assemblies such as the one that is you, or in sputnik diners, Greyhound escapes, stockroom reveries, Stratocaster apartments, frightened clinics, methadone lavatories—wherever the outscoured psyche gropes through pain and confusion for a word of holy communion... pages that situate a mesozoic tale in a paleozoic setting with such clarity and wit that if you read them with the *Task Force Report on Treatments of Psychiatric Disorders*, published, in 1989, by the American Psychiatric Association, you can find your favorite characters residing in both books, as I did when I bought it at the Strand Bookstore, 12th Street and Broadway, after two days of hearings at the 9/11 Commission down the block, a dull theatre of lies (aptly presented where *Inside the Actors Studio* was taped) that gave the novel this perspective: beside the black machinations of the Bush administration and the morning of ash for which it was so well prepared, pumping your pentup spunk into the meat of a watermelon looks like self-denial, and *Suttree* reads like *Lives of the Saints*... in such pages it is not only the hills that are alive with the sound of music: everything is, to a degree that is almost Disneyesque, as when a mockingbird warns our melonomaniac of the buckshot to come, and his watermelon orgasm makes the earth move.

If Suttree's father truly believes that, as he says: "There is nothing occurring in the streets" (14), what he means is that his son is a zero; demonstrating, of course, that he is himself a zero. But if he wondered what it's like at that level of disregard—the level at which everything, or most of it, is open—he has only to crack open his son's book and absorb a few pages. There he will find a magnificent *parv*ificence: the Tennessee talks and kisses, pieces of junk rear, condoms roil, a boat cradles, cars sulk, tires sing, engines cough, sumacs quiver, the sun fashions wheels of light, a sneaker plucks dimples, Knoxville—too predictably—rises, and, most memorably, bridge shadows "accommodate his [Suttree's] prone figure and pass on" (7). Noting that they, the shadows pass on, not Suttree himself, this, to me, is a scene out of *Fantasia*, more signaling from McCarthy that whatever else it is, this is a lyric in which life and death mingle everywhere, assuming each other's appearances, aping each other's molecular composition. Implying, of course, that you might get them confused—a dangerous situation that could lead to a shootout of suicides aiming, each, in the wrong direction. In a hardknocks place properly called Knoxville where *ruder forms survive* you might not ever be rude enough; or, if you are, that type of survival might well be insufficient for a man who hates, or needs to feel that he hates, his father and will not be denied at least a taste of the transcendence that is his birthright—especially in a world where the shadows of a bridge might reflect more vitality than he does.[5]

PLENARY

As this fictional talk was advertised as *plenary*, I went to learn what that could mean. I was sickened to see it in Oxford as follows: *In his speech to the conference plenary he appeared to be struggling.* How could I not take that personally? I wrote two more letters: one to my friend Jay Ellis, who was deep into his excellent *No Place for Home: Spatial Constraint and Character Flight in the Novels of Cormac McCarthy*; another to Bill Spencer. The note to Jay was a single sentence but that is all you need with Jay.

> Dear Jay:
> Is Suttree, like Augustine, practicing vice so that he won't be accused of virtue (e.g., being his father)?

My second letter to Bill went further.

> Dear Bill:
> How do you write a word about *Suttree*? After two years of grappling with the ruins of September 11, am I, now, to be defeated by a novel? I read the great scene of Suttree and Uncle John, I see Sut's hand rising up as a treaty to his uncle in disgrace, I choke up, I sob—all I can do is point. Pointing is not criticism, or even commentary—it's only enthusiasm. And so you must teach me, Master. Do I need to *compare*? I've no talent for that. During a writer's residency in the John Steinbeck Room, a drab hole-in-the-wall in a library basement at Southampton College where the windows above you showed your students' feet, I wanted to ask this man for whose "room" I held the key whether he saw *Cannery Row* and *Tortilla Flat*—at least a liking for them—in McCarthy's great novel, and whether he saw *East of*

Eden lurking around *Suttree* the way it lurks around *The Gardener's Son* and *All the Pretty Horses*... but Steinbeck would not be caught dead in that room, so my days of comparison were over before they began. And so, M of S (Master of *Suttree*), I await your instruction.

I sent the letters off, then kicked myself for not goading Bill to say something about *the wave* in Suttree. That wave to Uncle John is just the beginning: there are more, and more meaningful waves, in this novel than in a boxed set of *The Andy Griffith Show*—but that is not for me to say, that's for Bill or someone else in a piece called "Suttree and the Wave," just as, in a piece called "Suttree and the Walk," someone to needs to address the perapatetics of this novel using charts, maps, photographs, postcards, video, Henry David Thoreau, Jean Jacques Rousseau, Basho's *Narrow Road to the Deep North*, Gurdjieff's *Meetings with Remarkable Men*, *Black Spring*, *Ulysses*, *A Moveable Feast*, the 9-in-1 Sun Watch, and equally nifty pedometric and fluviomatic devices he or she would invent for verifying their observations, devices like the Spenc-o-matic Tellzall and the handy Knoxbillometer, devices I can market in my books the way the 9-in-1 was sold in the comic books of old. "Readers of *Suttree*—It May Save Your Life!"[6]

Jay fired back a near Elizabethan contempt for Suttree, who to Jay is—or was, at the authentic but not necessarily definitive moment of writing—a terrible father, a cold narcissist, and a nasty boozing Mother Theresa. Jay credited Bill for viewing his subject as a kind of sociologist, but he couldn't abide Suttree's faux selflessness, calling him a Christ-poser surrounded with "Garden of Gethsemane epiphanies."

"I haven't read much Augustine," Jay wrote, "but Suttree is surely the big sinner sinning his skin off so he can slither into a new and cleaner life." That life would of course exclude Jay who, as if the invitations were in the mail, asserted a preference for lunch with Lester Ballard over coffee with Suttree. That made the point. "Yes, there are passages in the book I have to admire," Jay wrote, "they just have to do with all the other characters!" Perhaps in the spirit of Augustine, Jay, with characteristically introspective honesty, concluded with a confession of his own. "As an author who is yet attempting to live a good bourgeois family life—to be a good father and good husband—I naturally would find that book poison. It is both too close, and too far, from my home." Not to worry. Unless under cover of that Vintage paperback, Jay—none of us—will ever meet Suttree, or *a* Suttree. No one that *I* have known, or that *you* have known, has gone his own way, despite the number who will tell us that they have. So much the worse for us.

Paulo Faria was kind enough to take my proposal seriously, but he too strove to protect his family from the book, for translating writers like McCarthy yields half the income than the pulp that he despises but on which he depends for his support.[7] Here I was taking food from Paulo's wife and three daughters, but with my plenary approaching in less than six months, the part of me that was *not* giving this talk was lit, now, like the director in Fellini's *8 ½*. *I really have nothing to say*, Guido explains, *but I want to say it all the same.*

With the best of intentions, Bill Spencer straightened me out about Suttree's height with no extensive peregrinations for me to pilfer. He even surrendered his notes on blue-lined, red-columned looseleaf paper with page citations about Suttree's appearance. A sheet from Bob Woodward about WMD or PDBs wouldn't have been more interesting. It was fascinating to follow Bill's thinking. But my heart sank when I saw this: "He's taller than four feet," based on the fact that a female dwarf who is "scarce four feet" looks *up* at Suttree on page 228—too tall to realistically read the wristwatch. It was time to invoke the Suttree Sign.

When Paulo asked me about the coldforging method that is mentioned in the Kid's dream of the Judge in *Blood Meridian*, I telephoned my friend David Munn, a blacksmith and sculptor in Waynesboro, Virginia, where I had gone to shoot David and his then partner, Fred Crist, as they fashioned an astonishing cross for St. Paul's Chapel, which is between Broadway and Church streets in Lower Manhattan, out of a shaft of tortured steel from one of the Twin Towers, and mounted it on a concrete base, also from the site and embedded with tiny flecks of legal paper on which you could read single characters of type, all that was left of lives that flashed away that morning. As I passed along to Paulo their professional observations, I marveled at the technological relay by which a translator in Lisbon, through a Long Island correspondent, receives clarification from Virginia metalsmiths in half an hour. I was even more impressed that this activity revolved around a paragraph of fiction. I felt a similar sense of wonder about a professor in Mississippi, at the end of a teaching day, filling up a sheet for a friend in New York with notations like: "Sut gives Harrogate one of *his* shirts. Probably means the shirt is a medium or a large but *not* bigger, because in Sut's shirt Gene 'looked less like a clown.'" What does all this signify? More than that you are studied, admired, beloved or believed, what it means is that you are lived—no mean trick for a writer these days.

FRENCHMAN'S BEND

It is an indulgence to drag in Jean-Luc Godard when it is a pair of Belgian brothers, Jean Pierre and Luc Dardennes, whose features *La Promesse, Rosetta,*

Le Fils, and *L'Enfant* come closest in the cinema of genius to anything in Mc-Carthy. But I cannot help thinking about Godard's *Vivre Sa Vie* (*My Life to Live*), an amateur masterwork that I watch at least a few times a year for mystification and inspiration. When a cop asks the pretty young prostitute, Nana (Anna Karina): "What are you going to do?" and Nana says: "I don't know, I... I is someone else," I think about Suttree, a man whose identity is everything in the novel, an exuberant, sprawling, dendrophagous, uncontainable *I* that demonstrates the positive power of demolition (how fitting that we leave the story with dumptrucks and grapplers), a power that I very much admired at Ground Zero, which is half a reason why, of all McCarthy's work, it was not *Blood Meridian* but *Suttree* that struck me as the least uncongenial to that site, and half a reason why I longed for McCarthy to travel up in time and make a great book out of this turn in civilization that we call September 11. When Nana's friend Paul recites these lines from a child's essay on birds: "Remove the outside, there's the inside. Remove the inside, you see the soul," I think again about *Suttree*—and, of course, McCarthy, for art, to me, is not self-expression, it is a motion beyond that to something truer, more terrific. It wasn't Godard, it was François Truffaut who, while shooting his first film, *Les Mistons* (*The Brats*), said: "It is impossible to create something—a film, a novel, etc.—that does not *absolutely* resemble oneself" (115). I would agree, but with a definition of self that encompasses the stargate in *2001*, the journey upriver in *Apocalypse Now*, the couch that is featured in *Beavis and Butt-head*, everyday life in *Fear and Loathing in Las Vegas*, the triple takes in Laurel and Hardy, Billy Bob's convulsive tic of the head in *Sling Blade*, the guitar break in "Aqualung," the barroom in *Husbands*, the war room in *Dr. Strangelove*, Coltrane's sax when he runs out of sax, and the city of Knoxville in *Suttree*. Which is why *Child of God* or *Blood Meridian* are as much autobiography as *Suttree* is said to be. Unless you conceive those works as, somehow, *less* McCarthy—and who would do that?

SUMMER OF SUTTREE

The first Summer of Suttree, the summer of the wristwatch, 1951, may have liberated McCarthy from Catholic High School in Knoxville, but it was a tough summer for talent. Pick anyone out of the hat. Have I mentioned Truffaut? In 1951, as mild a mannered youth as little François Truffaut went AWOL to dodge being shipped out to Saigon and to catch up on cinema in Paris. After turning himself in at the Invalides, he was confined to the Hôpital Villemin, where he wrote half a novel and went AWOL again. This time he was handcuffed, charged with desertion and tossed into prison, where-upon his head was shaved and sent to a cell in a German insane asylum. The French Army judged him a hysterical syphilitic unsuited to the colonies. In a moment that he dramatizes in *Baisers Volés* (*Stolen Kisses*), Truffaut was dis-charged for physical *and* moral inaptitude. No Indochine for him. Like Arlo Gutherie after him, he was not man enough to go kill Vietnamese. Truffaut was 19. For his own discharge from the service of Knoxville, did Suttree do much worse? For its own discharge from the service of *Suttree*, did Knoxville do much worse?

Dear friends, let's face it: Suttree had a ball in Knoxville. Like all non-conformists who arrange their lives to be constantly manhandled, Suttree shares every lonesome loser's preference for being chased, chiseled, pelted, polluted, incarcerated, evirtuated, hallucinated, even decimated over the in-conceivable hell of being ignored. Holding the truth of Suttree to be self-evi-dent is downright independent. *Proving* the truth of Suttree to be self-evident is self-contradictory. Twice in my own life I have lived on the water to lessen worlds that had become too numerous, but these were townless towns that were more trouble to reach than I was worth. The second episode followed a half year of homelessness, the basis on which I would ask you not to dismiss Suttree's often seedy situation as *a choice he has made*, and to warn you off de-fining his or anybody's limits of endurance. True, here is a man who, built to last like a Roman road, is so inured to swallowing shit that he has to go into the mountains to starve, freeze, break down and flounder around in order to re-recognize the taste. But a man who can endure being smashed into pieces might be broken irreparably by allegedly more gainful employment. Suttree is, like all of us, surrounded by the Judge, that man or that woman who will, quite reasonably and quite literally, talk you to death—and without neces-sarily saying a word. Still, if Suttree wanted to be left to his own devices, he wouldn't be living in one of the most distinguished dwellings in Knoxville, a sitting duck whose father can surveil his every move. But then comes a day when, instead of showing your father what for, you are fine without a father and your father, dead or alive, has become, like God for Stephen Dedalus, a shout in the streets on which you can shut the window, or from which you can drive away.

That same first Summer of Suttree, William Faulkner was staying at the Algonquin Hotel for theatre business in Manhattan as our handsome friend Gene Barry loaded his wife and infant son into a brokedown Kaiser Fraiser and drove out of the city to do *Annie Get Your Gun* in Louisville, Kentucky, before braving on to Hollywood, where Paramount Pictures put him into *The War of the Worlds* with the hot green deathrays from Mars. During the six-day drive to LA, Barry picked up a hitchhiker on Route 65. Not by chance is the car in my *Suttree* canvas a beatup Kaiser Fraiser. "I remember he had a look of desperation," Barry said, "as if he'd been waiting there with his thumb in the air for years, and yet… it was a look of urgency. He *needed* a ride, so that I said to my wife: 'I can't pass that guy. Let's stop, give him a break.' He didn't have a suitcase. Can't remember where I dropped him. He wished me luck in Hollywood, said he'd watch for me in the movies."

Of course, Suttree returns to Knoxville because, like many a young man who scouts out the percentages, he needs a little time to call his sins to remembrance, to bury at least one of the sons he has killed, to drown his father in the form of a cop car, to seat James Agee in the back of a Broadway cab, to speak to the oracle and the rainmaker—perhaps even to get himself eaten up alive like the Kid in *Blood Meridian*. When you are food you don't need to act brilliantly, or act at all. But there is a tipoff—in cards it is called a tell—on page 63 of the novel, when Suttree wakens at high noon—high noon!—and walks to the rail of his houseboat. As he leans on his elbows, scanning the Tennessee, a graveldredger passes, crawling upriver. From the roof of its pilot house a man waves to him. Suttree waves back.

In Sam Peckinpah's *Pat Garrett and Billy the Kid*, Garrett (James Coburn) is resting on the banks of the Rio Pecos when he and a man passing with his family on a keelboat draw each other into the sights of their Winchesters. The men are ready to shoot, and in a film like this there is no reason *not* to… but they *don't*—no, neither man fires a shot—so that you marvel equally at the restraint of Pat Garrett, the stranger on the boat, and Sam Peckinpah.

This is the same scene, as is any scene in which men are not killing each other. If a stranger waves at you, it is not that he will necessarily save your life, it's that he *is* saving your life. A wave is everything. You can either wave at a man or you can kill him. If Suttree jumped off the Gay Street Bridge that very afternoon, Suttree would, nevertheless, have had it all: he had the wave, which is what, at high noon in Knoxville, gets the draw on that dancing trickster judgment and enables Suttree to light out for California. Between that wave and the getaway car the path is sure, so sure that on page 63, Suttree has quite gotten away already. The world of the wave holds its own against the world of war.

Could this be a tale for our time? All I know is that Suttree could step off his house and he could fly anywhere, he just doesn't see it, and so he remains within the preterition of Knoxville's parentheses with all of its other obscene children, thinking that if he keeps off the lists and the registers he will not be elected for death either. But as the Judge will hasten to show you, that is a census from which there is no anonymity—*unless you get the wave*. The cup has been passed: Suttree has only to drink it. The novel is a four year, four hundred page preparation for receiving that beatitude, that dispensation for having as much of the universe on this side of eternity as the other. As Kerouac said, walking on water wasn't built in a day.

NOTES

1. My contributions to Paulo's translational projects are best summarized by the following note to him when, in August 2009, he was beginning his second attempt at *Blood Meridian*.

Dear Paulo:
Last night I had an extraordinarily vivid dream in which I found a series of maps, each one of a great book, and the series included a map of *Blood Meridian*. It was $29.95. I calculated what it would cost to buy one for me and one for you, realized I couldn't afford that, and bought a map for you. "I'll send it along with that book on the Southwest," I thought, "although this map is ten times better—what a find!—and what a time to be sending it!" It was not overcrowded as many maps are, in fact it was extremely readable, like those maps of, say, Paris that show you pictures of famous places so that you can find them as you walk. Now, today, I am sorry that I can't send it to you, especially as I've already bought it. I apologize for having lost it in the transition out of sleep. It's irritating that we take with us into the morning the foul emotions of nightmares, and yet we leave behind our valuables, such as a map of *Blood Meridian*.

2. In Richard Ellmann's *Ulysses on the Liffey*, he is writing about Stephen Dedalus (p. 9) when he quotes this line from untitled verse XIX of Joyce's "Chamber Music" (639).

3. When I drink to that jumper, I think about the fact that among those survivors who fled the South Tower before it was struck, some said that they did so because of a single sight: people who, assaulted by thousand degree temperatures, stepped into the air from the heights of the North Tower. In other words, they saw themselves and they refused that destiny.

In one of Dickens' best essays, "Night Walks," there is this compelling line that reminds me of *Suttree*: "But the river had an awful look, the buildings on the banks were muffled in black shrouds, and the reflected lights seemed to originate deep in the water, as if the spectres of suicides were holding them to show where they went down" (116).

4. Einstein would have appreciated the Stauer EMC² Atomic Watch, which apologizes for losing one second every 20 million years.

5. In *Edinburgh*, Robert Louis Stevenson's rendering of Old Town is reminiscent of Suttree's Knoxville, with a sense of what it takes to survive in such a quarter:

The great hotel is given over to discomfort from the foundation to the chimney-tops, everywhere a pinching, narrow habit, scanty meals, and an air of sluttishness and dirt. In the first room there is a birth, in another a death, in a third a sordid drinking bout, and the detective and the Bible-reader cross upon the stairs. High words are audible from dwelling to dwelling, and children have a strange experience from the first; only a robust soul, you would think, could grow up in such conditions without hurt. (37–38)

In making the point that social inequality "is nowhere more ostentatious than at Edinburgh," Stevenson begins a paragraph with these stirring words: "One night I went along the Cowgate after everyone was a-bed but the policeman" (39), precisely the sort of firsthand accounting you want to hear from him. He proceeds to describe his experience in *listening* to the life within a tall dark building, with "family after family contributing its quota to the general hum, and the whole pile beating in tune to its time-pieces, like a great disordered heart" (39). In *Visions of Cody*, Kerouac says about sitting and listening to the night in Jamaica, Queens: "The sound of the whole thing in general when there are no specific near-sounds is of course sea-like but also almost like the sound of the living structure, so as you look at a house you imagine it is adding its breathing to the general loud hush..." (9)

6. On this issue of perapatetics, try, for starters, Jay Ellis's *No Place for Home*, chapter 4; and Wesley Morgan's website *Searching for Suttree*.

7. In 2008–2009, Paulo Faria translated *Suttree* into Portuguese, a project for which he traveled to Knoxville, where Wesley Morgan and I watched him shoot check pool with Jim Long, a model for J-Bone in the novel, and meet with two other friends of McCarthy who appear as characters in the book: Walt Clancy, and John (Big Frig) Hannifin. The game took place at the Fraternal Order of Eagles on Walnut Street, opposite the Church of Immaculate Conception, where McCarthy and Jim had been altarboys. McCarthy's old friends looked good and they could not have been more accommodating. During a pre-game chat, we sat at a long table where Walt had a beer, I sipped white rum from a paper cup, and Wesley—who was kind enough to arrange this adventure—drank a cup of coffee. Recalling a sequence in the novel that was vexing for Paulo—

> Old Suttree, said Oceanfrog. He caint fade nothin.
> Why don't you put me on something?
> Shit. You got it all locked now. (112)

—I confirmed our conclusion about the meaning of *fade*. "That's right," Jim said. "If you can't fade the bet, you can't cover it." When I asked him about Harrogate, describing some of his attributes and schemes, Jim said: "No, I expect [McCarthy] made him up out of his imagination." When Paulo asked whether Knoxville was violent, Jim told us that it wasn't especially so, but when I referred to the scope of the brawls in the novel, he confirmed that when a fight broke out, everybody was likely to join in. In a discussion of Red Callahan—Jim was supposed to have gone with Callahan the night that he was killed—Jim and Walt agreed that Red was expected to be difficult, and "he didn't disappoint them." When asked whether they missed the old days, Jim said: "I suppose I do." Both men said that McCarthy—Charlie to them—never put on airs of being smart, but everybody knew that he was. Jim: "He'd sit there lookin out the window up at the sky. Teacher would call on him, he'd turn around like he didn't even hear what they were talking about. But he'd always answer the question right. They couldn't teach him nothin. He knew that. Everybody knew that."

The wood-paneled room for pocket billiards featured a sign dedicating it to "Irish" Jimmy Long, a painting of W. C. Fields holding a cue and an 8-ball, and a large framed still of Paul Newman as Fast Eddie in Robert Rossen's *The Hustler*. During the game, I was framing some tasty compositions of Paulo and Jim leaning over the pool table, but there was a problem.

JOSYPH: (To Jim Long) I've never seen anybody shoot so *fast*. I don't mean *hard*—I mean *you don't take time*. I've taken a hundred shots and I don't have a good one—I can't focus—you've taken your shot before I can get to it.

JIM LONG: I guess sometimes you fall into a rhythm. I was always pretty fast. Maybe I'd do better if I wasn't.

Jim remembered a Knoxville kid who was so good a shot that, to make the game fair, he had to play one-handed.

Suttree and the Brass Ring: Reaching for Thanksgiving in the Knoxville Gutter

GOOD FOR ONE FARE

One morning in Knoxville, Wesley Morgan—loyal townsman, studious *Suttree*an—held out a fist to me, smiling and wordless, urging me to receive. I placed a palm beneath him. Out dropped a little brass coin. On the face of it, raised over a crosshatched field, the city said:

KNOXVILLE TRANSIT LINES
1946

The reverse said:

GOOD FOR ONE FARE

This was Suttree's trolley token, the one that mercied him, the one that froze him to death. It was textured, it was worn by a thousand thumbs, it had a susurrant charisma, and it was lighter than the one in the book, for even a single sentence will outweigh brass, in this case seventy-five thousandths of an ounce. It had a milled edge, a little ridge twice the width of what you see on a dime. If you sheared off the border it would stack on a dime perfectly, a thing easily lost in even a small crowd of change. I secured it in six different hideaways, distrusting everybody including the Marriott maids and myself, until I hung it on my keyring and drove it to New York. Things don't interest me to own, but this coin fell perfectly into the class of exceptions: it was small and it was equally artifact and artifiction. Every thing is a piece of the past, we too, but when you secure an allegedly obsolete coin, key, or any old charm so that it sits with you in your pocket or sleeps in your coat, you are inviting a kind of communication beyond your control.

Four months passed before I properly noticed the letter **K** hitching a ride in the center of the token. Perusing the episode in which Suttree, too cold to live, seizes the gift of a thaw from the gutter of Central Avenue, a "small brass coin stamped through with a **K**" (177), I saw that if I had noticed the **K** in the token, I had not decoded it, and so I hadn't read it; and if I had, in fact, read it I had not comprehended or remembered it, for now I had to wonder: could Suttree's token have been minted differently than the one in my winter coat?

No, the letter was there, a double-junction **K** with the lower ascender connecting to the upper, configured in the coin so that I could slide it onto my ring in one of four separate spaces between the letter and its points of attachment. Nice touch, I thought, for a city with a silent **K** to store and display its missing letter in trolley tokens—and so pronouncedly. How could I have missed it? In "Mexico Fellaheen," Chapter 2 of Jack Kerouac's *Lonesome Traveler,* Kerouac's buddy, Enrique, cannot say **H** ("'Is Kard for me to pronouce'") and so he substitutes **K**. "When he said 'K' his whole jaw leaped out, I saw the Indian in his face" (24). When this coin said **K**, I saw the city and the novel in its face, and I thought that I might be seeing something else.[1]

Among the keys on my ring is a distinctly foreign one, the type that faces two directions and resembles a Dubuffet calligraphy. When the poet Carolyn Elkins brought it back for me from Dubrovnik, I received it with the prospect (not quite a promise) of basing a film around it, for which a plot was in my head before the week was out. Along with the **K** in Wes's coin—this **K** so clear-cut, so central to the civic, historical, economic, exonumic, and literary life of the brass (central to its streetlife as well)—had I also neglected to see *the assignment* in it?

I had wondered what had earned me this sterling icon, a ¾-inch concentrate of mid-century Knoxville, image of a scene that is so sympathetic to the life of every man for whom the winter is the world, a scene no writer could have composed half as well, a scene no writer would have bothered to write at all—excepting, perhaps, Miller, with whose *Tropics* the novel has a lot more in common than meets the eye, and, perhaps, Kerouac, with whom McCarthy has little in common, although it's a little that means much. Samuel Johnson, in his *Dictionary,* examples the word *troll* with a couplet from Swift: "How pleasant on the banks of Styx/To troll it in a coach and six" (425), a suitable song for Suttree's life along the Tennessee and along that other river and for any of us ensnared by the novel. In Old French or Middle English, *trollen* is to roll, circulate, or ramble, and so *trolley* has its roots both in dragging about (a fishing line) and strolling about (whorish, as with trollops): alternate ways of snagging a catch (or singing a song—which is a *catch* too—as McCarthy does in the novel) by a wandering allure. Wesley Morgan, Professor of Psychology at the University of Tennessee, is not unfamiliar with behavior modification and psychological suasion. With the study of objects and fetishes among his specialties, watch out. Through this charming periapt, was he, like a headman in the village, like Deep Throat in the D.C. parking garage, or like McCarthy himself, who is known to have answered questions—with John Sepich, for instance—not with answers but by handing out clues—consigning me to a search with a foregone conclusion? With Wes's miniature in my hand was I now in the palm of his? If a key is the power of Peter, what's a coin? Token = *teeken*, Dutch for sign, mark, *miracle*: ice-walker elevated to waiting electric transporter, taken for a ride; but even among atheists, gods are everywhere with all kinds of faces, some with several, so divine interventions can be two-faced, too—dirty old tricks of light, of time, of memory, of fate, of chemical imposture (false metal, or mettle), tricks of the devil in disguise... in other words, you, Sir, making an ass out of yourself. In French, *trôler* can be to lead, lead about—as on a hunt or a wild goose chase.

I was still in the throes of a larger assignment—Lower Manhattan and the September 11 attacks—but that magnitude, as an excuse, was self-defeating. If you can handle that, how can you complain about a five-cent coin? Dimesize objects can, however, betoken big things. Even the morning of no return had its very small coins and lower brass both behind and within the conflagration. *Suttree*, of course, is a different immensity, but I am more than humbled in its presence—I am troubled, for there can be a kind of terror in great art. Reading the book in a New York Starbucks, I broke down in sobs but it was not one of *Suttree*'s shattering insights or a surge of exquisite prose, it was a sense of the book's sheer impossibility—impossible to grasp, impossible to be—and in that infirmity the novel became confounded with Ground Zero, the sort of dream-conjunction with which I have learned not to argue. Is it not, after all, the same feeble imagination—an imagination formed, rather too much at random, around the accidental properties of childhood—that is commandeered for grappling with any of these outsized phenomena of art or catastrophe?

It can help to look at things very small—just don't expect them to remain that way. Even at the instant of assignment, Wes's little **K** was projecting and elaborating its ancient origins, for by a long, circuitous route the Roman letter **K** is derived from an Egyptian hieroglyphic denoting an outstretched (or open) hand. Facing each other at this event—a brain-bash for the novel in which his city speaks forever at its Falstaffian best—Wes and I were two of these ancient hieroglyphs, a North-South pair of Amer-Egypto-Roman **K**'s.

"That simple gesture, the upturned palm, is one of the oldest and most widely understood signals in the world," writes John Tierney in the Science

Times section of the *New York Times*. "It's activated by neural circuits inherited from ancient reptiles that abased themselves before larger animals" (F1). Tierney, it seems to me, is describing my stance in the face of *Suttree* and this *Suttree* assignment—but he is also describing Suttree in relation to the larger animals of Knoxville, the spirit world, and all the universe. In and around *Suttree*, every inscription is an encryption. If a life is but a dream, a dream is a life too, and Gestaltists would like to have it told from every angle, the better to hear who we are. In the case of a novel, which is a life and a dream too, Gestalt can be a path to a kind of critical cubism and a guard against the solitary confinement of character to sentences that bear the hero's name—although in this case they all bear his name.

I, Suttree, a once-pure planchet irrevocably annealed, overstruck, and circulated with Knoxville incused and inscribed in me forever, have been cudded, bagmarked, denticled, gouged, dropped into the gutter, spat on, shat upon, and snatched up by faithless and unworthy claimants who toss me down again.

I, Suttree, am a cold empty vessel that goes in circles; idle, now, on a cold empty street, manned by a colder, emptier captain till the drop of a coin sparks me on to one more round that will groan under the falling of the night.

Whitehead said that geography is half of character. For Suttree forget the half. The gutter and what is found there: that, then, must be character too. Nothing in any gutter is beneath a man's destiny. And where the coin is, he too can be.

I was sure that I had seen photography of the 11th, including amateur video that can still make me start out of my chair. But then I saw two pictures in an East Village gallery. It was an exhibition organized by Bolivar Arellano, a photographer with the *New York Post* on whom both of the Twin Towers had collapsed. Bolivar was not new to catastrophe—he had witnessed massacres, he had seen the Contras toss enemy infants into the air and machete them, *Blood Meridian* style, as they fell—and he understood the import of capturing—and showing—the atrocious *in detail*. Thus two pictures, not for every eye, behind the desk in the rear of his little walkdown gallery on 9th Street and Avenue A, pictures that ought to have shown, in journals and newspapers, that death on the 11th was a lot more than dust. But they didn't show that because they weren't to be seen—they were deemed beyond the pale. One shot was of an uprooted arm that, like the 20-ton beams that were reaching out of flatbeds and flying on the big Weeks crane at Pier 6 before the tug *Kathleen* brought them over their own Styx (the East River), left no doubt about the brutality with which it had been torn from its body. It was the very image of what a New York paramedic, James Creedon, told me he had found as he rushed toward the buildings along the Westside Highway: first a leg on the ground, then a hand "cut off toward the elbow, lying on the street with nothing around it, three blocks away from the World Trade Center, positioned exactly the same as the hand of Adam [in the Sistine Chapel]."[2] The other shot was of a handsome black woman, middle-aged, well-dressed, seemingly unbruised, unbleeding, lying face-down dead in the gutter. Since then, the concept of gutter—*found it lying in the gutter—belongs in the gutter—gutter talk—gutter mouth—picked you up out of the gutter—drop you back into the gutter from which you came*—has a more multiguous meaning for me. The gutter can be the last thing you see, the first thing you don't see. If a gutter is the long low wall where the street meets the sidewalk, Suttree is at that conjunction all the time, stepping up, jumping off, falling into it. Hammered under heels, ground under wheels, I, Suttree, am privy to the slush of every storm and every squatter in Knoxville; and I, Suttree, am an unswervable line drawn in concrete and stone where the world disregards me and yet I am Central.

Like a character in a comic to whom things happen fast, almost simultaneously because the strip unfolds in the flash of a few panels, Suttree takes the foundling **K** across Central Avenue to a trolley that departs, instantly, with the hero in a seat and at least, farther up, two black men standing. ("At this Station of the Cross," you will say, "here is Suttree the Savior in company with a pair of 'thieves,' both hanging, of course, in what the author calls an *archaic craft*, reminding us that...") When they reach the end of the line and Suttree, wanting the warmth of the return, remains seated, the driver—who incorrectly calls him buddy (he's anything but), not Buddy—explains how "fares is one way" and how the tokens are priced at six for thirty cents, "Or you can put in a dime" (178). When Suttree confesses, or protests, that he hasn't any money—fantasizing, perhaps, that the cold might have warmed the heart of the monster, volatizing a legal notion new to the Knoxville night: *extenuating circumstance*—this hardlesson cop, teacher, parent, priest, plantationer, judge—or, to coin a phrase of Ambroise Paré, this executioner chiming carols on Suttree's back (82)—delivers the most hateful line in McCarthy: "This would be a pleasant world if everybody could ride and ride" (178). Meaning: *I am your father (I am Death)*; and meaning, of course, that no Knoxville streetcar would ever be named Desire and this is *not* the place for depending upon the kindness of strangers; that you, who want to cheat back the city that has cheated you for years and who shouldn't have to get off with all the rest of the Knoxville niggers and are asking not to suffer needlessly, *do* need to suffer needlessly, so: find a job, take a bath, and keep that wreckage out of my streetcar forever.

In the theatre we speak of *given circumstances*, realities of situation printed in black and white on which we base the composition of a scene. Actors act authors, who put themselves, literally, on the line with unshakable premises to ground the improvisation we call theatre. Defending the interlineations, annotations, storiations, babewyns, amphigorics and other marginalia with which excitable ham readers such as myself are prone to score our mental (and therefore schizophrenic) copies of *Suttree*, we have only to point to a line like: "The driver watched him in the mirror" (177) and blame it on Mc-Carthy for providing such stimulating *given circumstances* on which to found the improvisation we call reading. For years now, some of the best minds in McCarthy have been spreading the strange rumor that McCarthy won't tell you what his characters are thinking, or feeling. Puh! His characters tell you that all the time (if you read them), so why do you need it from McCarthy?

For sure, the driver watches Suttree, out the driver's window, snatching the coin out of the gutter.

For sure, the driver smells him as he enters and enrolls himself, further confirmation that his passenger is a pig.

For sure, it is galling to see Suttree ride—and by the luck of the gutter-draw—and for sure he follows Suttree's movements in the mirror to better keep that connection of contempt.

For sure, he can't wait to show that lucky son-of-a-bitch how far his luck will take him.

If you are wondering how to determine the most hateful line in McCar-thy, take the character you most want to kill and find the line that makes you want to kill him the most. And yet the entire beat world of the episode neces-sitates the driver, who could, perhaps, have played the same part in exchange for a soulslapped brood in Kerouac—but never in Hemingway, where the driver would have scorned his lucripetous mandate and let the hero ride for free... would have made special stops for him that weren't on the line... would have discussed the condition of the cables and the tires and the temperatures in fonder foreign cities... would have seen that his passenger was fortified in dress and in drink and would have asked about the fishing—in other words, where McCarthy's Knoxville couldn't exist.[3] Here, this ordinary streetcar psycho is telling Suttree, more obviously, that no one lives forever—but he has picked the wrong man, for it is not true for Suttree.

It isn't, however, what the driver gets wrong, it's what Suttree appears to have gotten wrong in which I can see my assignment as presented in the coin. I say *appears to have gotten wrong* because Suttree might have been telling a lie. It doesn't seem so. "I thought you could ride as far as you wanted on one token" (178) he tells the driver, and it has the ring of truth, for Suttree is nothing if not naïve. No need to wonder what the Thanksgiving streets were made to hear during Suttree's long trek home, many miles, in killer cold (six degrees). For me there is more in this walk than in all of *The Road*. McCarthy's choice of words for it—*maudlin, muttersome*—constitutes an atmospheric/emotional weather report that ignites into a great monologue on contact. One does, however, wonder whether Suttree's soliloquy cursed the coin too, ruing the moment it caught his eye. In Shylock's extremity his ducats and his daughter are interchangeable: lost treasure in two forms.[4] Suttree's token: with what other villainous currencies, counterfeited by knaves and foxes and by that breed of betrayers *who live in homes*—with what tangle of undoers was that **K** made to commingle, and how deep into time, and into what scoldings and schoolrooms and Sunday supper arguments and insults in front of his friends and walks to the barbershop when he wished he could have bought a revolver instead of a crewcut do you think it might have reached? And how, one wonders (by what marvel of aprosexia), could Suttree have lived such a long life in Knoxville, around and upon its trolley system, without having comprehended its rules?

That he also makes the mistake of imagining *a hand out* will buy as much mercy as *the symbol of a hand out* suggests that Suttree's trouble is more than trolley-trouble: he doesn't understand what Ezra Pound (and Henry Miller after him) called *money and how it got that way*. The **K** in the coin isn't a Knoxville hand held out in charity, or held out *for* it—empty, like that of the blind beggar whom Suttree passes "sitting in the empty feastday street" (177), presumably in the gutter—no, it is a hand held out with a token in it,

GOOD FOR ONE FARE,

one ride to the end of the line. In other words, it is a picture of Suttree himself—but as a Before, not an After. With this failed bid for charity, Suttree is back in the gutter again, blind, with a hand out to no one, hitching a ride that isn't there. If, by the intrinsic nature of **K**, every **K**-picture is to evoke a **K**-parable, this, then, is a story of municipal commerce, not the compassion of Christ. In *Rocky*, when that Philadelphia fighter is told, by his friend's kid sister, Adrien: "It's Thanksgiving," Rocky says: "To you, to me it's Thursday" (41). The trolley episode is the story of a man who both knows and forgets that it's Thursday. McCarthy's savviest characters can get dumb fast if the plot calls for it, sometimes incredibly but not so here. This lapse into magical thinking is just another turn in the sweet circle of torture to which Suttree seems so wonderfully committed.[5]

REPETITION

Konstantin Stanislavsky, director of the Moscow Art Theatre in Chekhov's day and the author of *An Actor Prepares*, founded his work on a precept concerning one's reliance on artistic inspiration: good luck is a grand thing, but it cannot be counted on, and so *one needs to have a method*, especially for getting out of a tough scene alive. It applies just as well to coming in out of the cold. To have a home truly you need a method of return. But in the way that he makes things better for himself, Suttree makes them a hell of a lot worse—a fair description of his life. This close to zero, where every block is a killer and every step is an invective, venturing abroad without a method of return is tantamount to not knowing how not to die.

Why is it, then, that when the trial of the night is at its worst and he is on the streets in six degrees of Thursday, Suttree appears more alive than in the protectorate of the trolley? If, for his rabid Republicanism (as we would now call it), we want to drive a stake into the heart of the heartless freak who refuses Suttree (six times—one for each degree), by what emotional logic does the hero, as the beast's ejectamentum, appear more properly in his element? I think of those glorious lines in *Tropic of Cancer*: *...and for friends I had the streets, and the streets spoke to me in that sad, bitter language compounded of human misery, yearning, regret, failure, wasted effort* (184)... or *The earth in its dark corridors knows my step, feels a foot abroad, a wing stirring, a gasp and a shudder* (282)... and I am reminded that the streets of McCarthy's Knoxville are paved, in part, with the stones of Miller's Paris. I think, too, of another great walker and what it meant for him to put one foot in front of another. "The chivalric and heroic spirit which once belonged to the rider seems now to reside in—or perchance to have subsided into—the Walker," wrote Thoreau, "not the Knight but the Walker Errant. He is a sort of fourth estate—outside to Church and State and People" (Walking 594).This is one of the meanest of walks, but, as I suggested earlier, Sut's a walker through and through, and in a strange and even fearful asymmetry, he exemplifies—even here—Thoreau's saunterer.

> I have met with but one or two persons in the course of my life who understood the art of Walking... who had a genius, so to speak, for *sauntering*, which word is beautifully derived from "idle people who roved about the country, in the Middle Ages, and asked charity, under pretence of going *à la Sainte Terre*"—to the Holy Land, till the children exclaimed, "There goes a *Sainte-Terrer*," a Saunterer—a Holy-Lander. They who never go to the Holy Land in their walks, as they pretend, are indeed mere idlers and vagabonds, but they who do go there are saunterers in the good sense, such as I mean. (Walking 592–593)

The novel is not simple. Neither is Suttree. For one thing, it is no more likely for him to hitchhike the KTA (Knoxville Transit) than to hitchhike the TVA of McCarthy's father. He might as well have asked the mayor to buy him a drink, or his father to defend Harrogate. For another, McCarthy's work hates houses and—as we see in Carlos Castaneda's novels of Don Juan, where the Don, literally, climbs into a car head-first on hands and knees because to him it is a dwelling, a kind of cave—the trolley is a municipal domicile, genus of jails, schools, cemeteries, dormitories, hospitals and other madhouses, hell on wheels for McCarthy, where the streetcar becomes "a trolley of dolls or frozen dead" (179) and where one is always safer (i.e., more alive) in restless streets of danger, destruction, dissipation, disintegration. As Thoreau said: "It requires a direct dispensation from heaven to become a walker. You must be born into the family of the Walkers. *Ambulator nascitur, non fit*" (Walking 594). If, like poets, walkers are born, not made, what are they born to do, where are they born to go? Thoreau's entire body of work answers that. So does McCarthy's.

Suttree is called a kind of *Huckleberry Finn*, and there is no question that Mark Twain would have loved it as much as his wife, Olivia, would have hated it; but I see more of *Walden* in the novel.[6] In the final chapter of *Walden*, you cannot read a paragraph without finding a sentence that says *Suttree*.

"Why level downward to our dullest perception always, and praise that as common sense?" (347)

"A living dog is better than a dead lion" (348).

"Humility like darkness reveals the heavenly lights" (351).

"It is life near the bone where it is sweetest" (352).

"There is a solid bottom everywhere" (353).

"The life in us is like the water in the river" (356).

Much like Thoreau, Suttree might be that rare kind of renunciate who has his retreat—Thoreau's cabin at Walden Pond, Suttree's houseboat upon the Tennessee—but who also thrives on walking meditation, for Thoreau the woods of Concord, for Suttree the Knoxville streets and the uriniferous dives to which they lead him. Are we not, in both cases, privy to an experiment? At the conclusion of *Walden*, Thoreau says: "It was not always dry land where we dwell" (356), a line he could have used, and McCarthy could have used, as an epigraph. The third to last line in *Walden*, "Only that day dawns to which we are awake" (357), is a gently revolutionary sentence, one that is translated and turned into an order in *Suttree*: "Fly them" (471). When Thoreau tells us: "I left the woods for as good a reason as I went there. Perhaps it seemed to me that I had several more lives to live, and could not spare any more time for that one" (345), matters of life and death are presented in a manner one would have to call relaxed, and that is an understatement about an understatement. *Suttree* brings more than whiskey and women to *Walden*. There is, at last, a spirit of urgency and a sense that, for this particular beast, the jungle itself has been circurated.

A few months after Suttree's Thanksgiving, Allen Ginsberg, living across the street from the New York Port Authority in a small furnished attic room, jotted in his journal (perhaps on peyote): "people really can't stand much reality" (12), a shrewd observation that doesn't, however, apply to Suttree, who can't get enough of it. Returning home after he has reached the end of the line is not something that will save Suttree, it is something that will kill him: the hero will disintegrate, finally, into ash, for in Knoxville he runs out of reality, perhaps the worst of all deprivations. McCarthy is hardly a tranquilist, but he is discerning about, even a connoisseur of, sound and fury and, as he proves in *Outer Dark*, in *Child of God*, in *Blood Meridian*, he understands the role of repetition in the transforming quality of violence for better and for worse. One of *Suttree*'s stunning accomplishments is the bravura management of repetition, a repetition that takes you to the end of a man's rope. Every new chapter says: *more*. At the end of *Suttree* (allow this confusion), Thoreau says: "I did not wish to take a cabin passage, but rather to go before the mast and on the deck of the world" (346). What Queequeg learned among Christians, Suttree has learned among savages: *it's a wicked world in all meridians*. For Suttree, all of Knoxville, including his houseboat, has become a municipal dwelling, where even another brawl is another imprisonment. He needs a boat now that moves. Fast.

At the conclusion of *Torture*, a book by Edward Peters that has become, to all our shame, more important since it was published in 1985, Peters offers a caution to "societies in which the presence of torture transforms human dignity itself" (187). As every novel is a society, sort of self-contained, sort of self-governed, but with every one of its readers in its social contract, we can apply this to *Suttree*. An interesting book could be written enjoying much of McCarthy's work in terms of different understandings and gradations of torture. In the final sentence of *Torture*, Peters maintains that a society that includes "both victims and torturers ultimately leaves no conceptual or practical room for anyone who insists on being neither" (187), a stimulating summary of why *Suttree* needs to end as it does, for its hero insists—not prefers—Peters' verb is irreplaceable—*insists*, in spite of himself, on *being neither*. If this appears to rewrite *Suttree*, see *victim* and *torturer* as flip sides of a coin and say that the ending arrives at the insistence of the story itself.

Time passes in *Suttree*, but nothing and no one develops—excepting, perhaps, time itself in its running out. People fart around, they raise a little local hell, they marinate, they bombinate, they get carted off either to jail or to the morgue. Watching for people to grow in this version of Knoxville is like watching for adventure in Warhol's *Sleep*. But even in *Sleep* a man turns over if you watch for long enough, and in *Suttree* repetition, which has been on the warpath, is not without lasting effect. As in *Outer Dark*, where the shift in Culla's consciousness is hinted at in two lines of dialogue—lines to-taling sixteen words—the seachange in Suttree is only a single sentence. He himself hardly shows it (although, if you are ornery enough, you might make a case that the entire book shows it). At the novel's last page it is you, reader, not Suttree, who contains more multitudes: your population has doubled. For Suttree, getting out of the novel is the only way of getting out of Knoxville alive. It's just as well. McCarthy and Suttree might have "learned" from *Henry IV* that it's one thing to turn your back on seeming dissipation or to run from a reckoning that bears your old name, it's quite another—and quite a mistake—to spurn the forms and figures of that life in the same profligate pages just because, being awak'd, you do despise your dream and would ban-ish your misleaders (see *Henry IV, 2*, V. v.).

And yet... we *could* say that Suttree does, in a sense, return from, and to, the end of the line over and over; that he does ride and ride, with that little Kafka **K**, whenever a reader starts the novel again. With each return to page one, Suttree and Knoxville are warm, they haven't inflicted those wicked bruises upon each other, they haven't torn each other's limbs off, or blown out each other's brains, there is no call for trolleys and we can forget about the fact that the '46 tokens were the last ever minted, for on August 1, 1947 in the much paler world of blood and bones, a trolley draped with flags and banners announcing **THE LAST RUN** rolled along the crowd-lined streets of Knoxville commemorating the end of an era, the streetcar era that started on May 1, 1890, when the first of them trollied down Gay Street.

Well, *you* can forget. Thanks to Wesley Morgan, these facts and the vicissitudes of Cormac McCarthy's fiction daily tinkle to my attention, so that I walk around wondering what it will take for us to see that the notion of anachronism is unfair to fiction, for any "historical novel" is as much a fantasy, an original compound, an assemblage of found objects as any other novel, and that a token for a system that ended in 1947 *could not possibly have been used* for that system in 1951, unless... an author *makes things up*.

JUNK

On assignment, my work is just beginning. With the coin in my hand this morning, I thought that perhaps, after all, Suttree does understand the rate of exchange, and that the price of the trolley ride is not the token at all, it's the miserable walk home—steep, but so is everything. At least, for his troubles, he got to see a few things, with his view from the trolley window making a motion picture of Knoxville—not bad for a Thursday night in a fundamentally filmless life.[7] As I film the **K** today with a macro lens, the crosshatching resembles the cablework on the Brooklyn Bridge, and the inscription reminds me of the wording around Barthman's Clock, one of the most surprising timepieces and one of the finest things in Lower Manhattan, a marvel that, embedded in the sidewalk of William Barthman, a 19th century jeweler who was still, until recently, at the corner of Maiden Lane and Broadway, I delighted to see aglow from the top of the South Tower and that, after it collapsed, I was heartened to find still glowing as I approached it, and to have its face again under my feet, and its time. For me, the survival of the city, of civilization, was partly in that archetype of urban enterprise, of Yankee ingenuity, of Downtown civility that gave you, with the time, a compass to set you straight in your direction, a good thing to have in the neighborhood of Wall Street, a good thing to have a stone's throw from the Federal Reserve, a good thing to have where the Bill of Rights resided.[8] In the lens of my camera, as on my editing screen, Wes's trolley token fills the frame completely. There, it is not small at all, it is monumental, and it, like Barthman's Clock in the same size frame, contains and projects the teaming power of its city and becomes its only image. Handsome, sturdy, astonishing for the life and the death to which it attaches. A sidewalk clock, a token in the street: as good as any where to start an investigation.

To start a book, too. I have written short stories, even entire novels based on things that, at the moment of purchase, attracted me as incidentals— notions—little nothings. Who knows but that this coin (or something like it) might have contained this delightful masterpiece for Cormac McCarthy— *before* it was written—as much as it contains *Suttree* for me now. We do as much a favor to the oddments of junk that we liberate from abject desuetude as to the sketches, photographs, films, and recordings in museum archives we are sometimes compelled to seek out and disinter, even if only by looking at them alone. When I was walking in a Knoxville railway yard with Paulo Faria—the dedicated artist of transculturation whom you met in the previous chapter—I was not being a charmer when I gave him a rusted metal I.D. plate that had fallen from some railroad machinery and told him to rub it whenever he felt out of sorts with *Suttree*. "This is the novel right here," I said. "This is the whole city. This is Suttree himself. This is junk, he's junk, this whole city is junk, it's a book about junk. Forget the rest. You can leave now—you can go back to Lisbon, or go to LA." In the same spirit, I shipped off to Lisbon a rusted old spike that I picked up for him on a deserted flatcar in a Knoxville railway siding, thinking it contained at least as much vocabulary as a CD-ROM of the OED. Perhaps, then, I *was* being a charmer in the way that Wesley Morgan and Carolyn Elkins were charming: I was attempting to soothe, allay, invoke and entreat in the name of some power inherent in the object. In the song "Diamonds On the Soles of Her Shoes," Paul Simon says: "She was physically forgotten/Then she slipped into my pocket/With my car keys." By putting it into his novel, McCarthy picked that coin out of the gutter and gave it to you, to me, to Wesley Morgan, to Suttree. And things like that—which know us, and know much more than we do—can be counted on to give back, always.

Carolyn Elkins had sent me that Dubuffet of a key because she knew that my Paris keys had brought me no luck and that I had switched, in desperation, to a Victor Hugo medallion I had bought from a *bouquiniste* on Quai des Grands Augustins—*only to lose the medallion*, leaving me to wonder whether I ought to forget luck. Yes, but not for the reason I supposed. For those of us situated to wonder about our luck, that is luck enough and we should consider it a charmed life. Suttree's token—perhaps what it's saying is: *Sut, you're alive, so take another ride. The Big Bang dropped me here as much as it did you. Reach for me, reach for it.* Or else it is quoting *Walden*: "However mean your life is, meet it and live it; do not shun it and call it hard names" (350). I had thought that I was photographing the coin in order to see it. Now I begin to wonder whether it isn't really the first step in filming McCarthy's novel. One will have to pay for the rights, but I can read my permission in the coin. On the screen my little token is a star, the first to be cast. With it, Wesley Morgan, like Suttree, was buying himself a seat to see the show.

NOTES

1. If the machine on which McCarthy typed *Suttree* was similar or identical to the machine (or machines) on which he typed the manuscripts I have seen, including work from the '70s and a complimentary letter about Wade Hall's "The Continuing Vitality of Southern Literature: Six Books by Cormac McCarthy and Heather Ross Miller" (*Twigs*, V, 273–292, 1970), McCarthy would have typed the sort of **K** that is in the trolley token (double junction, lower ascender connecting to the upper). Whoever typeset the novel for Random House did *not* choose, for the sentence in which it is mentioned, a **K** corresponding to the form of the **K** in the coin. However, we ought to go easy on Random House, for they did publish the novel, and possibly McCarthy himself (who must have proofed the galleys) didn't care. When you can purchase *Suttree* with an unabridged narration of it pocketed in the back on a bonus CD, an alternate ought to offer you a Knoxville token which will talk up a storm, and it will serve as an Erratum for page 177.

The subject of McCarthy's typewriter is an example, in miniature, of how difficult it is to do any kind of history or biography, even with access to a firsthand source such as the subject himself. In December 2009, when McCarthy's light blue

Olivetti Lettera 32, which he bought in a pawnshop for fifty dollars, was auctioned at Christie's, the highest estimate for the sale was $20,000, but the typewriter sold to an unnamed collector for $254,500. McCarthy's share of the sale was donated to the Santa Fe Institute, of which he is an enthusiastic member. Before the auction, Wesley Morgan pointed out that McCarthy was incorrect in the authentication statement that he wrote about the machine and that was issued by Christie's for its potential bidders. "I have typed on this typewriter every book I have written including three not published," McCarthy wrote. "Including all drafts and correspondence I would put this at about five million words over a period of 50 years" (Cohen). On November 10, Wesley wrote to me as follows:

> The *Knoxville News Sentinel* ran a story about Cormac's typewriter and the fact that it is coming up for auction at Christie's on December 4. There are some problems. First, there is an undated letter, circa 1964–1965, from Cormac to Albert Erskine in the Mc-Carthy Papers in San Marcos (Box 1, Folder 1) that says that his typewriter is a "Royal Portable, Quiet Deluxe model, vintage 1958." Second, the Olivetti Lettera 32's weren't made until 1963 or 1964, so Cormac could not have bought one in 1958 as he states in his letter to Christie's. Lastly, there are *at least* two type fonts used on the manuscripts in the McCarthy Papers. I wrote to [McCarthy's brother] Dennis about this. Dennis talked to Cormac...

On December 1, in an article by Patricia Cohen in the *New York Times* called "No Country for Old Typewriters: A Well-Used One Heads to Auction," Cohen wrote: "Speaking from his home in Santa Fe, Mr. McCarthy said he mistakenly thought that the typewriter was bought in 1958; it was actually a few years later. He had a Royal previously, but before he went off to Europe in the early 1960's, he said, 'I tried to find the smallest, lightest typewriter I could find'" (Cohen). Curious to see whether the correction would have made its way to Christie's, Wesley checked its website on the day of the sale, but nothing had been altered. The day after the sale, December 5, Randy Kennedy wrote an article in the *New York Times* called "McCarthy's Type-writer Sells for $254,500," in which she refers to the Olivetti as the machine "that Mr. McCarthy said he bought in 1963 for $50 and used to type all his novels" (C2).

2. My conversation with James Creedon can be found in *Liberty Street: Encounters at Ground* Zero, and he is featured in the film *Liberty Street: Alive at Ground* Zero.

3. The driver might also have found work in Charles Bukowski.

4. Even in Hebrew, **K** is well suited to Suttree, for when it entered that language the Phoenician *kaph* was not an open hand (or the palm of a hand), it was a fist.

5. If the breed of Gestaltists I have invited into this essay are reading McCarthy's work, they will notice that the pretense to see Suttree from the driver's point of view is more a device to reimagine this driver, on whom I have heaped so much abuse, from Suttree's (or my) point of view, while I ought to have tried to see the driver (allowed the driver to have a say) *as Suttree himself* ("I, Suttree, fend off beggars while I take another lap on the round to which I am sentenced, even on Thanksgiving," etc.), and I ought to have acknowledged that it's Thursday for both of them. After all, even Death is only doing his job, looking toward a little time off.

6. Although it was first published in 1992, I did not read "The Imprisonment of Sensibility: *Suttree*," by Thomas D. Young Jr. until this book was going to press, when I was delighted to see that Young, too, has observed a connection to Thoreau.

7. Just before the trolley episode: "He [Suttree] went on toward the town, a colorless world this winter afternoon where all things bear that grainy look of old films" (177).

8. Barthman's Clock was installed at the corner (literally, *in* the corner) of Maiden Lane and Broadway in 1899, a block east of the World Trade Center/Ground Zero site. The original clock was square. For a time James Madison lived on Maiden Lane. In 2006, Barthman moved a few doors up Broadway and is no longer on Maiden Lane. The clock is still in the corner.

· 3 ·

Suttree Sutured:
His Short Stay in Knoxville General

THE SUTTREE SYNDROME

This is simplistic, but it's something I need to say: *Suttree* is yet to be *properly* ranked as one of the greatest of the greats. Susan Sontag proposed viewing literature as "criticism of one's own reality, in light of a better standard" (179). For me, the standard of *Suttree*—and of Suttree—is one of the best. But the novel is even neglected among McCarthy enthusiasts. One reason, perhaps, is that critics seem to love intellectual acrobatics and, compared, say, to *Blood Meridian*—whose loquacious, cerebrational fat man, the Judge, gives them a field day—*Suttree* can be viewed as less of a brainteaser. It might also suffer from the prejudice—one that afflicts some of the smartest of academics and writers with at least one foot in that world—against acknowledging with too much praise a novel that is rated as too autobiographical, the *too* deriving (I suppose) from a species of peer-reviewed dementia according to which X, Y, and Z (one can fill in the blanks) are more worthy of regard than lesser novels or novel-like books such as *The Sun Also Rises*, *A Moveable Feast*, *Tropic of Cancer*, *Tropic of Capricorn*, *A Thief's Journal*, *The Subterraneans*, and *Suttree*, about which it is apparently better to smile and say: "Yes, yes, but no—*I think not.*"

But there is something else working against the novel, something I have yet to put my finger on and that contributes to what I will call, for now, the *Suttree* Syndrome. Here are four divergent examples of the *Suttree* Syndrome.

In his conversation with me about *Blood Meridian*, which is in this book, Harold Bloom, one of the smartest, most passionate of readers, says: "I had read *Suttree* and admired it a lot, though it's *very* Faulknerean." And: "*Suttree* was a marvelous book, though so close, at times, to *Absalom, Absalom!* as to be almost embarrassing." Suddenly, in the course of a single word—*Suttree*—the brilliant Professor Bloom had taken leave of his critical senses. Had the discussion continued on this course, I would have imitated Picasso who, in the young Paris days when he packed a revolver, startled a reactionary discussion about Cézanne by bringing the gun down on the table, saying: "One more word and I shoot!" Perhaps I ought to have said: "I admire *Blood Meridian* but it draws an awful lot from Sergio Corbucci's *Navajo Joe*." Or: "The Judge is interesting, but there's rather too much Wolf Larsen in him." Or: "Awful lot of the trial from Joyce's Nighttown in the Judge, wouldn't you say? I mean, can one read his denunciation of Reverend Green without thinking, at least, of Alexander J. Dowrie and 'the man called Bloom is from the roots of hell, a disgrace to Christian men. A fiendish libertine from his earliest years this stinking goat of Mendes gave precocious signs of infantile debauchery recalling the cities of the plain...' etcetera (492)?" I had not yet suffered De-Lillo's *Underworld*, a stinker that the generally acute Professor Bloom had the temerity to place in a league with *Blood Meridian*, but at least I should have probed into what he could have meant by comparing *Suttree* to *Absalom, Absalom!* Was he so intoxicated with the Judge as to confuse Suttree with someone else? I have done that. For the second time this year, I was listening to *Cancer*, thinking about the difference between Miller, who reflects that he can never convey to his wife his contentment at being a proofreader in Paris, and Suttree, who wouldn't need to explain his emotions or his situation to anybody. Does this, I wondered during a cranial collapse, have anything to do with his being a Southerner? I turned off the book, sat in the car, and gave myself a talking to. "*Who's* a Southerner? Certainly *not* Suttree." In the *New York Times* ad for *The Gardener's Son* ("It's off-Broadway television."), the lowercase *s* in its description of McCarthy as "an acclaimed southern novelist" is probably inadvertent, but that's about as Southern as I can allow for him: he's been working *down there*, not up here.[1] And Suttree is no more Southern than McCarthy, a Rhode Islander, is Southern, or I, a Long Islander, am Southern. He is even less Faulknerean and so is his book. If you need to call Suttree a name, call him a transcendentalist.

When I volunteered to write a blurb on *Child of God* for Abby Werlock's *Facts on File Companion to the American Novel*, I asked Ms. Werlock about *Suttree* and she told me it was not on the list. The sensible Ms. Werlock embraced my suggestion to assign it to Bill Spencer—but why did I need to pry open a list that had welcomed *Interview with the Vampire*, *Looking for Mr. Goodbar*, *Pet Sematary*, *Showboat*, *Tarzan of the Apes*, and a host of other indisputably minor works in order to make room for this towering masterpiece? Was it partly to do with the critical reception of the novel, which had ranged from the somnolent to the insentient, or the fact that reviewers had written it up (written it off) as *a Southern novel* in the tradition of William Faulkner (with whom, as I've said, it has very little in common), and suggested that we have, in *Suttree*, a variation on something we have seen, and seen it done better? Over the course of the *Suttree* Silver Jubilee, I developed a hunch about the professional Faulknereans who gathered in Knoxville to celebrate Sut, so I posed the following query to around half a dozen of this learned society: Is *Suttree*—or any work by McCarthy—as good as the best of William Faulkner? The answer was no.

In the year it was published, 1979, *Suttree* was not awarded the Pulitzer Prize. Neither was any novel. The award for fiction was given to *The Stories of John Cheever*. The Cheever is a remarkable collection with more minor master-works than most practitioners would dream of achieving, but that is what the book is, a collection of undeniably good fiction. *Suttree* is more than fiction. *Suttree* leaves *fiction* in the dust. *Suttree*—like *Naked Lunch*, like *Cancer* and *Capricorn*, like *Howl*, like *Ulysses*, like *The Subterraneans*—is a step and a half beyond literature, thus beyond the reach of Pulitzer, in the way that *Husbands* is a step and a half beyond film and thus beyond the Academy of Motion Picture Arts and Sciences. In any case, *Suttree* was not nominated.

I had hoped that the panels and publications that were organized around the novel's silver anniversary would help to rectify this lapse in appreciation, a subject that, in itself, deserves more serious commentary. But I have been sad to see that the anthology that had promised to materialize has never seen the light of day. The *Suttree* Syndrome again! Even Bill Spencer, formerly my favorite *Suttree* aficionado, dropped the ball when entrusted with converting the celebration into a booklength document, as did my buddy Rick Wallach both before and after Bill, letting it languish, helpless, in limbo for years. Is this any way to treat a masterpiece? At last and at least the collection appeared, several years later, as an issue of the *Cormac McCarthy Journal*, but that is not a book, and I am left wondering what dark trickster forces are lurking behind the *Suttree* Syndrome, hoping for fresh faces on the Suttree scene who will do for the *Suttree* Syndrome what Bill Spencer once did for *Suttree*.[2]

Meanwhile, I want to look at a sequence in the novel that, even when *Suttree* is properly revered, is likely to remain undercelebrated. Join me, if you will, for a preemptive strike against episodic neglect, and let's look at Suttree in the hospital. Having recently read, at last, the work of René Girard, a Catholic thinker (or thinking Catholic) who, because of his work on violence, used to be a favorite of McCarthy criticism, I did find a sentence, one, that didn't annoy me, and I will imitate my friends in the academy by quoting it. "Let's face it," Girard said to James Williams, "readers, including academic ones, usually read texts pretty simplistically" (267). I shall try, then, not to become another proof of Monsieur Girard's observation.

In fact, since I've started reflecting on it, the hospital episode has followed me, nipping at my heels, leaping up to my knees for a stroke on the snout. At my elbow as we speak, there is a marmalade jar with a cracked lid made at the Dresden Works of Lancaster & Sandland in Hanley, England, a jar that I bought, after it had traveled over decades, in Point Pleasant, New Jersey—bought because it is, for me, Boswell's indelible *London Journal*, Picasso's masterpiece *Les Damoiselles d'Avignon* (which he called *Las Chicas de Avignon*), and, most importantly, the hospital episode in *Suttree*. All for five dollars—the jackpot.

The images on the jar represent *The Cries of London*. On the cracked lid, a girl in a scarlet dress with a lowcut bodice is striking a dancer's pose to interest a gentleman in her "Fine black cherries." I can't identify the street, but there is a short wall or a pillar that's convenient for the leaning of a wench during the heat of a Boswell night, with or without his pig's bladder protection. The second image is a girl in a red dress asking a gent who is walking a spotted dog: "Who'll buy my lavender?" Her lands are full of lavender, her basket is full of lavender, the gent's Dalmation is sniffing the word *lavender*. In the third image, another dogwalker is leaning on the cart of another lowcut moll who is offering up "Sweet oranges." From her breasts to her waist, her body is a vase. The bonnet over her curly brown locks is decorated with scarlet ribbon. St. Paul's is in the distance—we might be on Fleet Street. The fact that there is a dog in every scene—even on the lid there is a stray—tells us that the boys on Clough Street, Hanley were taking no chances. Quaint London streets, fetching irresistables, handsome young gentlemen of leisure—*and dogs*. Two of the men have their hands in their waistcoats, poised to buy—they've been fetched, all right. The man on the lid is in another state: he has kept his hands on his cane behind the arch of his back. He might buy black cherries, but he is going to buy the girl in the bargain. *He's safe.* He might be in for a dose of the clap, but he knows what he's buying and is calculating where she can take the trouble to him. When *he* reaches, he will reach for everything *and he knows it.* It's the man who imagines he is buying *lavender* for his wife or his fiancée, the man who decides he should wet his summer whistle with *an orange*, the man who enters the Barcelona bordello on Calle Avinyó missing the skull on the table because Picasso removed it for him to fend for himself, the man who decides to relax for a while in the perfumed breast of a hospital bed—it's these men who might not make it through the year. Good luck to all of them... and thanks to the hospital episode for yelping and dancing at my boots and for buying the jar for me. In my jar there is no marmalade: in it is the nurse from Knoxville General, offering an orange, offering lavender, offering heartfelt Tennessee love, offering inlaws who won't call the sheriff and won't want to kill me, offering eternal life—offering, offering...

THE HOSPITAL EPISODE

There is not much to say about Suttree's short stay in Knoxville General, to which he is taken after his skull is cracked open in a brawl at a dive called the Indian Rock. Despite the opening, no obtrusive light appears to have entered. Suttree is treated, he dreams, he urinates, he chats flatly with a pretty flirtatious nurse, he steals orderly clothing (perfect disguise for a drunk and *dis*orderly), and he discharges himself by walking out the door in stolen shoes that are too small for him. He doesn't fornicate in his bed the way Tenente Henry does with the English nurse's aide Catherine Barkley while the fourth floor sleeps in *A Farewell to Arms*. He isn't labotomized and smothered under a pillow like McMurphy in *Cuckoo's Nest*. In McCarthy a hospital, however hospitable, is for leaving, so Suttree takes off as soon as he finds his legs. There are no dead spots in *Suttree*, but this episode is hardly a highlight.

Originally, I had marked this scene because of a weakness it shares with McCarthy's *The Stonemason*. The conversation between Suttree and his nurse, Miss Aldrich, recalls the kitchen banter between stonemason Ben Telfair and his wife Maven. Both of these conversations are as normal, as domesticated, as close to chatty and cute as anything in McCarthy, and chatty and cute are not McCarthy's strong suits. In *The Stonemason* the writing is flat enough to remind us that genius is not an open house. In Knoxville General the dialogue may be the weakest thing in the novel, but at least it is unobtrusively so. Mostly. Lines from Suttree such as "This tastes like wet mattress stuffing" or "It looks like where they lock up dangerous incurables" (191) briefly threaten to undermine the enterprise, not as much for being cute as for being poorly written—infelicitous—among the few such lines in the novel. You can read them, aloud or in silence, in every kind of tone, with every accent and inflection you can muster—still, they don't scan, they don't lift, they don't sing—and you don't want to hear a bad line from Suttree because in the moment of speaking them he *can't* be Suttree, and in such moments you wonder whether he isn't the character you thought that he was when he was speaking properly in the verse of the everyday, the poetry of little nothings. "Let me have a Redtop" (184) is all that you need to hear from Suttree, or: "What the fuck are we fighting?" (186). "It looks like where they lock up dangerous incurables" is some other McCarthy who needs to keep his hands off the novel. Happily, he does.

Still, thinking that *Suttree* is a mature twenty-five and is certainly strong enough to defend itself, I was going to have a sympathetic lunge at these pages... but I have since come to see that, although there isn't necessarily more to this scene than meets the eye, it offers up strengths that are more significant than its faults. In Proust's *On Reading* he refers to a local church "whose sculptures did not sleep at night" (23), something that I have found true of *Suttree* whenever I look for a while at an episode in isolation: its figures will not sleep and they keep me awake with them.

DADDY WATSON

During the time that Suttree is out cold, the narrator turns quite naturally to an evocation of Knoxville. In its tone and in its second-person address—"When you asked for the shop of the heart's apothecary we thought you mad" (192)—this interlude recalls the prologue of the novel, further demonstration that Suttree the man—who, like one of the novel's namesakes, Sut Lovingood, "kin git into more durn'd misfortunit skeery scrapes than anybody"[3]—is only one layer—the manifest content—of the *Suttree* dream that includes all of the city; or, to put it another way, that Cornelius Suttree isn't a character in a landscape, he is a character who *is*, or at least includes, the landscape. [Of Joyce's Humphrey Chimpden Earwicker, Anthony Burgess said that "he is not only a builder of cities, he is a city himself" (19), and one can say of Suttree that he is not only a fleer of cities, he is a city himself.] Then, barely five pages after one of the most painful injuries in literature—Suttree's skull caving in under a floorbuffer—the hero is on the streets again headed for the Corner Grill. At 8:45 that night, Suttree explains his injury to the death-besotted derelict Daddy Watson, who gives Suttree the time. "I make it eight forty-six," Daddy Watson says after consulting his railroad watch. "We all got to go sometime" (193), a juxtaposition of lines that will resonate with readers who recall that the 767 which, at 470 mph, penetrated six upper floors of the North Tower, made its mark at 8:46:26, reminding us, as does the entire scene with Daddy Watson, that even after you walk out of the House of Death itself, Death, or one of his roadmen, will stroll down to the riverside and come knocking for you.

As to why Suttree asks Daddy for the time, you could say that he wants to reorient himself... or you could say that it is really half a tease and that he likes to see the railroader yank out his big old watch... or you could say that, in the spirit of Daddy Watson, he wants to know whether it's time for him to go. Perhaps I shouldn't have called Mr. Watson *derelict*. As a lookout for Death he is industrious enough, even if only as a blind for loneliness. You only have to be a little shy to find it easier to say: "I just wondered if you were alive" than to say: "I just wanted to see your face, hear your voice, feel the warmth of your existence for three or four minutes." I have gruffed up friendship for much of my own life, have left messages saying: "I just wanted to see if you were dead or alive," or: "Just making sure you haven't joined the Booth Brigade." It's a short step from there to: "Allowed ye'd gone under" (87), or "Allowed ye was dead" (192). Daddy's assumption that Suttree is dead is always derived in the same way: he didn't *see* Suttree, which for him could only mean one thing. And if it's legitimate to wonder whether someone is alive if you don't see him, it has to be legitimate to wonder whether *you* are alive if *he* hasn't seen *you*. Daddy Watson has developed a charming little ploy to elicit life-affirming conversation. If whenever you imagine that I am dead it turns out that I am not, that is reassuring indeed. When Daddy tells Suttree "If I'm goin to cross that river tonight I'd as well start now" (194), he is speaking about going home across the Tennessee, but he is also thinking about all the way home.

When I attended an exhibition of the Portuguese painter Paula Rego, I was shocked to see a friend of mine, the English writer Tony Rudolf, dying and dead in some of her paintings. Poor Tony—and poor me to have learned about his passing in the Yale Art Gallery, gazing upon his limp white corpse. They had lived together, he had taken ill, she had painted him unto death. What a noble mind was here overthrown. When I called him in London and spoke to him a few days later, he was more alive for me than he had been for many years because I'd thought—almost for certain—that he had gone under. Tony's resurrection was a reprieve for me too. If Tony can die such an untimely death—a death as certain as art can make it—and then live to talk to an old pal on the telephone, why too can't I?

The bluntness with which McCarthy vacates the sexual enticements of the hospital—"She winked at Suttree. I'll see you tomorrow," followed by: "But he was afoot and gone by fall of dark" (192)—is so striking that the reader might feel cheated, even pornographized, for there is the bed, there is the handsome wounded man who did his wee wee like a good lad, there is the nurse eager to nurse, and if Suttree, if the novel, are going to pass on *that*, what kind of deadbeat companions *are* they? This, for me, is comparable to John Grady Cole not visiting the Alamo when he seeks out his mother in San Antonio. With lines like "Her soft breast against his elbow" (190), and "Soap scent of her hair and her breast brushing across his eyes" (191), we are assured that Suttree is not immune to the feminine properties at work. *We* are not immune, and when I suggest that we are a little pornographized, I mean that it is hard not to think if *that's* the deal, put *me* into the ward.

But we mustn't miss the fact that Nurse Aldrich resides in a morgue. Or underestimate it. When it was revealed to me that Ferne's Harness House, the Long Island nightclub in which I had been performing, was once a mortuary, I would rather not have heard that this was where they brought the bodies in and that was where they laid them out. After that description I could never quite separate the sets I had played from the slabs or the tables that the corpses had been laid on, so that even today, decades later, I would have to tell you that I once had a gig in a funeral parlor. When I lived a few blocks from a large funeral home on Hillside Avenue in New Hyde Park, I used to cut into the street whenever I passed it, and once, after a blizzard, I positively ran from the snow that was blowing from its roof. The scene with Daddy Watson, which one could say completes the Indian Rock episode, is a reminder of what the hospital adventure is about, and in fact Daddy Watson's behavior is predetermined by Suttree's behavior with the nurse. If Suttree had stayed and played house with that delicious flirt, Daddy Watson would not have passed into the night and over the bridge: he would have attended the death of the hero in Knoxville General. When, toward the end of the tale, Suttree is admitted to St. Mary's Hospital, deathly ill and delirious, he makes this strangely elliptical comment: "To wish to lie down here is to entertain the illusion that kings may worship" (452), by which he sounds so much more like McCarthy than Suttree should sound that Suttree can only be channeling his biographer, who wants us to know that for Suttree it is only through the extremes of deprivation that he shall enter the Kingdom of Heaven. If this is an announcement that he doesn't belong there or that he doesn't deserve to belong there, the house of St. Mary becomes a safe house and, in a way, a gate to salvation, for Suttree bolts as soon as he hits the bed, and St. Mary enables him to visit other places across the universe without harming himself further. When Suttree, just out of the wilderness, is nursed by Mrs. Long, he doesn't mind it at all, but this is not an institution, this is the home of J-Bone's mother where Sut is more likely to be scolded than seduced. When McCarthy tells us, about the steady round of visitors: "None asked if what he had were catching" (298), it is one of the more endearing expressions of why Suttree commits himself to their society; but on another level, *all* of them know that it is, in fact, catching, catching them all, and so—what is there to wonder about?

Forty years later, a study undertaken at Harvard Medical School and reported in the *Journal of the American Medical Association*, found that hospitals are among the most dangerous places to be, a finding supported by the following statistic: in 2004 alone, 98,000 people died in hospitals from malpractice or from other non-disease related causes. We could say that Suttree is ahead of his time, but who of us, with or without statistics, has not wanted to keep away from hospitals, if only to keep away from our mortality? When I was young I stated it bluntly: "I'm afraid I'll catch death." For that reason, in all his long life Picasso never visited a friend in a hospital. Also, in fairness to Knoxville General, we shouldn't forget that the hero takes to the streets *after* he has been seen and properly treated. Without the sutures of Knoxville's surgeons, *Suttree* might have concluded on page 187.

Of course it is possible that Suttree does, in fact, die. Remembering the story of Lazarus imagined by Oscar Wilde—when Jesus asks him why he is crying, he says, in effect, *did you not bring me back to life?*—we could cynically say that Suttree bolts out of the hospital *because* it has saved, or returned him to, his life. But I don't think that he dies, at least not technically, for Miss Aldrich would have mentioned it. Nor is it Miss Aldrich herself, or sex, woman, girl, femininity, vagina, mother, or any combination thereof, that would have killed Suttree if he had remained. The handsome hero and his nurse might even have tied the knot and, unlike the starcrossed couple in *A Farewell to Arms*, lived a long life together, bred a swell family, grown to be Granma/Granpa Sut. It is just that if a McCarthy man remains in a hospital, any hospital, *for his own good*, as it would have been, too, for John Grady Cole, he is signing his own death warrant. My friend Donavin, whom I mentioned earlier, was so badly injured in a motorcycle accident that he was sirened off to the nearest hospital and hitched to IVs and other painsaving devices, from all of which he disconnected himself and split the scene the way Suttree splits it and John Grady too, knowing that the saving of life is death for him. It is partly this instinct, in high fidelity, that galvanized Donavin on September 11 when he was under the Twin Towers and flew from both collapses. In fact for Donavin, for John Grady Cole, and for Suttree in spades, you can define death precisely in these terms: death is wherever they want you to be, death is wherever they are taking care of you, death is wherever you can place your trust in them, death is wherever you are wanted passionately, death is where they wouldn't harm a hair on your head, death is where you need not worry about a thing, death is hospitality, death is where all your bloody wounds will be healed, death is the best of professional assurance, death is the finest of life support systems, death is a transfusion of someone else's blood, death is a steady intake of oxygen, death is a basket of fine lavender, death is the sweetest of summer oranges, death is where the ivory thighs are parting for you alone, death is where all of you is perfectly understood, death is where nothing of you will ever be rejected, death is another new shirt in the closet, death is the c-note waiting for you on the mantelpiece, death is the *promised*, the secure, the fail-safe, the unsinkable, the inflammable, the *uncollapsable*, death is where the randy Miss Aldrich will take your pulse tomorrow under clean white sheets, death is where Daddy Watson, content in his neurotic confidence, will abide in the reception room, with all the time in the world, waiting for the visiting hour.

NOTES

1. This poorly designed ad appears on the same page in the *Times* as John O'Connor's rave review of the film.

2. See Jay Ellis's *No Place for Home*, chapter 4.

3. This quotation from the work of humorist George Washington Harris (1814–1869), who wrote for the New York sporting paper *Spirit of the Times*, is taken from an electronic edition of Harris's collection *Sut Lovingood. Yarns Spun by a "Nat'ral Born Durn'd Fool."* The story in which it appears is "Sut Lovingood's Sermon. Teaching Ye Cat-Fishe Tavern," p. 172 at docsouth.unc.edu/southlit/harrisg/gharris, a website of the University of North Carolina at Chapel Hill called Documenting the American South.

II

BLOOD MERIDIAN

The night in day's clothing.

—McCarthy

• *4* •

Blood Music:
Reading *Blood Meridian* Aloud

1.

*T*o be awake is to read life for all it can say to us, and this is equally true of reading books. Of course wide-awake reading is not necessarily one's feet stretched out, bright pages in our lap, a cup of matcha or a foamy cappuccino driving off the winter chill and nothing but the eyes in motion. Sometimes the book stays at home—warm, windless, dry—while the reader is out walking the world, finding it there, or else sounding it in those fathomless worlds below.

"I had an idea that a Man might pass a very pleasant life in this manner," wrote Keats to his friend Reynolds. "Let him on a certain day read a certain page of full Poesy or distilled Prose, and let him wander with it, and muse upon it, and reflect from it, and bring home to it, and prophesy upon it, and dream upon it... A doze upon a sofa does not hinder it... Nor will this sparing touch of noble books be any irreverence to their Writers..." (73). What Keats did not say is that for Keats to walk abroad and give a page this sparing touch of idle dreaming could bestow a greater wealth upon the page than ever it gave its gentle reader. None of us is ever Keats, but his suggestion can be turned to some account. "Books," Whitman said, "are to be called for, and supplied, on the assumption that the process of reading is not a half-asleep, but, in the highest sense, an exercise, a gymnast's struggle" (76). I agree, but I do not see why an enlightened half-asleep cannot be part of that struggle. Often my researches tend to tumble into a doze upon a sofa, or a nap upon clover that, as Keats would say, generates "ethereal finger-pointings" (73).

Now, for example, pondering *Blood Meridian* in the dark of a New York night, I doze into a dream, on a Pacific shore with a powerful sun setting,

51

in which an altercation causes me to bump Keats's elbow, making it bleed. Thinking: "I'm being bled on by Keats's arm!" I brim with satisfaction over the privilege. Is this anything but a dream about the peaceful (Pacific) artists' colony Yaddo, where a problem (altercation) with this piece about a book that is *all* altercation and is subtitled *The Evening Redness in the West*, has moved me to take a walk, chance upon a volume of Keats's letters, and discover a fine page by the tubercular-bleeding (and now *Blood*ing) Keats to help me to fashion this introduction?

Thank you, McCarthy, for placing me on such intimate terms with Keats, for even if Keats were alive today—well, if Keats were alive we would kill him, but before that—how else but by dreaming could we meet him? This is the kind of thing that can happen when you wander past your bedtime, take a book to heart, and read it with your eyes wide open to the night.

2.

Shortly after reading *Blood Meridian*, I began the novel again. This time I read the entire book, every word of it, aloud. I did this partly to treat myself to the pleasure of speaking its darkly poetic prose, partly to follow a hunch that to feel the vibration of every sentence in muscle and bone was to alter—perhaps deepen, perhaps confound—my understanding of this unusual, undeniably challenging novel and, perhaps, of McCarthy's work as a whole. With a head-long sureness that is something beyond the human, something that—given all that is burned away in its path—is closer to arson than to art, *Blood Meridian* invites us to envision a character who is unique in contemporary American letters: not the Judge, who is thrilling enough, but this McCarthy guy with a pen and a typewriter who appears to be taking no one's advice, is writing without concern for the literary police of either the left or the right, and is happy to go to the devil on his own terms and, like Blake, to walk in Hell delighting in the fires of genius—or, once again like Artaud, to burn at the stake, signaling from the flames—but with a smile on his face and a congenial pose, in a Knoxville motel, for the lens of Mark Morrow's camera.

McCarthy's appetite for characters who lean toward the brute, the bloody, the brawlerous, the chronically monosyllabic, the psycho- and socio-pathic, is a propensity the reader needn't share in order to marvel at the talent at work. Few readers, few authors, would feel at home in McCarthy's milieu, and fewer would not envy McCarthy's genius in rendering it. But when an exquisitely textured novel that is driven by some of the most impressive prose of its day features no major character who isn't, literally, a slaughterer, and scarcely a thought or a deed, in over 300 pages, to inspire a wisp of hope for the human race, it is natural to ask questions about that talent and to wonder whether one is perceiving it rightly, or judging it fairly. One gluts upon a baroque of thieving, raping, shooting, slashing, hanging, scalping, burning, bashing, hacking, stabbing... and as sumptuous as it is, McCarthy could not pretend that he has written a cheery tale or shown us men more likely to lift us up than to lay us low. Every great writer knows the world well enough to know when they are provoking it, and every provocateur should be so lucky as to find that the world is provoking him back. This being the first McCarthy novel I had read, I was less than half through it when, duly provoked, I made an initial lunge at why a writer would want to be siring all the bad boys in this book with none to believe in, none to look up to. Is this a sideshow, I wondered, to the body of this man's work, or is this *the event*, and is he, Beckett-like, another aggrieved Irish Catholic striking back at the god of his youth because it has vanished, or because it won't? Had he, perhaps, drunk too much out of the Faulkner flask, a brew of a hundred proof that could easily induce a cirrhosis of outlook? Rude, fractious finger-pointings, not at all ethereal—meaningless today—but they derived from drinking McCarthy's bitter brew of Southern Railroad gin and Texas medicine, and by the time I had finished the novel I was convinced that this curative-intoxicant warranted further and better attention from me. And so I initiated a special investigation, opened my lungs, and began to speak *Blood*.

I had conducted this experiment on other works that had posed special challenges. I generally found it productive. It is an inconvenient experiment and a slow one to perform on any book, chiefly because of its impracticability in the places where we read, such as trains, jets, banklines, waitingrooms, cafes, partnered beds, or wherever else there is likely to be an underappreciative audience. It is also demanding beyond the customary exactions of silent reading, for the concentration necessary for reading aloud well is peculiar to that act, is generally undeveloped, and draws upon a reservoir that is easily drained, even for a wizened theatrical ham such as myself. "I would no more force my reading than my writing," Whitman told Horace Traubel. "I read by fits and starts—fragments: read in moods: no sequence, no order, no nothing" (155). I too am a fit-and-starter, a leapfrogger, a skip-the-beginninger—even, increasingly, a backwardsman; but reading a book aloud is all sequence, continuity—*stickwithitiveness*. There is, on the other hand, incomparable delight in being the sole breathing instrument by which a succession of artful English sentences sounds good. The phrase *sounds good* bristles with new meaning. With you as the sounder, you are required, in a sense, to *become* the book as the bearer of its voice and, by extension, become the storyteller, with emphasis on the *teller*. Of course reading a tale in such a way that it won't be told unless we say it is not as demanding as a book that won't be read unless we write it, but long days of small talk, or weeks of silent reading, are nothing to an hour of making a book sound as great as it really is.

At the time that I began this experiment on McCarthy, I was reading aloud the book that my good master Thoreau concluded at Walden, which is not, as is commonly thought, *Walden*, but his first book, *A Week on the Concord and Merrimac Rivers*, a central piece of the "private business" he went to conclude "with the fewest obstacles" (23). Like McCarthy, like any committed writer, Thoreau needed to flee the voices that surround us, he needed to close the door—not on the world, but on the things that keep us from it—and he needed to scribble. He scribbled a fine, sturdy, wholly American book that was published the year in which most of *Blood Meridian* takes place—1849—and he laid the foundation for one of the best books of all. Although it records an excursion on two rivers, *A Week* is *not* a breezy volume, and I had never had an easy time approaching it, despite having acted the part of its author on the stages of New York for several years. To put it plainly, I couldn't get through it. To put it plainer, I could barely begin it. On a nightly basis I was recreating Thoreau, in a play entitled *An Hour at Walden*, unable to read the book that he had written there—a most unthorough impersonation indeed. But now, as I spoke it, it was thrilling me with passages of astonishing richness and power that I might never have noticed because I would not have made it to that part of the journey, or would have arrived in the wrong condition. Thoreau's *Week* was now taking me two years, but that week having been said, I would have lived it. "Not the book needs so much to be the complete thing," Whitman said, "but the reader of the book does" (76). When, at the end of the Sunday chapter of *A Week*, Henry and his brother John—who was shortly to die of lockjaw with Henry as a witness—put themselves to bed beneath an oak tree on the riverbank, Thoreau puts his prose to bed as well, and perhaps too the memory of his brother, and you cannot speak these pages without feeling your own voice, your own spirit, put to bed at the same time. When it happened to me, perched over the coast of the Long Island Sound, the sound of my own voice became a channel in which I traveled to Henry and John's Massachusetts, and Henry and John's Massachusetts traveled to me, and the eyes of every peaceful evening closed upon us all. In November 1847, writing about *A Week* to his friend Emerson, who was lecturing in England, Thoreau said: "Wiley & Putnam, Munroe, the Harpers, and Crosby & Nichols have all declined printing it with the least risk to themselves..." (Norton 1852). I can understand that reluctance. From a week such as this, one never returns.

Also around this time I had bought, for a scandalous five dollars, Volume Two of the first U.S. edition—published in 1837 with the first English edition—of *The Posthumous Papers of the Pickwick Club*, "edited" by Boz.

Excited that this small brown waterstained volume was really *it*, the book in which this country first read what has come to be known as *The Pickwick Papers*—that vast ancient treasury, so bright in my youthful reading—I decided it might be fitting to read this Dickens aloud as well, just as it might have been read to the Hegerman clan gathered anights in its Norwich, Long Island, parlor by Mr. Elbert Hegerman, the book's first owner, after he brought it back from C. J. Fulsom, Bookseller and Stationer, at 40½ Fulton Street in Lower Manhattan. Dickens and McCarthy: is there not a kinship between these worddrunk progenitors? Was there, I wondered, a parlor in all this country in which the assembled would be read to from *Blood Meridian*? At least for the course of a few months, on the same night, in this small singular theatre of Peter Josyph, there could be found these distinguished, distinctly different authors—Cormac McCarthy, Henry David Thoreau, Charles Dickens—sharing a bill for private performance.

3.

Of course you cannot read aloud for even your own ears without interpreting your text, and while literature is generally not sold with speaking instructions, suggestions will inevitably arise. What often happens—I am speaking now of narrative, not of dialogue—is that you are conscious of a number of ways the writing seems to work so that it rings right to the ear while, at the same time, making sound sense to the listening mind. And *it feels right in the mouth*. When I wrote the above sentence, I accidentally typed *feels right* as *feels write*, which is, perhaps, a better way of stating what I mean: the prose feels as if it were written to speak that way. Reading aloud for oneself, one can fluctuate at will from one to another orchestration. With *Pickwick* and *A Week*, a variety of options arose for every passage. Reading *Blood Meridian*, I noticed something peculiar. There seemed to be no two ways of reading this book's brilliant prose. As often as I wandered, the book brought me back to one approach, and that approach seemed to apply equally well to the whole novel. Nothing else sufficed because everything else sounded flat wrong. What, I wondered, did that right sounding betoken? I had a few ideas, but while I was sorting them out, or urging them to sort themselves out, I conducted a different kind of experiment.

4.

Reading the book this second time supported my surmise that spitting was a mode of self-expression. Virtually every time a character spits, he is feeling something that he will not say; or, rather, something he says clearly, but through spit instead of words. I marked off each instance—doubtless the first marginalia of spit—and after thirty or more (my total was forty-four), I wondered precisely what species of spit we were talking about. Not much of a champion spitter myself, I essayed different approaches, observing which, if any, felt or looked like *Blood Meridian* spits. I spat into sinks and toilet bowls and parkinglots and railroad tracks and lawns, I spat out the door of my car, I walked on the beach and spat in the sand and into the water, I spat on stones and abandoned rusts of pipes and cranes, I spat into stormbeached concrete cisterns, I spat in the wind, I spat in the woods, I spat in the rain, I spat in the town and in the city on Manhattan avenues, I even tried spitting through my teeth the way a boy, Bobby Reese—one of my heroes when I was six in Jamaica, Queens—used to spit from a great distance beautifully aimed precision streams wherever he wished. It was largely for this virtuoso spitting, along with a bearish talent for shimmying up trees, that I idolized this boy. Decades later I was still envying him, still trying to spit like Bobby Reese (only now, of course, in the cause of literature), until it was pointed out to me that Reese could spit that way because of a space between his two front teeth. I stopped trying to replicate those wonderful Reesean jets, but I would not be contented until I had struck a spit worthy of *Blood Meridian*, the problem being that *my* spits were only about spit. An expressive spit commands a force behind it, a focus, a finding-of-target. It has *aim*. Did that, I wondered, partly derive from chewing tobacco?

At the time of my spit researches, I had not yet spoken to Brad Dourif about his role as Bobby McEvoy in McCarthy and Richard Pearce's *The Gardener's Son*, during which conversation we talked spit. "It's all in the chewing tobacco," Brad told me. "He [McCarthy] *loved* the tobacco spitting—he just *loved* it. We used to talk about it, about the rhythm of it—*it has a rhythm*. I mean, it *points* things. Somebody'd say something, you go—" and here Brad demonstrated, dryly but convincingly.

It points things—nice way of putting it. And it makes an unmistakable sound, too, not like any other. Chaw is mentioned in *Blood Meridian*, but no one is seen spitting it specifically. Tobacco, then, would be a presupposition—a pretty sure bet with these guys—but not a certainty. In any case, tobacco was not enough of an answer to settle me. *Puttt!* A thewing not to be sneezed at, a pointing not to be settled too easily. Was the requisite here, perhaps, a long resistance to, distrust and dislike of, verbal effusion? Was this, then, a book of men for whom confusion and contempt could best be vented through the speechless forms of their own spit, or the draw of another's blood? If so, the monumental figure of Judge Holden—lawlearned scalphunter, polyglot child-rapist, fearless killer-genius who speaks well to all occasions, audited by his largely uncomprehending gangmates—would be the one major exception; but then, in the annals of literature, Judge Holden is an exception to everything. With what wonder does one hear this eloquent monster speak his mind—or whatever is there inside his great shining Shakespearean skull. More than by his twisters of knowledge and rhetorical provocation, we stand before the Judge and are blown, and blown away, by a force more rare: the private energy of joy—unsharable, unsappable—the sheer vitality of a man who is living a grand life. In any case, throughout *Blood Meridian* the Judge, who so plentifully passes sentences, does not spit once, although he certainly does draw it, and other juices, out of others. If McCarthy's pack of losers had been given the book devoted to them, what could they have done but to spit in the face of its loquacity? If, on the other hand, the great fat hairless diablo had read it to them aloud by the flickering camplight, the chronicle of their own misdeeds lit by the "will to deceive that is in things luminous" (120)—that light which is enemy to the ones who live in darkness—would they not—after, of course, a great rain of spits hissing into the flames—have listened attentively?

5.

My third experiment was a reading of two iconic American Westerns: Zane Grey's *Riders of the Purple Sage* and Owen Wister's *The Virginian*. The results, as they pertain to *Blood Meridian*, were exactly nil. If these novels are, by any accounts, definitive American Westerns, *Blood Meridian,* although it is set in a mid-19th century Southwest and Mexico—I do not say *the* mid-19th century Southwest and Mexico—is decidedly not a Western. It is equally true that in *Purple Sage* it is purple—drastic overwriting—that ruins the book; that *The Virginian* ought to have been a masterpiece but is not quite; and that *Blood Meridian*, which you might say should *not* have been a masterpiece, is. A memorable line in *The Virginian* is: "You must break all the Commandments *well* in this Western country" (312). Wister's Virginian ought to look to *Blood Meridian* if he wants to see what that looks like. But then, Wister's Virginian could ride the world forever, rocking back and forth in time, running horses into the ground, and never encounter the Glanton gang, for despite its historical sources, despite its epilogue (the novel's one false note) of fencing in the open West, *Blood Meridian* is not for me a novel about 19th century America, nor is it a novel about 19th century Mexico, because it is not about the 19th century.[1]

   To qualify something I said earlier, *Blood Meridian*'s 1849 is not really *the* 1849 in which *A Week* found a publisher, Mark Twain worked on his brother's *Hannibal Journal,* Melville sailed off to a London that was publishing *Redburn* and *Mardi,* and Poe taught Richmond "The Poetic Principle" before dying in Baltimore. I understand that there was a Glanton gang, but I also know that the world of the Glanton gang in this book is not a world in which the Glantons of record, or anyone else of record excepting McCarthy, has ever walked. The boys in the dream we know as *Blood Meridian* are even less John Glanton's boys than the Keats in my Keats dream was John Keats. In *Blood Meridian*'s 1849 the Judge fiddles, but a provincial English fiddler of that year whose gigs were local dances and weddings, a Dorchester schoolboy named Thomas Hardy, would not have been able to play them because the 1849 in *Blood Meridian* would not have allowed Thomas Hardy to have been born.

6.

Although McCarthy's next novel, *All the Pretty Horses*—which, despite its mystique of blood and ambiguous moral logic, does, with its incredibly cunning hero, have a great deal in common with the classic American Western—went on to win the National Book Award, its author was still a comparative unknown. But my researches were hardly taking place in a vacuum. I had recently mailed a copy of *Blood Meridian* to one of my favorite living authors and dearest of friends, Richard Selzer. Rick Wallach, who introduced me to McCarthy, had sealed it in a priority pack and dispatched me to post it at once to Selzer's address. "Let me know as soon as you hear from him." A commander of armed forces under siege could not have awaited more eagerly his reports from HQ than Rick awaited Selzer's response to McCarthy. Less a man than a force of nature, Rick craved *everybody's* response to reading the novel. In the famous Sammy's Rumanian Style Restaurant near Delancey Street—easily the craziest place to dine in Manhattan—I had seen Rick produce a copy of *Blood Meridian,* thrust it upon our waiter, and coerce him—in the middle of Christmas Eve—into reading a couple of paragraphs. In a Miami carpet store, when I called Rick's attention to a clerk reading a book during her break, Rick animated the girl in conversation, drove away with his carpets, and three hours later he returned with three stacks of reading assignments, on top of one of which was *Blood Meridian.* No flirtation or followups—he was being an enthusiast, being an educator.

For Rick's sake I prodded Richard Selzer in every letter. "I'm saving the Cormac McCarthy for the very next reading venture," Selzer wrote to me at last. "Right now I'm finishing a so-so-ish book by Jean Giono—at one time an idol of mine, but no longer." The following week he wrote: "Yes, Yes, Yes, I'm beginning *Blood Meridian*. Stop nagging me. I read three pages—it's wonderful. I'll take it with me to Cleveland on Friday." I relayed this intelligence to Rick, but I could report no appreciable operations until two weeks later, when there was this:

> Feb 24. Felled by a stupid cold. So I am 200 pages into *Blood Meridian*. McCarthy has more sheer talent than anyone living. I'm knocked flat by the range of language, imagery—the richness, the mastery of lore. Only one trouble: the violence is there for its own sake. He revels in it. No single character arouses our affection, or, for that matter, our interest, as we know almost nothing about them. They are devoid of feelings, reduced to members of a primal horde. But then, the technique is enough. He is a genius—also probably somewhat insane. As for me, I'll go on insisting upon the essential benevolence of half the human race, and the possibility of love, redemption, grace—all of that. I have heard he is a recluse; I'm not surprised; it's just as well.[2]

Probably Selzer's sense of McCarthy's reclusion derived from journalists who believe that if a writer will not talk to the press, he does not talk at all. Rick, predictably, could not agree about the gratuity of the violence, but he already knew that it was not the book's violence but the gratuity of its affection that troubled me. Knowing that I valued his perspective on McCarthy, Selzer soon sent me a lengthier response.

> In the matter of Cormac McCarthy, and it is a most serious matter, I must say yes and no. McCarthy has more of the writer's gift than any other living writer of my ken. His power and scope of language is of a sort that comes along as often as the century plant blooms. Line after line unto the many thousands testify to his genius. Then why am I hesitant to proclaim, to venerate? Perhaps it has something to do with the profound pessimism of the novels, their belief that the actions of man are predestined, and that man is innately corrupt. There is no speck of human warmth, of love, of a sense of home—rearing of young, taking and giving shelter—there is only the mindless mercenary impulse toward slaughter. *Blood Meridian* fairly reeks with the accumulation of gore. Massacre after massacre is described with lipsmacking relish. Its characters are clones of the same murderous One. Most of the violence is egregious, rising out of some manic cruelty and flung in the face of the reader with all the bravado and defiance of a smart-aleck teenager, as if written by an author whose emotional development had been arrested at an early age, before compassion and tenderness could burnish what had been dull and rough. It is not that I am revolted by the awful facts of blood and flesh. On the contrary, I confess to a certain fascination with the wound. As Emily Dickinson wrote: "'Tis so appalling—it

exhilarates—/So over Horror, it half Captivates." It is that McCarthy has an insatiable need to depict it for its own sake. The satisfaction he gets from this seems to me quite sexual, however disguised. Unspeakable as the purpose and end of life may be for McCarthy, he has chosen to speak it all, again and again—and again—until the civilized gorge rises.

When later I sent him *Child of God*, Selzer's reaction was similar. "I continue to be astonished by his mastery of language, his flamboyant style, his unerring and novel imagery," he wrote. "And I continue to be nonplussed by his egregious love of depravity and violence for its own sake. What a waste! All that great gift laid at the feet of cruelty. The necrophiliac scenes—just the idea of there being more than one!—are so disturbing as to be unforgettable. That scene wherein he leads the men into the cave and entraps them is marvelously wrought, as is the scene in the shooting gallery. McCarthy could have been the finest writer of our time, but, after all, this is literary jerking off. Sorry, I can't genuflect before this guy."

Neither did I, but I did take McCarthy to church. As a result of Rick's P. T. Barnumizations, a member of my theatre had read the novel, and we debated it under a tall extension ladder while installing a huge expressionist altarpiece, *St. Jerome in His Study*, which I and another artist, Kevin Larkin, had painted for turn-of-the-century Church of the Advent on Broadway and 93rd Street in Manhattan. Even as Kevin climbed to the top of the ladder, the old austere church, which was only as austere as you can be when you've had Tiffany as your glazier, reverberated with references to the Glanton gang and the Judge. The story of the lion that was accidentally transferred from another saint to Jerome did, of course, apply to Jerome, for like McCarthy and all writers of importance, Jerome *must* have had a lion in his study (McCarthy certainly had a Lion in his study, for that dog in Faulkner's "The Bear" has more in common with McCarthy's people than any of Faulkner's men), and how could I not wonder what a roar would have erupted from that crusty patron saint of translators if we could read him a Vulgate *Meridian*? What, for that matter, wouldn't I give just to hear the book in Latin! Would it not resuscitate, forever, that lost and wondersome language? Given the wild world in which he lived, Jerome would not have been aghast at being awash in the novel's bloodshed. But what would Jerome have thought of the way McCarthy would have us root for one vile killer creep over another?

If old Jerome were Rick's friend, he certainly would have read the book, with or without a translation, because everybody in range of Rick learned that they *had* to read it—if, that is, they expected to cross his threshold again. Like the madly anti-Semitic Degas, who would peer out of his door and ask: "Dreyfus—for or against?" as a way of determining who to admit, the madly pro-*Meridian* Rick posed the question: "*Meridian*—reading it or ain't?" The novel did not exist in the form of an audiobook, but one could hear an abridged version just by being around Rick, who had learned several passages—the Judge's denunciation of Reverend Green, for example—well enough to perform them verbatim, as if rehearsed for the stage—which, in a way, they were. John Sepich, who had kindly shown us his then unpublished *Notes on* Blood Meridian, flew to Long Island from Peoria, Illinois, to spend a couple of days discussing the book with us, and following John's cue, we were reading *My Confession: The Recollections of a Rogue* by Samuel E. Chamberlain, a member of Glanton's gang and a likely source for at least the bare bones of the Kid, whom you could call the book's hero if you can use that word for a boy who kicks in the brain of a stranger and then burns a hotel before riding out with scalpers, rapists, and killers, and who meets his conclusion, possibly—depending on how you imagine it—being eaten alive in a shithouse. We were also reading the rest of McCarthy, including his early stories, "Wake for Susan," and "A Drowning Incident," which, exhumed from his college magazine, show from their very titles that McCarthy was not rehearsing for light comedy. Here, then, was a real discovery we were welcoming into our midst, who as yet was underread and unacknowledged and whose work had become our daily bread, for which we gave thanks, for at last, upon we scroungers for curbside crumbs, McCarthy had bestowed an entire loaf. In *Tropic of Cancer*, Miller wrote: "I believe that today more than ever a book should be sought after even if it has only *one* great page in it: we must search for fragments, splinters, toenails, anything that has ore in it, anything that is capable of resuscitating the body and soul" (257). To have found an entire book that, like *Cancer* itself, was filled with ore on every page was a mercy out of the blue, an unexpectedly beautiful, if demanding, revelation.

7.

I was reading aloud from the middle of the novel, during a cold winter's night, the rough waves pounding under my window, when the book slipped from my hands and released me into a lucid dream of standing in an enormous garage gazing up at a violin that was walking across the top of a big boiler. There were other striking components to this nifty little vignette, but its focus was on the violin and the wonder of how it could walk like that. My perplexity dissolved when I saw that the violin was two things at once: a violin, and a brown Chihuahua that was nipping away at the instrument, impelling it to move across the boilertop. I awoke in the clear knowledge that here was a dream of *Blood Meridian* and the intellectual challenge it had posed.

Chihuahua City is one of the principal towns in the novel. Most of the book's adventurers are, like Chihuahuas, lowdown dogs, and men who doggedly press on across a boiling desert terrain. They themselves are also boilers: steeled machines of tight containment, combustible, likely to burst or *be* burst at any moment. In *Blood Meridian*, is not McCarthy's prose exquisite enough to shame a nation of versifiers, and am I not exploring McCarthy's language, trying to grasp how it moves, and what is moving about it? The well-crafted violin is moving because it is driven by—by what? Bite. Teeth. Dog's teeth. The novel's rabid doggery—ferocious people, landscape, notions—gives bite to McCarthy's melodic prose, empowering it to move and thus to move the reader. In the exhibition of saints that included *St. Jerome*, we had displayed a Tibetan saying: "Where there is veneration, even a dog's tooth emits light." McCarthy's prose is nothing if not venerative, and fueled by a stern, testamental inexorability that bows to no scruple, shies from no catastrophe, and rejects, or tends toward rejecting, all overt narrational personality—which is why, compared to *Pickwick* and *A Week*, it discourages, even punishes, too much latitude for vocal improvisation, providing, as it does, an unswerving template for its oral interpreter.

Such a monumental contract between the writer and his text must, by its nature, run the risk of appearing forced, portentous, overblown, for *we did not write this way*, not *nearly* this way, at that time in that century; nor do we write this way now. McCarthy's achievement in this regard—I mean the extraordinary mettle of his prose—was, for the longest time, typically underappraised, as if an author's book could be divided from his language. If its weakness is that it tries too hard, that is not a fault, because there is no easy way to such an utterance: McCarthy could not have achieved it without trying too hard, without, in a sense, forcing it, for out of what would it arise naturally? There wasn't a trend or a dimension of life in these United States that was *not* geared against it. The novel was published in 1985. Read aloud from any page, then look at what was published in that year. To steal a formulation from Thomas À Kempis: *They show fair letters, but McCarthy declareth the sentence.* A writer could not summon the language of *Blood* without hurting himself into it. If a man attempts a precipice, pay him out as much rope as he needs. Strain is here a necessity. What does it matter if it shows, what do we care if what we are given is too much? Better that than, as with most recent novels, nothing at all. Melville made too much *Moby-Dick* so that his English publisher could release it in three volumes, but could just enough *Moby-Dick* still be *Moby-Dick*? If there is too much *Blood Meridian*, why am I reading the book for the fifth time?

On a simpler level, one reads *Blood Meridian* aloud and one is tempted to stop and say, as Joseph Campbell said after reading aloud the Cyclops in Joyce's *Ulysses*: "What a—what a show!"[3]

It is easy to say that out of a strong sense of self and of his fathers—among the famous we can hear, or imagine that we hear, Ishmael, Twain, Conrad, Crane, Joyce, Hemingway, Steinbeck, Farrell, Faulkner, not to mention his greater great grandfathers, Heraclitus, Apollonius of Rhodes, the King James Biblicans, and the prelectors of *Beowulf*—McCarthy has forged a voice that is original; but what this misses is that McCarthy doesn't *need* to be original. We are all thieves in the night. The difference between *derived* and *derivative* is the difference between escaping and being caught. McCarthy gets away with so much for one reason: he has genius. How can *All the Pretty Horses* sound so much like Hemingway without consigning McCarthy to his legions of pretenders? The answer is that in *All the Pretty Horses*, McCarthy *is* Hemingway: he is what Hemingway might have been had he lived to be Cormac McCarthy and write that book. To see how badly Faulkner failed at meeting the challenges for the absence of which he once, in a remark he later retracted, ranked Hemingway fifth, not first, among the best of his contemporaries, try reading *Absalom, Absalom!* aloud. *Listening* to the novel makes its failings more apparent, especially the fact that its prose is abominable.[4] Any Mississippian would have been shot in three minutes for its run-on forever sentences. What my experiment on the language of *Blood Meridian* demonstrated is that it does not *sound* forced, *sound* strained, *sound* indulgent; it sounds soul-stirring—as if finally your voice were getting what it has been promised—because the book is not an attempt at epic prose, it is the achievement of epic prose, which, as with those crustier, ancienter epics, is best read on the tongue. If thrilling eloquence is tonic to the psyche, reading it aloud makes it buzz through the body. Speaking, and speaking *about*, such a resounding success are different things. In the case of *Blood Meridian*, it doesn't hurt to do both.

8.

Blood Meridian is a novel about force, and this, as Simone Weil pointed out in her marvelous essay, *The Iliad, or, The Poem of Force*, is the soul and the sole hero of Greek epic, in which "those who have force on loan from fate count on it too much and are destroyed" (14). When the late novelist Jerry Badanes gave it to me in pamphlet form, I was astonished at how much of this rare gem of Weil's—written, from the heart of her heart, during the fall of France in 1940—applied to *Blood Meridian*—with, of course, the exception of Judge Holden, who is exempt from the idea that the retributive power of fate will, ultimately, reduce to tears the practitioners of force—unless we think of Holden himself as Fate. It is tempting to quote Weil's entire argument, but one passage—translated by Mary McCarthy—will have to suffice. She says of the epic protagonist:

> Since other people do not impose on their movements that halt, that interval of hesitation, wherein lies all our consideration for our brothers in humanity, they conclude that destiny has given complete license to them, and none at all to their inferiors. And at this point they exceed the measure of force that is at their disposal. Inevitably they exceed it, since they are not aware that it is limited. And now we see them committed irretrievably to chance; suddenly things cease to obey them.[5] Sometimes chance is kind to them, sometimes cruel. But in any case there they are, exposed, open to misfortune; gone is the armor of power that formerly protected their naked souls; nothing, no shield, stands between them and tears. (14–15)

The novel is also a national epic, but an epic of that country called McCarthy where there are two authentic heroes working together magnificently: the dreamer, the imaginist, the envisioner; and the teller, the one with the words, the one with the *epos*, the one with the music. Howsoever the great Judge fiddles, we remember that he himself is being fiddled and that all the coveted world he tries to trap, name, possess in his black journals of bad science is itself a book in which we can shutter him in darkness by closing it, all of the Judge's power merely a song sung by another. Imagine comparing the Judge's journals with Thoreau's. "The freedom of birds is an insult to me," Holden says, Fatelike. "I'd have them all in zoos" (199). For the earth to be his, nothing should exist without his knowledge and permission. In an exciting sequence the Judge, using a formula from his journal, manufactures gunpowder to save the gang from advancing doom. But of course applying a practical formula is not the doing of science. And when Thoreau says that the earth that he knows will *not* bury him, he has a different survival in mind, understanding that the earth that is worth knowing is an earth that would bury no one. Suttree is on the same wavelength: as he is driven to Mrs. Long's through McAnally Flats, watching the excavators and bulldozers "reared against the cokeblown sky" the way I watched them for months at Ground Zero: "He knew another McAnally, good to last a thousand years. There'd be no new roads here" (463).

9.

This is a roughneck novel indeed, but like a photographic reversal, as if it were written from Death's perspective, *Blood Meridian* can be seen as a positive book, for Death relishes men who add to his legions abundantly and with such healthy hearts, and surely it's an enjoyable book to read, often a highly amusing one. I have said that the Judge is enjoying himself. It's more than that: much like Suttree, he's having a ball, and that is a joy to watch. References to the light, as in the above "will to deceive that is in things luminous" (120), are characteristically negative, which is fitting in a novel with an epigraph from Jacob Boehme that *sorrow is a thing that is swallowed up in death, and death and dying are the very life of the darkness*. For the great glutton Death, who is the ultimate *comedos*, devourer, life is all *comedia*, festival. The epigraph to this section, "The night in day's clothing" (59), taken from McCarthy's *The Sunset Limited*, could serve as a description of the Judge—and of the novel. If the Judge neither looks nor feels like the night, that is because McCarthy enables us to see him as he sees himself, and thus not a figure of darkness at all. It is partly for this reason that I can't quite accord with Professor Bloom when, in the conversation to follow, he sees Judge Holden in the violence and terror plaguing us every day; or with John Sepich when, in one of the pieces expanding his revised edition of *Notes*, he says: "Face the judge. Find a way to stop him" (152). I admire both men for taking the Judge into the world, into their own lives and into the life of the nation. As a postscript to one of John's letters to me, he wrote: "Lit theory or life? That's the McCarthy challenge." I am delighted to see that John overcame what was perhaps an overdetermined personality, broke out of the shell of research, and spoke some of his mind, publically, about this exotic, enticing, pox'd whore of a novel with which he has slept more than any of us. As with the responses of Wesley Morgan and Bill Spencer to *Suttree*, the typed essays and concordances, the handwritten letters, the scrawled slips of note paper that John has sent to me are the record of a mind whelmed over by a single work of art. The difference between the published *Notes* and the pile that I have before me is this: in the book I can read John's thoughts, but here I hear him thinking aloud. "Just wish I'd quit having *thoughts* about the novel," John wrote to me after five pages of "Chamberlain Analogs." Not much hope for that. Both John and Professor Bloom have taken the Judge a step beyond interpretation, and that's refreshing. Some forms of interpretation have a crowding effect, making it hard to breathe a book. As Thoreau said: "There may be an excess even of informing light" (Walking 621). Applying the Judge is a way of reading the Judge, a way of understanding him. But if I take any instance of violence or terror—say, the September 11 attacks, a subject with which I have grappled as an artist for nearly a decade—I do not see the Judge in the religious hysteria, the political, corporate, and tribal opportunism, the sexual sublimation, the blind subjugations, the cheesy and complacent reportage, or, really, in *any* dimension of national and international life surrounding those events. Nor do I see them in the Judge—not unless by abstraction to the point of deformation. If I am honest with myself, the answer is: "No—that's not him." I am thus tempted to say that this way of understanding the Judge tends to do so by misrepresenting him. But it does so honestly, for perhaps that is, after all, the only way to wrestle with the Judge: to compose or composite your own version of him and to understand *that*. Judge Holdens who are not in McCarthy—including the Judge with whom I begin this book, the one I have traveled to McCarthy's Knoxville—seem to me too much more and too much less than the one in *Blood Meridian*.

Our first sight of the seemingly ageless Judge Holden reveals a connoisseur of chaos; in one of the last, we can imagine him, vampire-like, swallowing up the body and soul of the Kid, as if to nourish his eternity on the Kid's thirst for violence; or, if you take the Judge at his word (God help you), on the Kid's resistance to it—which, in any case, at least means it is something to which the Kid is keenly alive. War, the Judge says, "endures because young men love it and old men love it in them" (249). Like the candlelit shadow of the dancing bear in the book's stirring finale, which "might have gone begging for referents in any daylight world" (326), the Judge, in fact the novel's entire populace, might also have gone begging. My dear old buddy John Sepich has breakfasted, lunched, dined, and midnight snacked on this witch's brew of a novel, ransoming his life to these greedy, extortionist pages... but despite the historical sources John's fine and fascinating research has revealed to us, little of John's authenticating has led me to read the book all that differently, partly because, unlike the pilgrim traveler to whom John compares the pilgrim reader, I cannot define my destination and possibly don't want one; I cannot see the book in the light of day; and, anyway, historical charts and compasses don't ever seem to fully apply to my *Meridian*. About Queequeg's island, Ishmael says: "It's not down on any map; true places never are" (150). John's superb work helps me to read another *Blood Meridian*, the daylight *Meridian* that is lucid in John's *Notes* but tends to fade when I open up McCarthy, because for me the poetic whole has little or nothing to do with the sum of its traceable parts. As surely as it was made from those sources—and John has devoted a life to showing that it was—it has just as surely sprung from somewhere else, and has transcended to something beyond. As helpful as it is to be shown the way to the borrowed facts, I am left to wonder about the borrower—and so, I am sure, is John. About *Ulysses*, Richard Ellmann said: "Joyce wrote his book out of fact, and also out of fire" (xiii). To paraphrase McCarthy's description of the Judge: whatever its antecedents, *Blood Meridian* is something wholly other—as indeed a *novel* should be. Here are the manifest sources for McCarthy's dreams: but what are the sources for his *dreaming*? There is a lot of incident in Chamberlain's *My Confession*, but it is in his dreams of the Judge—"Holden seemed to be hovering, crawling around me" (330)—in other words, the Judge of Chamberlain's own imagination—that I can see the most compelling inspiration for the Judge in McCarthy.

This is a spirited fairytale of the night, one of the most consistently nightly novels of its century, a century that pissed away oceans of surrealist ink evoking a night that never was. *Blood Meridian*, unapologetically, takes its very life from the darkness, and to read the book aloud is to be exhilarated—exhaustingly—celebrating the other half of energy. If, as Blake said, Milton was better at writing the Devil because his Devil was more to his liking than his God, McCarthy must have recognized that to show us a kingdom of darkness by shining upon it the light of his brilliant prose was a fitting, perhaps a necessary, challenge for his development as a writer. In McCarthy's best book, *Suttree*, "an enormous lank hound" arrives out of a meadow by the river "like a hound from the depths" (471) and sniffs at the patch of pavement where Suttree has hitched out of Knoxville forever. Is the river the Styx? "Somewhere in the gray wood is the huntsman," McCarthy tells us, "and in the brooming corn and in the castellated press of cities. His work lies all wheres and his hounds tire not" (471). We hear in the book's last lines: "I have seen them in a dream, slaverous and wild and their eyes crazed with ravening for souls in this world. Fly them" (471). If we sliced open that highway hound sniffing after Suttree, what would pour out would not be blood, but *Blood Meridian*, McCarthy's next book.

Lovers of *All the Pretty Horses* who cannot read *Blood Meridian* ought to consider that McCarthy might not have been able to write *Pretty Horses* in the fashion that pleases them were it not for his having written *Blood Meridian*. There are infinite paths to a novel before it is finished, but once it is done there was always only one. In the world of *Blood Meridian*, *All the Pretty Horses* tries to be born—in other words, the Kid tries to become John Grady Cole; or, more accurately, a kid becoming John Grady Cole tries to happen—but in this book there is no quarter for such an event and the likes of John Grady Cole cannot exist until, in 1949, a hundred years later, new territory appears that, although nominally similar in topography, and dangersome, and at times bleak and bloody, is never *Bloody*, and is actually an entirely different world.

In *Blood Meridian*, the sense of what we could call *virtue becoming* is best dramatized in a scene in which the Kid—at 28 a kid no longer—is moved to save the life of a Mexican woman, the sole survivor of a massacre. Or so he imagines. This leathered and beshawled old crone has, he discovers, been dead for many years and is entombed in her cave, and so there is no one on whom to bestow this act of kindness. The dead woman's shawl "was much faded of its color yet it bore like a patent woven into the fabric the figures of stars and quartermoons and other insignia of a provenance unknown to him" (315). How could they be known to him? Despite numberless nights under a clear wide sky, such starlit entities are not among the knowns or even the knowables in the Kid's dark passage. We are told on the first page: "He has a sister in this world that he will not see again" (3), but that is because his sister—all of his other half—cannot survive in such a place. It is not that the Kid must die in order to make way for John Grady Cole, it is that the Kid's entire world must pass away.

Our sense of identification with the Kid derives from McCarthy's skill in making us breathe the life of his people, but he is supported by the device of dropping the Kid from the narrative when the gang is engaged in violence, and bringing him back when it or he has become a victim. As one of the Glanton boys, the Kid could not have absented himself from carnage, but we seldom see him at it personally. If we had watched him at, or joined him in, the gang's atrocities—even as a consenting witness—this gesture of kindness by an adult and now adulterated Kid would not mean the same to us. *Blood Meridian* is not—nor, probably, is it meant to be—a hundred percent reversal against the light of moral action. To intrude at least a sense of impending virtue, without which we might not care to read the book at all, McCarthy employs a sleight-of-hand, relying on the reader's lapse of scrutiny and a willingness to not give the book's massive brutality *too much* thought. In this regard, the novel does, in fact, bow to scruple and is, ironically, insufficiently violent. The Kid says to one of the gang: "What's wrong with you is wrong all the way through you" (66), as if what's wrong with the Kid is not; and when he later refuses to kill a wounded comrade, or risks his life to draw an arrow out of the leg of another thug, are we not to feel that compared, say, to Glanton, the Kid is at least a slightly better sort?

Perhaps he is, but upon reflection—which the book does not encourage in this regard—in deed the Kid is as bad as the rest of the gang. After all our relations had been butchered, how touched would we be that after years of lonesome wandering the Kid just *might* think twice before another scalping adventure? How many times must I hear about the Kid, now the Man, having a bawl over a dead old buzzard? It was I who brought it up just now, but let's not be stupid about it. The Kid bawls. In Chamberlain's *My Confession*, even the Judge bawls a bit. You can bawl too. You can bawl *with* the Kid—take your handkerchiefs to the jailhouse and all bawl together as the Kid sits waiting for the noose. I will take his picture and, like the photographer in *The Gardener's Son*, give the Kid a cut of the sales, payable after they spring the trap. Do you see what you sobsisters have done to me—turned me into a lawman. All right, then, I am the lawman. I understand that you want to discuss the transformative power of age, experience, loneliness, reflection, empathy, and (I am about to gag on this) *the possibility of redemption* in the Kid or the Man... and that you'd love to have long, fruitful talks and seminars about the Kid in terms that are, perhaps, best summarized in Shane Schimpf's bold and thoughtful "Overview" in his *Reader's Guide to* Blood Meridian: "He alone in the novel represents what is supposedly noble and good in man—our capacity to empathize with another person and show mercy" (3). *Have* those talks about your beloved Kid—that's what the novel is for—just let me lock him up first. For me to become a lawman reading *Blood Meridian* is perfectly consistent with the wonderful schizophrenia the novel can engender. That's not all it engenders. Last night a cricket leaped out of its pages. This morning it was a homonculus. Two weeks ago it was on the passenger seat as I drove through the Midtown Tunnel when out rolled a lit cherry bomb. One can only hope that whatever comes out of it will not come after us. But when you read it right you become a firewalker. The coals beneath your feet are still burning, but you can relax and enjoy it.

O shipmates, what I have heard in every port about the Kid and that cave! As lovers of good books, we have a vested interest in first rate writing, and as lovers are wont to do, we want to defend its creations. I have heard perhaps one too many sympathetic readings of the Kid and other members of the gang; not, mind you, for their effectiveness as characters, which is inarguable, but for their behavior, which is, of course, insane. But love *will* make us mad, and McCarthy—with the Kid, with the gang, with Lester in *Child of God*—works us toward a sympathetic joining with these killers. Of course McCarthy is not admiring criminals—he procreates in words and punctuation—but his prose will, at times, admire criminal characters, as the *filmmaking* in films such as *The Godfather* and *GoodFellas* admires the beautiful mobsters on the screen, or as *the prose* in *No Country for Old Men* will admire the manufacture and use of weaponry. As every imaginist knows, part of the bargain we strike with the public is this: if we cherish their commitment to *as if* when they like the results, we ought not to demean it with an *only* when they do not; in other words, if characters are real enough for X to believe in them, they are real enough for X to be concerned with how they are treated by the techniques that have brought them to life. When beautiful words create an enemy to the law, my job as a reader is not to confuse my longing to loose that prose on the world in which I live with a longing to keep its subject free in the world of the novel. But we read in order to care, and with outlaw protagonists we have to be on *some* side of the coin or we might not turn the pages. A way to keep readers *behind* them is to make the opposition—whichever side of the law it is on—a little less attractive. Do you want the viewer to take the side of Don Corleone and his newly recruited son? Cast the parts with Brando and Pacino, make the crooked police captain the meanest son of a bitch, and give the part to Sterling Hayden. That accomplished, they will soon be rooting for mobster extortionist-killers.

In *Blood Meridian*, when the owner of an eatinghouse, Owens, refuses to serve Jackson, a black member of Glanton's gang, unless he moves to a separate table, Owens loses his brain to Jackson's revolver. McCarthy's prose does *not* put us behind Owens here, chiefly for the reason—an absurd one in the light of the gang's mission—that Owens is presented as a segregationist. Strange integrationists, these killers of every type of "nigger." But we also despise Owens because he is not willing to act on his convictions—meaning, he is not a cunning survivalist, not a master of his trigger, at which Jackson is unhesitatingly swift:

> He simply passed his hand over the top of the revolver he was holding in a gesture brief as a flintspark and tripped the hammer. The big pistol jumped and a double handful of Owens's brains went out the back of his skull and plopped in the floor behind him. He sank without a sound and lay crumpled up with his face in the floor and one eye open and the blood welling up out of the destruction at the back of his head. (236)

This and scenes like it trouble me, not because they are lurid entertainments, not because McCarthy relishes such descriptions of bloody ruin and so do we, but because every writer's prose has an ethos, and at times McCarthy's prose, for all its genius, is so admiring of the quick over the dead that it is ethically bereft. A detail completing this sordid scene is key to McCarthy's perspective: "Brown rose and retrieved his pistol and let the hammer back down and put it in his belt. Most terrible nigger I ever seen, he said. Find some plates, Charlie" (236). If this sneering kind of bravado about cunning criminality feels familiar, that is because for the last fifty years it has been progressively easy to find at the movies.

When soldiers who naively try to enforce the law are bullied away, again McCarthy's prose aligns itself beyond the law. "The lieutenant seemed stunned at the baldness of these [the Judge's] disclaimers. He looked from the judge to Glanton and back again. I will be damned, he said. Then he turned and pushed past the men and quit the place" (237). The law here, spoken or otherwise discharged, is the law of force. There is one more encounter in which Holden, the bulliest pitcher of rank cerebration since the puppets of Ayn Rand, a man who shoots sophistries like shells from a Gattling gun, assaults the lieutenant with law and philosophy—really a mockery of both—forcing the lieutenant and his men to drop out. The message is clear: this weakling army is no match for *these* boys. When, at the Yuma ferry, Glanton at last meets his match and (as foretold by a gypsy fortuneteller) the gang, hungover from a night of drunken revels, is decimated by Yumas, the Judge deflects his assassins with a howitzer under one arm and a lit cigar in the other. Again, McCarthy aligns us not with the Yumas—*of course* we are not with the Yumas—but with the Judge; and in fact the scene, the entire novel, *is fashioned to make us root* for the Judge. But when the Kid is later besieged by the Judge, McCarthy puts us behind the Kid. Ultimately, however, they are all ruthless marauders, so why should we care for any of them?

McCarthy is such a master that we can't help ourselves: we care whenever he wants us to care. But in this play of moral perspectives, the novel has, at times, the feel of a boy's game that makes me wonder whether it isn't perhaps a book of profound writing that, because it means to shift our sympathies constantly, is not a fundamentally serious book. I would not want to suggest that we should not *take* it seriously, only that we might be disappointed when we do. Despite its virtuosity and its bold imagination, I cannot shake a sense of emotional stinginess, a kind of aridity, at its core. For a novel about violence, of which we suffer too much in our cities and our wars, its dialectic is curiously inert. For a novel about blood, it seems to have been written in little of it. I agree with John Sepich that the novel is, in some ways, an unfriendly book, but for me it has to do with the fact that in and around Manhattan we are out here being shot at, mugged, raped, driven off the roads, and, most recently, raided and incinerated by terrorists, and when a man writes about thugs we take it seriously and hope to be *engaged*, which is not the same as being enthralled or entranced; and when the behavior of those meant to enlist our sympathies reminds us of the monsters we will encounter out on the streets this afternoon when we take the book awalking, one's reservations become a matter of life and death.

Profiting as it does from the ploy of confusing, and diffusing, the reader's response to criminality, even to barbarism, can one feel comfortable giving the book to a young reader, one, say, living without guidance in a jungle like Manhattan and turning to fiction to seek it there? Like most of us, I would recommend the book to a young *me*, not to a young *them*. Unqualified resistance to institutions of every type, along with a singleness of purpose that refuses to be denied, is one of McCarthy's identifying concerns. In McCarthy there is much walking out, walking off, walking away. I like this: all Americans need to walk, *really* walk, a lot further. In his "Walking," from which I have quoted earlier, Thoreau was on to this early, as he was to so much that is killing Americans. But for me the admiration of raw cunning—especially that of the outcast—typified in the chapter in *Child of God* in which the cipherous psycho-killer makes fools out of his captors, is one of the least attractive traits in McCarthy's work. And I am with my friend Richard Selzer in that there is no one in *Blood Meridian* I give a damn about.

This reflection does not, however, entirely suit the reading experience, for one would sooner spend literary time with these boys than with more likable sorts in lesser novels; not because their lives are more sensational, but because McCarthy is going where writers ought to be going and taking us with him. Whitman would have read it with interest. "I say in the future of these states must therefore arise Poets immenser far," Whitman wrote, "and make great poems of Death" (68). Well, there is McCarthy all right: immenser far. *My Confession* concludes with Chamberlain instructing Judge Holden to put a full day's ride between them. McCarthy has put a full day's ride between all of us and *Blood Meridian*. That's a good thing. Too much of what we read is too easy to grasp, too familiar, too affordable—too absorbable into the flow of another day. We need such books as cannot be read on the train without making us want to leap into the fields. We need more books that make us disrespected, inexcusable—dangerous. About McCarthy, Richard` Selzer once told me: "Such people live at a different intensity than the rest of us: they are driven by demons of unimaginable fury." Henry Miller understood the kind of artist we have in McCarthy. "A man who belongs to this race must stand up in the high place with gibberish in his mouth and rip out his entrails," he wrote in *Tropic of Cancer*. "And anything that falls short of this frightening spectacle, anything less shuddering, anything less terrifying, less mad, less intoxicated, less contaminating, is not art. The rest is counterfeit. The rest is human. The rest belongs to life and lifelessness" (255).

What I most admire about this novel is that, in a culture that is falling faster than anybody can catch it, it protects and defends my beloved English language, is a repository for language and an exemplum of how to use it to render the wonderful. It feels almost mean to discuss McCarthy's sleight-of-hand when *Blood Meridian* can generate the realest of magic. Selzer once told me that his standard for good fiction, borrowed from *Hamlet*, is that it turns us into "wonder-wounded hearers" (5.1.257). *Blood Meridian* wounds us with wonder as few novels can. We take our wonder where we may. Where the language is exalted, there I make my stand. We should be wary lest we become too querulous with our singers, of whom McCarthy is one of the best, for the danger is always there that they will hear us.

But must we, I wonder, check our *ethos* at the door to fully enjoy McCarthy's *epos*? It is wonderful that McCarthy sees Lester, his killer-necrophiliac, as a child of God like all of us, and dares us toward the same understanding, for we cannot be rightly blamed for who we are. But would McCarthy treat him so kindly if, God forbid, one of his own offspring had joined that gruesome collection? Perhaps this is an unfair question. Lester *is* one of McCarthy's own, and, anyway, part of the purpose of fiction is that we can be better there—certainly more compassionate—than anywhere else. Mc-

Carthy brings us a very wide world, *alive*, in ways that enlighten its darkest moments with staggering beauty. I only question whether at times he might be prankstering at the heavens through the medium of his readers; bleeding hearts for characters scarcely worth the ink; and falling short where even the hardest-working writers can fall short: with respect to his own tremendous potential. There is tension in *Blood Meridian*, but little drama, for drama is the conflict of conduct, and conduct, as Wallace Stegner rightly defines it, is more than merely behavior, it is behavior with a palpable moral dimension to give it shape. Ultimately, this lack of drama separates the work from its companions in the pantheon of great American novels. And yet, unquestionably, it has made its place there. Could it be that what I am saying is that I want Cormac McCarthy to do everything? If I am, it is only because I feel that he is, perhaps, one novelist who can.

10.

Having heard that there was something about McCarthy in *The New York Review of Books*, I drove to the town of Saratoga Springs to pick up a copy. I was parallel parking when a meaty punk kid pulled his van directly behind me, as oblivious to my intention as he was to everything else in the world of reason. There was room for my maneuver, but after awakening to the fact that he was standing behind a car that wanted to park, he fulminated with rage, pounding his horn and shouting for me to stop, calling me every sort of name. He sprung to the passenger window, cursed me, jerked his head back, and spat at me.

He was a few yards away, but his ammunition, flying from window to window, reached its target: my face. During the automotively mobile interview that followed, I addressed him rationally, impressing upon him the fact that he had done me an injustice, insisting that, for all his will to *settle* this affair in a parking lot (he actually called me "bub"), all that had to be settled was in his mind. This made the fellow frantic. "Shut up!" he shouted repeatedly, keeping alongside me down Broadway. "Shut up! Shut up! Shut up!" I, of course, left him, thinking: "You wanted a *Blood Meridian* spit—you found one."

NOTES

1. A hint of the wide divergence on this issue can be gleaned from this exchange with Paulo Faria in August 2009, when Paulo was translating the novel a second time.

Paulo Faria to Peter Josyph

Dear Friend:

Thanks a lot for sending me that book on the Southwest. I have been reading *Doniphan's Expedition* by John Taylor Hughes, one of the books Cormac McCarthy allegedly read before writing *Blood Meridian*. As you surely know, it describes the conquest of New Mexico in the war of 1846. At a certain point in the campaign, General Kearney receives a deputation of Apaches and exhorts them to embrace "peaceful pursuits" and to "desist from all robberies" (68). The venerable Apache sachem replies: "My skin is red, my heart sunburnt, my eyes are dim with age, and I am a poor Indian, a dog, yet I am not guilty. There is no guilt there [putting his hand on his breast]—no! I can look you in the face like a man. In the morning of my days my muscles were strong; my arm was stout; my eye was bright; my mind was clear; but now I am weak, shriveled up with age, yet my heart is big, my tongue is straight. I will take your counsel because I am weak and you are strong" (68). I think the essence and poetry of *Blood Meridian* is contained in this short paragraph, don't you agree? "I will take your counsel because I am weak and you are strong." Meaning: I will die to give way to you, because that is the law of nature, that is the law of the universe. Innocence and guilt don't matter here.

Peter Josyph to Paulo Faria

Dear Paulo:

Re: *Blood Meridian*, I am not so sure that the book, great as it is, has any meaning at all, or that, if it does, the meaning relates in any way to American history.

2. This and all other Selzer quotations are from Richard Selzer's private correspondence with me. For a sampling of his epistolary art, see *Letters to a Best Friend*.

3. One can hear this by listening to *Joseph Campbell on James Joyce: Wings of Art*, Tape 2. It is a nice detail that Campbell is reading from a *Ulysses* that he bought from Sylvia Beach at Shakespeare & Company as a young student in Paris in 1927. Campbell's relish for Joyce is evident in every word, but the lure of reading works of genius aloud, especially those that are brewed for the tongue, sometimes results in diminishing returns in a teaching environment. Campbell's talks on Joyce have this in common with Harold Bloom's talks on Shakespeare. In both cases, the temptation to read aloud becomes increasingly irresistible until, during the last quarter of their respective seminars, these masters of explication are seduced into behaving as if these difficult texts are self-explanatory.

4. Gore Vidal has said that Faulkner's style reminds him of his grandfather's speeches in the Senate. See *Views from a Window*, p. 187.

During the *Suttree* Jubilee in Knoxville, I discussed my reaction to the prose of *Absalom, Absalom!* with the eminent Faulknerean Noah Polk. In an admirable display of patience and fortitude, Noah countered with the offer to read a few pages of it aloud. Although I had already listened to the book in its entirety, the narrator was *not* a man of the South. Someone rustled up a copy for Noah, and that night a few of us were treated to a special kind of music. It did not turn me around about the book, but it left me with the conviction that if I read the novel again, Noah will have to read it to me.

5. McCarthy says of the gang: "Notions of chance and fate are the preoccupations of men engaged in rash undertakings" (153).

· 5 ·

Tragic Ecstasy:
A Conversation with Harold Bloom
about *Blood Meridian*

During the making of a series of documentaries called Acting McCarthy, *I asked Harold Bloom to speak with me on camera about* Blood Meridian, *which Bloom had placed on his Western Canon along with McCarthy's* Child of God *and* Suttree. *He also discusses it in the chapter on* Othello *in his* Shakespeare: The Invention of the Human. *When he agreed to the interview, he said of the novel: "I yield to no one in my admiration for* Blood Meridian. *I think there is no greater work by a living American."*

On the day of our conversation, which took place in Bloom's home in New Haven, Connecticut, on February 6, 2000, I brought Bloom a copy of John Sepich's sourcebook Notes on Blood Meridian. *I also showed him Samuel Chamberlain's* My Confession *in the deluxe edition, published by the Texas State Historical Association, containing color reproductions from the pages of Chamberlain's memoir, including paintings of Judge Holden. Bloom was so delighted with this book that I advised him to keep it. In return, he signed and gave me a bound, uncorrected proof of his soon to be published* How to Read and Why, *in which an entire chapter is devoted to* Blood Meridian. *Bloom has also written about* Blood Meridian *in a chapter on McCarthy in* Novelists and Novels.

The most remarkable characteristic of the interview for me cannot be conveyed on the printed page. This is the quality of thoughtfulness personified. It was audible in his speech, visible in his manner, which enacted the Zen saying: "Stand still, dance inside." Conditions were far from ideal—we had never met before, floodlights were shining into his eyes, he was coming down with a cold, it was late in the day with not much time to spare (dinner partners were waiting for him)—but Bloom was so wholly absorbed in thinking about the novel that it became, in a sense, the ground on which we met, and he made me at home there. I never had the impression of being instructed by a man who had worked out all the answers. Toward the end of My

Confession, *Chamberlain writes: "I was no longer troubled with dreams of Holden"* *(330). I couldn't imagine this would ever be true for Bloom. For him, the issues of the novel remained open, and I felt as if we were probing them together. What Thoreau said about his meeting with the philosopher Henry James reminds me of Bloom. "It was a great pleasure to meet him," Thoreau wrote to Emerson. "It makes humanity seem more erect and respectable.... He is a man, and takes his own way, or stands still in his own place. I know of no one so patient and determined to have the good of you. It is almost friendship, such plain and human dealing" (Norton 1849). Slouched back in a chair with shoeless feet on a stool, his hand moving at times to rub his chest the way that a man might stroke a beard or pinch a brow, Bloom's beautiful Falstaffian face shone with a rare light that was not the result of video equipment.*

JOSYPH: I understand that your first attempt at reading *Blood Meridian* was not entirely successful.

BLOOM: As I say in that little book that I just gave you, I was first given *Blood Meridian* many years ago by Gordon Lish, who is quite mad. Gordon loved it, simply because he loves anything that shows how violent America really is. I read about half of it, and although I was very impressed, I couldn't go on because I started to have nightmares. I began it a second time and *again* I didn't get through it because I started to dread the slaughter too much.[1] But then the third time it all came together. Since then I must have read the book scores of times, and of course I've taught it many times now. But I find my students and some of my friends have much the same reaction. There's a lot of initial resistance, until suddenly it meshes. You see what you might call the aesthetic justification, the rationale, for all that horror. After all, it is, technically speaking, what you might call the only successful holocaust novel. The holocaust is of the Native Americans of the Southwest, but it is certainly a holocaust. When I wrote the section on *Blood Meridian* in *How to Read and Why*, we were learning the full horrors of what the Serb paramilitaries were doing to the Kosovans, and I couldn't help comparing the two. It's hard to take.

Didn't you have that reaction the first time around?

JOSYPH: I was inebriated by the language.

BLOOM: Well, the language intoxicates me also, but the language provides problems. Even though he gets away with it, there is something beautifully precarious about it. The Faulknerian element in the rhetoric, the Melvillean element and the Shakespearean element are always there, and he decides to handle it by just bringing it forwards rather than concealing it. Quite frequently it works remarkably well.

Remember in *Moby-Dick*, where Ishmael and Queequeg have signed on to the *Pequod*, and Elijah, the prophet, accosts them and warns them not to sail on that ship? In the same way, before the initial expedition in *Blood Meridian*, the one headed by Worth, which comes to disaster, the Kid and a companion are warned by a crazy old Mennonite. And the parallelism is almost precise, down to some deliberate verbal echoes. It's McCarthy's own defiance of his indebtedness. And he makes it work.

JOSYPH: In thinking about *All the Pretty Horses*, I asked how McCarthy could get away with sounding so much like Hemingway. The answer was: because he *is*, in a sense, Hemingway.

BLOOM: Yes, yes, there is that element. *All the Pretty Horses* is certainly his second best book. I regret that the other two books in that series, *The Crossing* and *Cities of the Plain*, seem to me interesting failures, but failures.

JOSYPH: I was saddened by *Cities of the Plain*. Similar character doing much the same things, making much the same mistake, but McCarthy just didn't have the energy—he had nowhere to go.

BLOOM: Well, he really burned it out in *The Crossing*, and yet something in him wanted the trilogy.

JOSYPH: Where had you been in your reading of McCarthy when you encountered *Blood Meridian*?

BLOOM: I had read *Suttree* and admired it a lot, though it's *very* Faulknerean. I had read *Child of God* and thought it was pretty good also. I hadn't read *The Orchard Keeper* or some of the others, and I had shied away from *Blood Meridian*. Even before my two attempted readings, I think I tried the first five or six pages and said: "No no—I'm not up to this!"

JOSYPH: Even among McCarthy scholars, *Blood Meridian* has an almost legendary status. You can sense this whenever it's introduced into a paper or a conversation, as if it were more than merely a novel.

BLOOM: Well it *is* more than a novel. It's an attempt, like *Moby-Dick*, like Whitman's *Song of Myself*, like *Huckleberry Finn*, at being the ultimate American saga. And maybe it is. *Blood Meridian* is not only the ultimate American Western. Together with some things of Pynchon—*Mason & Dixon* is an awfully good book—I was very heartened by it—I had been discouraged, because Pynchon had been so marvelous, particularly in *The Crying of Lot 49* and the best parts of *Gravity's Rainbow*, and then came that awful thing... that I even repress the title of...

JOSYPH: *Vineland.*

BLOOM: Yes—I couldn't stand it, I couldn't believe it was by *him*! I even publicly said I didn't think he wrote a sentence of it—you know, some friend of his did it as a contract-breaker or something. What is it? It's pseudo-Kerouac, and Kerouac is pseudo enough by himself, so you don't need an imitation. But *Blood Meridian* is not only the ultimate Western. Even more than Pynchon, or any of the poets who are still alive, like Ashbery... if I had to speak of one work of imaginative literature by a living American, I would have to call it *Blood Meridian*. Once you have done that, you're in trouble. What do you do to match it? None of the other books by McCarthy is at all like it.

JOSYPH: What is it about *Blood Meridian* that's so extraordinary? You said to me over the phone: "It has no weaknesses, only strengths," implying that it succeeds at what it is about. What *is* it trying to do?

BLOOM: What it does, whenever the tension even begins to fall off, is to very skillfully take you away from the center, which is the relentless drive of Glanton and the Judge. The Kid cannot be called the center, his consciousness is too intimate, he fades out too often, quite deliberately. But McCarthy finds ways, much subtler than they seem at first, of giving you side stories. Like Brown going to have his gun fixed, or the extraordinary interlude of the breakup of the Yuma ferry and everything connected with it. There is a surge of narrative propulsiveness and power in the book, and an astonishing charge of language, which, finally, in spite of its clear Faulknerian and Melvillean affinities and sources, goes back beyond Faulkner and Melville to *their* source—particularly Melville's—in Shakespeare. Which is why I think Iago shows up so powerfully in the Judge, and I found, in writing a book about Shakespeare (*Shakespeare: The Invention of the Human*) and writing about *Othello*, that I couldn't really talk about Iago without bringing up the Judge. Not that the Judge is a Machiavel—far from it—but that the Judge is a pyromaniac who wants to set the whole world on fire with warfare and blood.

JOSYPH: And he is, in a sense, immortal, isn't he? It certainly ends that way.

BLOOM: It ends that way. And yet, unless I misread, in that strange, italicized epilogue, there is that man who is traversing the plain, and he's holding a two-handed instrument. I didn't say so in *How to Read*—I was writing, I hoped, for very common readers indeed and I didn't want to overburden them with associations and allusions—but McCarthy, who is profoundly allusive and very erudite, undoubtedly has in mind that great moment in Milton's *Lycidas* when you are told that the corrupt clergy and the whole corruption of England will be cleansed by "that two-handed engine at the door" (105).[2] That two-handed engine, that implement, is being wielded by a figure striking fire that is imprisoned in the stone, which is clearly a Promethean motif. The Judge is off in the meridian sunset. That figure is at dawn. Clearly there is an opposition. There is, I think, a hint—a hint, but a real one—I don't know otherwise how to interpret it—that a kind of new Prometheus or Promethean figure is rising up at the dawn who will move west and perhaps challenge the Judge, although we do not actually know that. That would be the only thing that might keep the Judge from being immortal.

Certainly the Judge is immortal in the normal sense of age. The Kid— who *was* just a kid, a teenager, when he joined the Glanton gang—is at least forty-five when he is murdered by the Judge. What ages the Judge? Nearly thirty years have gone by and the Kid is now in full middle age. The Judge would have to be seventy-five or eighty years old, but he looks exactly the way he always looked, and clearly he has the power and endurance that he's always had, that terrifying strength. There's that *horrible* implication, which is very hard to evade and has got to be taken as deeply hinted, that the Judge, who opens those great arms to embrace the Kid, violates him and then smothers him in the muck. That is the way the murder is done, a ghastly moment in its implications. But since the Kid is pretty tough himself, it would take pre-ternatural strength—really, inhuman strength—to accomplish that.

JOSYPH: What is it that he wants from the Kid, and does he get it?

BLOOM: This is an *ex post facto* explanation on his part, but he *says* that he's looking for a son. His relationship with the Indian seems to parody the relationship that he wanted with the Kid. But the Kid, from the start, evades him. The Kid is, of course, remarkably disengaged from his own father at the beginning of the book, and seems to have a sure sense that he wants to stay as far away from the Judge as possible. I suppose the Judge wants discipleship, with everything that might be involved in that.

There is a very powerful but, in the end, I think misleading interpreta-tion of *Blood Meridian* by a very fine fellow named Leo Daugherty,[3] that the whole thing is to be read in terms of Gnosticism, with the Judge as one of the archons, one of the evil demiurges ruling this world. In a very great pas-sage, which may be a dream vision, when the Kid is in jail, McCarthy warns you not to use *any* system, including the Orphic system, for interpreting the Judge. Don't try to reduce the Judge to his origins. Don't try to make this a Gnostic fable. Don't try to see the Judge as the hierophant or the priest or even the demiurge of some heterodox vision. I think he's right. I think it would lessen the imaginative force of the book if you could so reduce the Judge. The Judge has no ideology except blood, violence, war for its own sake. And that is what makes him so astonishing a figure, so frightening and foreboding.

I think of the Judge all the time, you know, when I read about some Aryan Nation gang armed to the teeth out of the Dakotas or Montana, or the blowing up of a federal building, or some nuts, fully armed, breaking into a school and opening fire. The United States has two special characteristics, I think, from 1800 to 2000, two full centuries now. It is both gun-crazy and God-crazy. The American religion is all mixed up with guns. In that sense the Judge can be called the high priest of one version of American religion.[4]

JOSYPH: He's an awfully good justifier, isn't he?

BLOOM: He is an astonishing rhetorician, the ablest in all of American literature. You would have to go to Shakespeare, to someone like Ulysses in *Troilus and Cressida*, to find someone who is a better sophist than the Judge. Or you have to go to Iago. It's that astonishing a gift. And there *is* something Shakespearean, at times, about the Judge. Some of my friends, some of my students, resent that in the Judge. They feel that he is *too* wordy. But of course McCarthy very subtly accommodates that by having the expriest, or Toadvine, or other characters like Brown, simply say: "Holden, you're crazy," or: "Why do you go on like this?"

JOSYPH: Or they spit.

BLOOM: They spit. And yet they are spellbound. They go on listening to him, as I think any sensitive, alert reader is mesmerized also.

After all, what are the great things in the book? The landscape, which is more astonishing, perhaps, than the landscape in anything *except* Shakespeare. It's a controlled landscape which goes beyond, say, what you'd find in the high Romantic poets, it's that astonishingly done. Better than Faulkner. Maybe not better than Darl Bundren's visions of the landscape in *As I Lay Dying*—and it is somewhat indebted, I think, to Darl Bundren's visions—but that much landscape, and that astonishingly beautiful, as well as menacing. There is that, and the Judge's rhetoric. And the whole sort of sublime mad trajectory of the book. And, finally, that great dialogue in the bar, if you can call it a dialogue, because the Judge is doing almost all the talking. But what the Kid has to say, even though it's laconic, is *immensely* forceful, down to the final: "You aint nothin," and the Judge says: "You speak truer than you know" (331).

JOSYPH: You mentioned earlier that the Kid disappears from the narrative intentionally. There's almost a sleight-of-hand in the book.

BLOOM: Yes.

JOSYPH: Here's a boy who's part of a gang in which, as with *any* gang, if you don't participate the way that *they* do—

BLOOM: You don't last.

JOSYPH: You don't last.

BLOOM: You don't last.

JOSYPH: By implication, he's guilty.

BLOOM: O he *is* guilty. On the other hand, how subtle McCarthy is about that. I cannot recall any place in the book where the Kid actually slaughters anyone. He always fires, as it were, in self-defense, or simultaneously with someone else firing or making a menacing movement with a knife. I think he is dropped out because McCarthy doesn't want to show you what is developing in him. But he finally does show it when the Kid desperately tries to come to the aid of the Indian woman who is already dead. Very striking moment in the book, which indicates that an enormous change has taken place.

JOSYPH: Let me give you a counter-example. In *Lonesome Dove*—

BLOOM: This is, after all—let's face it—to compare a minor Western with the greatest instance of a Western that could be imagined, but go on.

JOSYPH: The two ex-Texas rangers have discovered that a partner of theirs, from the old days of rangering together, is riding with real killers.

BLOOM: Sure, sure.

JOSYPH: They've stolen horses and done a *Blood Meridian* deed of burning some farmers—

BLOOM: Yes, okay.

JOSYPH:—and so the two friends track him down and string the guy up. Just before they do it, they say: "Ride with an outlaw, die with him" (572). It seems as if at some point in *Blood Meridian*, McCarthy really wants you to be *softer* than *Lonesome Dove*: he needs you to *forgive* the Kid for what he's done. Otherwise, he's got nobody to go up against the Judge.

BLOOM: He does have, I repeat, that mysterious figure at the end, who evidently is being prepared to go up against the Judge. But it's quite true. Although the expriest is willing to argue with the Judge, there is only the Kid.

Of course the Kid is handled strangely. He is hardly allowed a personality at all. He finally shows, in his laconic way, considerable moral force and courage in the last confrontation with the Judge in the bar, and we can begin to intuit that a personality has been developing there. But McCarthy does not want us to identify with him. And while it's always a terrible shock to realize how badly he dies, one is, in a sense, insulated from that. It's not as though we feel Huck Finn has been raped. We don't love the Kid. We don't really empathize with the Kid. I think we admire him, finally, but only toward the close. And of course we have the mystery—which is not fully explained by McCarthy, and which is worth a lot of cogitation—I'm not sure one will ever solve it—the mystery of what it is, finally, that the Kid means to the Judge. He clearly means more to the Judge than he does to the reader. But the Judge is not able to fully articulate it, though he does say to the Kid: "Was it always your idea that if you did not speak you would not be recognized?" (328). Which implies that the Judge *has* recognized him as someone who matters, someone who is implicit, although we do not know what the burden of that implicitness is.

JOSYPH: There's that line in the film *Hud*, where Hud says to the girl who he's failed to seduce and who he's even failed to force: "I'll remember you, honey—you're the one that got away." I get the sense, not so much that the Kid is resisting the Judge's approach to the world, but that the Judge is saying: "You're the same as I am but you don't want to acknowledge it, you want to *pretend* to be different."

BLOOM: Maybe, maybe, but it's fascinating that we're both omitting what probably is most unforgivable in the Kid as far as the Judge is concerned. The Kid has an excellent chance to find out whether the Judge is mortal. The Judge passes three times, I believe, in front of the Kid, buck naked and unarmed. The Kid is an excellent shot. The Kid presumably could have dispatched him and would ultimately have saved his own life had he done so. He's been urged by his sidekick to do it. *He will not do it.*

Now, why he will not do it we have to surmise, and again surmise is almost endless. I think it ranges from scruple at killing a naked, unarmed man, all the way to a kind of spiritual fear that maybe you can pump bullets into the Judge and it won't touch him at all, he is so uncanny. But we don't know that. This is mere surmise on my part or any reader's. I think the Judge bears out what you're saying, but I think he transcends it. It is, as it were, a demoniac form of a temptation of Christ. Not that Christ is involved in any way in this book. But the Judge does pass back and forth, offering a temptation to the Kid, and he cannot forgive the Kid for not having taken it up.

JOSYPH: It's almost as if, by not shooting him, the Kid has disproved him. The Kid knew that if he shot the Judge, the Judge would then be right, because the Judge is saying: "That's what we all are, that's what we're made of."

BLOOM: I can grant that and not argue with it, but it's larger than that, I think. There are transcendental elements in it also. The great thing about the book is that, even though McCarthy deliberately cuts off any traditional explanations of a negative transcendence, such as a Gnostic explanation or a Manichean explanation or an Orphic explanation, still, the intimations reverberate; still, there is the extraordinary sense that the Judge is not just preternatural. There is something Homeric about the book after all. There is also something which reminds one of *Jason and the Argonauts*, though in a terrifying, negative sense.

It is an old tradition in Homeric romance, or Hellenistic romance following Homer, that these mortal questers will have a concealed god in their midst, a Hercules figure, someone who is at least half mortal, half immortal. That these heroes in *Blood Meridian* are thugs, bestial murderers, doesn't make them different from epic heroes throughout history. As Shakespeare demonstrates so well in *Troilus and Cressida*, the heroes among both the Acheans and the Trojans are commonplace criminals. But to introduce a divinity among them is an old stroke.

McCarthy's originality is, I think, more a question of temperament, ever, than it is of material. Though I haven't yet read the original text of the

Chamberlain—I will now, now that you've been kind enough to give it to me—I *have* read accounts of it. It is very Shakespearean on McCarthy's part to have taken his plot from a source. Shakespeare had every possible literary gift except one: he couldn't make up a plot. In the two plays for which he has no sources whatsoever—*The Tempest* and *The Merry Wives of Windsor*—nothing happens. They are plotless, as it were. Shakespeare had no interest in making up plots. I suspect that in all of McCarthy's novels except *Blood Meridian*, what most gets in the way is the plot. Even in *Suttree*, or *All the Pretty Horses*, one feels that not enough happens, that too much is somehow contrived. One doesn't feel that in *Blood Meridian*, but that's because history has given him the main line of his narrative and has, indeed, given him his characters. Only the Kid is really his invention, and he doesn't allow the Kid to be a full-scale invention, though his elaboration of Holden is so baroque, so extraordinary, that it transcends any possible source.

JOSYPH: In Chamberlain there isn't much of Holden. You'll also see that Chamberlain's a mediocre writer.

BLOOM: He wasn't a mediocre person, though. He led a rather extraordinary life.

JOSYPH: I want to ask you about the relation between the novel and the history of the West in this country. You mentioned the epilogue, which has always bothered me. It's been interpreted as a process of digging holes, of setting dynamite to build a fence: the closing in of the West.

BLOOM: No, no, no, that's a very bad interpretation. That two-handed implement is, as I say, doing one thing and one thing only: it is striking fire which has been put into the rock, clearly a Promethean motif, and he is clearly contrasted with creatures who are either goulish human beings, if they *are* human beings, or already are, in fact, shades, looking for bones for whatever nourishment that might bring about. The contrast between striking fire and looking for bones is extraordinary. And I cannot see that as any kind of allegory of anything that has happened to the American West.

Allegory is always a mode of irony. They are really two words for the same thing. Any great literary work has a certain intensity of irony in it, but the mode of irony in *Blood Meridian* is almost purely rhetorical. The irony is always a question of the deliberate disproportion between the extraordinary language and the carnage.

JOSYPH: I don't see *Blood Meridian* as being about any West that ever existed in the American past.

BLOOM: O no no, no no no no—

JOSYPH: It has as much to do with the West as *Apocalypse Now* has to do with Viet Nam. It's a vision—

BLOOM: It transcends. Whatever the holocaust that was visited on the Native Americans—and it was horrible, the decimation not just of *a* people but *several* peoples—one rather doubts that the particular nightmares that are being rendered so vividly by McCarthy are anything but his own nightmares. It is a very individualized mode of perceiving carnage. It depends upon grotesquerie. It depends upon distancing. In order for the reader to stand it, it has to be stylized to the most extraordinary degree. The entire book is a stylization.

I'll be very interested in looking at that book on the sources (*Notes on Blood Meridian*), but already, sight unseen, it reminds me of the *endless* collection of books—encyclopedias—on the sources of Shakespeare's plays, which are *terribly* self-defeating documents from any civilized, humane, literary point of view. You read these *amazing* accounts of sources, and you finally say: "This has to stop." Because the sources, say, of *King Lear*, or *Hamlet*, or *Othello*, are almost infinite. They never stop. You *can't* stop them. Shakespeare had the mind of a cormorant.

JOSYPH: Someone went so far as to tell me: "I found the source of the bear in *Blood Meridian*! I found it in Hawthorne!" I said: "Are you forgetting that McCarthy's a *writer*? That's what writers do—they *imagine* things. Can't there be *another* bear?" They need, somehow, to diminish imagination, to reduce it to something else. Why are people so uncomfortable with admitting—

BLOOM: The sublime. Shelley, who is a very wise literary critic in his way, defined the literary sublime as that which persuades the reader to give up easier pleasures in order to absorb more difficult pleasures. That is what *Blood Meridian* does. Like *Moby-Dick*, or *As I Lay Dying*, it's a work of transcendental and very difficult pleasures indeed. And it *tries* to make them as difficult as possible. The difficulty of the book is not just the carnage, it's not just the baroque language. The difficulty is the total conception of the book. It finally conceives of itself mystically.

For me, in some ways, the most important passage in it is not actually written by McCarthy, it's the great epigraph by Jacob Boehme, a passage from *Six Theosophic Points* that I can see he's altered slightly but decisively.[5] I know Boehme very well. As an old Blakean, I would have to know Boehme very well. I find him a fascinating writer anyway. But the attribution of what Boehme calls the *Ungrund*, a kind of negativity that is the basis of all our existence, that darkness that is the necessary companion to the light, is simultaneously affirmed and yet dialectically denied by Boehme. And that is very much the transcendental scheme, as it were, of *Blood Meridian*. To affirm the darkness, to affirm the horror, but ultimately to transcend it and to suggest that, even though we are alienated from it and cannot get to it, there is the final parable of man striking fire from the rock and whatever that intimates. The aesthetic achievement of the book is to bring about a negative transcendence, and that is quite Shakespearean.

It's not individual tragedy as it would be in Shakespeare. McCarthy is not of *that* eminence. I don't think he could realize an individual tragedy like Hamlet's, or Macbeth's, or Lear's, or even Iago's. And Holden is in no way a tragic figure. But the book, somehow, achieves a kind of tragic ecstasy. Very difficult to describe except in purely aesthetic terms.

JOSYPH: That quotation from Boehme helps to answer the question: "Why is the novel so enjoyable?" If you are *of* the darkness, everything is reversed, so there's a tremendous exuberance in the book.

BLOOM: Exuberance is clearly a key word there. There is a terrifying method of exuberance to the book. Finally, I suppose, it has to be regarded as some mode of mysticism, as Boehme is a mode of mysticism.

JOSYPH: You mentioned Blake. Blake said that Milton wrote best about the Devil.

BLOOM: Yes. Shelley also said, magnificently: "Satan owes everything to Milton." And Judge Holden owes everything to Cormac McCarthy. Not that Holden is a Satan. That's too simple, too reductive.

JOSYPH: I want to read you a passage from Simone Weil.

BLOOM: I have mixed feelings about her, but go on.

JOSYPH: She wrote this in 1940 about the *Iliad* in a pamphlet—

BLOOM: Yes, *The Poem of Force*. It's a remarkable essay. She has the insight that Achilles more than kills, he murders precisely as an attempt to eradicate death, almost as though he would destroy death by inflicting so much of it. It's a very strange piece of work.

JOSYPH: Let me ask you if you hear anything about *Blood Meridian* in these few sentences. "Since other people do not impose on their movement that halt, that interval of hesitation, wherein lies all our consideration for our brothers in humanity, they can conclude that destiny has given complete license to them, and none at all to their inferiors. And at this point they exceed the measure of force that is at their disposal."

BLOOM: Yes.

JOSYPH: "And now we see them committed irretrievably to chance."

BLOOM: Yes.

JOSYPH: "Suddenly things cease to obey them. Sometimes chance is kind to them, sometimes cruel. But in any case there they are, exposed, open to misfortune" (14, 15).

BLOOM: What that could be applied to is, I think, the greatest single moment in the novel, perhaps transcending even the encounter between the

Judge and the Kid at the end. It's that marvelous moment when they come riding into the Mexican town that first sent them out, and they've gone mad already and they're bringing with them the scalps of Mexican villagers. When they ride out, within a couple of days there's a price on Glanton's head and so on. But as they set themselves toward the west, their horses are described as "tragic mounts," and they themselves are described as "infatuate and half fond," *fond* in the Elizabethan sense of mad (185). The meridian is invoked quite explicitly, and you get a great phrase about "the distant pandemonium of the sun" toward which they are moving (185). That moment is very close to the moment that you've just quoted from Simone Weil. Interestingly enough, she herself goes on to say that although it holds for the others in the *Iliad*, it doesn't hold for Achilles. For him it is never chance. For him it is design. And I suppose I would not put it beyond the ironic powers in this astonishing book that the Judge throws a terrible light back upon Achilles, although the Judge is, of course, a negative theologian of violence.

I guess he is a prophet, really, whether one likes the phrase or not. And it transcends the American West. I think of that great subtitle: *or The Evening Redness in the West*, which means the sunset, but it doesn't just mean the Western United States, it is also a kind of elegiac look at Western consciousness, as the other epigraph, from Paul Valéry, enacts when he's talking about the self-destruction of European consciousness, the decline of the West, although he doesn't use exactly that phrase. Of course it is most deeply true. Even though we live in a relatively protected environment, for which *something* be thanked, we cannot pick up the *New York Times* without reading about the latest Hutu-Tutsi massacres, or the Serbs on another berserk lunge, or something ghastly happening in Afghanistan, or the horror that the Russians are slaughtering man, woman, and child. No one is going to prove Judge Holden wrong. The entire chain of human history from the beginning to now is a confirmation of the Judge.

JOSYPH: I get the same feeling from you that I got from my professor of Blake, Professor Leonard Dean. Although Dean had taught him for years, Blake was still troubling him: it hadn't resolved. When I spoke to him years later, he was in the same condition: Blake was still completely alive for him, still disturbing him.

BLOOM: I will probably teach *Blood Meridian* another half dozen times or so. In the rest of my career I don't think I will come to the end of it. I *would* like one conversation with McCarthy, though I am sure he will always keep a good distance away from me. One would want something to help solve the mystery of why this astonishment was possible for him only that once. He is a great puzzle, I think, aesthetically, because *Suttree* was a marvelous book, though so close, at times, to *Absalom, Absalom!* as to be almost embarrassing. It is true that there is a whole series of major American novelists who have only the one great book. There are very few who have more, like Henry James, or Faulkner, who had one great phase which lasted ten years, during which the five really top books were written. James is able to go on for thirty-five years and there are masterpieces at every point.

JOSYPH: But you would rank *Blood Meridian* very high?

BLOOM: I repeat: we have remarkable living American writers of narrative fiction. I've mentioned Pynchon. Philip Roth is a close personal friend, but aside from that, in the last ten years he has written eight astonishing books, the very best of them, *Sabbath's Theatre* and *American Pastoral*, almost unmatchable. And there is Don DeLillo's one great book, *Underworld*. As marvelous as those three are—Pynchon, DeLillo, Roth—they don't match *Blood Meridian*. I keep trying to get Philip Roth to read *Blood Meridian*. He won't do it. He takes a glance at it and says it's not for him.

Remember, I'm talking about *living* figures. William Faulkner is dead. If I had to vote for *one* work of prose fiction by an American in this entire century that just ended, it would have to be *As I Lay Dying*. In this course called How to Read and Why, which I probably won't teach any more now that the book is coming out, I have always taught *Blood Meridian* at the end of a sequence that starts with *As I Lay Dying*, goes on to Nathanael West's *Miss Lonelyhearts*, then to Pynchon's *The Crying of Lot 49*, and culminates with *Blood Meridian*. Not that they are in any way equivalent, but because of the negativity that is involved in the four works, the essential darkness of the vision. There was a time I would have thrown in Flannery O'Connor's *The Violent Bear It Away*. In one of her letters, O'Connor says that the two American novels in her century that she most cares for are *As I Lay Dying* and *Miss Lonelyhearts*. I suspect that had she lived to read *Blood Meridian* she would have been very impressed indeed.

JOSYPH: What would Shakespeare have said about *Blood Meridian*?

BLOOM: *(Laughing)* He might say: "I wrote that in *Titus Andronicus*." He'd be wrong. But no, I think he'd be too shrewd to say that.

It's not like any particular Shakespearean work. The book has its landscape. The book has its language. The book has its aestheticized violence. What the book primarily has is the Judge. One cannot get away from the Judge. The difference between this book and everything else by McCarthy, or everything else by anybody still alive in the United States, is the Judge. It's the Judge who, finally, can't be absorbed. You can understand absolutely everything he says. You can memorize everything he says, as I practically *have* by now. But his ability to frighten you, to shock you, to turn you inside out and to simultaneously fascinate you and horrify you, never ceases. In that sense, he is the real bedrock of McCarthy's genius. How he was possible for McCarthy, I don't know.

JOSYPH: Is *Blood Meridian* filmable?

BLOOM: I am sure that if Mr. Tommy Lee Jones wants to, he will make a film of it.[6] I wish he wouldn't. I certainly won't go to see it. Do you remember John Huston—who was, after all, a terrific film director—do you remember his ghastly *Moby-Dick*? It was bad enough that he had the impossible Gregory Peck as Ahab, which was terrible miscasting, but he had a beautifully sensitive Ishmael in Richard Basehart, and he had an amazing Father Mapple in Orson Welles, and he had a very good Queequeg, whoever that actor was—[7]

JOSYPH: Welles, by the way, was terrified of delivering that speech—afraid he'd forget it, or he wouldn't do it well—but then he did it in one take.

BLOOM: He does it very beautifully, with an extraordinary Shakespearean music. But then, it's a very Shakespearean speech. But think of the disaster of that film!

Besides, there is the other problem. You can see a lot of stylized violence in different Hollywood epics, but if you really tried to convey the precise quality that McCarthy is getting through to you, I don't think spectators could take it. I think you'd start having defensive laughter. It's beyond one's capacity to absorb visually.

JOSYPH: That Comanche raid—you need to imagine it, not see it.

BLOOM: Yes, that's of course one of the most astonishing things in the book. The *amazing* historical anthology of garments they are wearing and the weapons they are using. They're out of Blake, really. They are a visionary procession. They can't be regarded naturalistically.

There is the heart of it. Here is a book in which everything that counts most is, in a sense, preternatural. Even if you could bring Sam Peckinpah back from the dead and make him permanently drunk, you wouldn't have a director who could manage it.

NOTES

1. When I discussed *Blood Meridian* with Ted Tally, he said: "I had trouble finishing that book, just because of the sheer relentless realism of it. 'O ho hum, another slaughter of another village of innocents,' you know?" Coming from a writer whose Oscar-winning screenplay, *The Silence of the Lambs*, concerned a cannibal who helps a female FBI agent to capture a killer who makes women into dresses, Tally's remarks testify to the power of *Blood Meridian* to disturb even the unsqueamish reader.

2. Concerning the line "But that two-handed engine at the door/Stands ready to smite once, and smite no more," Roy Flannagan, editor of *The Riverside Milton*, says: "No scholar has been able to determine exactly what the 'two-handed engine' is. The image has become perhaps the most famous crux in English literature. The best-informed guesses are that the engine may be some sort of weapon, such as the 'huge two-handed sway' of Michael's sword in *Paradise Lost*" (105).

3. See "Gravers False and True: *Blood Meridian* As Gnostic Tragedy," by Leo Daugherty.

4. In conversation with Brian Lamb on C-SPAN's *Booknotes*, September 3, 2000, Bloom made the same application of the Judge but with a rhetorical difference that gave it a different force. After saying that the novel carried a "deep, implicit warning for current American society," Bloom confirmed that the Judge has, indeed, never died. "He is responsible for those horrible posses we have out there in Idaho. He is responsible for those people who blew up the Federal Building. He is responsible for these mad people who break into schools and shoot children. We are a country that has had a kind of perpetual ongoing religious revival since the year 1800, and, simultaneously, we have been completely gun crazy for the last two centuries. And, in some sense, that's what McCarthy's great book is about."

5. As it appears in *Blood Meridian*, the quotation from Jacob Boehme is: "It is not to be thought that the life of darkness is sunk in misery and lost as if in sorrowing. There is no sorrowing. For sorrow is a thing that is swallowed up in death, and death and dying are the very life of the darkness."

6. At the time of the interview, actor-director Tommy Lee Jones was in the pre-production stages of filming the novel. Bloom's regard for Shakespeare showed its fervor when I asked him about casting *Blood Meridian*.

BLOOM: Presumably Mr. Jones intends to be the Judge.

JOSYPH: Maybe Glanton.

BLOOM: Glanton. Well, maybe he is planning to take the horrible John Malkovich and make *him* into the Judge. That would be typecasting, I suppose. I must say I loathe Malkovich. He is a good actor, but he was recently quoted in the *New York Times* as saying: "What's all this fuss about Shakespeare? Thornton Wilder's *Our Town* and Tennessee Williams' *The Glass Menagerie* are as good as anything Shakespeare ever wrote." Poor poor man. If he really does believe that *Our Town* and *The Glass Menagerie* are on the level of *Anthony and Cleopatra*, *Lear*, and *Twelfth Night*, poor fellow, poor fellow—he is sadly lacking in education.

7. In the film *Moby-Dick*, Queequeg is played by Count Friedrich von Ledebur, an Austrian aristocrat who was a friend of John Huston. In the photographer Cecil Beaton's diary, in which he calls Ledebur a "great gentleman... wise and understanding and forgiving..." (76), one finds him not on the *Pequod* with Ishmael and Ahab, but on a yacht called the *Siëta* cruising the Greek islands with a party that includes the Baroness Cécile de Rothschild and Greta Garbo.

· 6 ·

Blood Bath: A Conversation with Rick Wallach about *Blood Meridian*

Since discovering Cormac McCarthy in 1992, Rick Wallach has been one of the foremost promoters of his work. He has written extensively about McCarthy; he edited Myth, Legend, Dust: Critical Responses to Cormac McCarthy, *and with Wade Hall he co-edited two editions of* Sacred Violence: A Reader's Companion to Cormac McCarthy. *He co-founded the Cormac McCarthy Society, organized its first conference, and has played major roles in most of its subsequent conferences here and abroad. He has also been a vitalizing force on the forum of the Society's website. The following conversation took place in a bathroom of the Menger Hotel in San Antonio, Texas, in 1999 when it was thought that Tommy Lee Jones was going to film* Blood Meridian. *For a reason I can no longer fathom, I asked Rick to speak to me, on camera, while immersed in a bubble bath. The talk exemplifies the eloquence with which he has spoken about McCarthy on many occasions both public and private. I have augmented our initial conversation with additional exchanges, which I have incorporated into the body of the text.*

JOSYPH: What is the Blood Meridian?

WALLACH: I think Blood Meridian is an oblique reference to the 96th parallel, which Frederick Jackson Turner defined as the boundary of the horizon of the West. Beyond that, the laws and regulations of civilized America didn't apply. When the rougher and readier among us went out and carved the malleable proto-matter of the new civilization from the wilderness, the 96th meridian followed them westward, so to speak. About the time the book is set, that meridian would run mighty close by Nagadoches, which is where the Kid meets the Judge for the first time. It is also, I think, the psychic limit of civilization, the point past which human fealty to the repressive mechanisms of the civilized psyche begins to disintegrate and give way to the unbounded gratification of the libido.

JOSYPH: Why is *Blood Meridian* important?

WALLACH: I don't know that it *is* important, really. We probably *lend* it importance because we want to believe in a point beyond which we still have license to succumb to our unconscious natures. We want there to *be* a point at which the repressive mechanisms—which hurt, after all—could be lifted, and we could give unbounded expression to our quest for gratification. I think *Blood Meridian* is a massive edifice of wish-fulfillment, a sort of memory palace where all of our unmet drives are stacked up before us in highly baroque fashion. It is, if you will, a cheat in some ways. We can observe our own bestial natures with the security of deluding ourselves that they've been posed for us like artifacts. I think that's the general attraction of artifacts of violence in our culture: a way of contemplating our own violent selves in the hope that the time spent in contemplating them will be deducted from the time spent indulging them.

JOSYPH: What is the relationship between *Blood Meridian* and *My Confession?*

WALLACH: The relationship between the diary of Samuel Chamberlain, or the concoction of Samuel Chamberlain—it depends on how accurate you think Chamberlain was, and especially whether you think Holden ever existed—is the same relationship, say, as between an extremely successful primitive organism and its highly evolved descendant many generations later, but a descendant that evolves to fill an ecological niche which itself is fragile and subject to massive and rapid alteration by environmental considerations that would destroy even such a specialized organism. I think that what happens in *Blood Meridian* is that all of the possibilities, all of the lessons, all of the exempla from *My Confession* that were posed in order to shock and titillate, are re-presented in highly expanded and interrogated form. They are opened out—pried open—by language, and all of their possibilities, implications, and ramifications are examined and set in language, that language being a semi-archaic language that only works within its own context. *Blood Meridian* was an anachronism even at the moment it was written, and we can enjoy it as an anachronism the way we enjoy seeing an artifact in a museum. It's livelier, of course, because the language is so gorgeous, but it's an archaic language. It jars against everything that the *New Yorker*, Gordon Lish, bare-is-better school of language—which is the dominant school in our culture since Hemingway— would recommend. So, *Blood Meridian* was evolved for a cultural niche which had already been transformed by environmental considerations, like some prehistoric creature in a B-movie that is preserved on an island and then destroyed by a volcanic eruption as the heroes escape in a small boat.[1]

(Reaching for the faucet) I want to avert a catastrophe. Let me run the water for a second.

JOSYPH: Is there a believable relation between Glanton and Holden in the Chamberlain diaries and those characters as they appear in *Blood Meridian*?

WALLACH: Even though the actual story of his life is lost in speculation, Glanton was constructed out of a good deal of historical material—newspaper articles, firsthand accounts, witnesses, etcetera—and so you can think of him as closer to an actual figure in Chamberlain. For Holden there are no references other than Holden—I mean, Chamberlain.[2]

JOSYPH: How does the Kid function in the book for the reader?

WALLACH: The Kid in the book is such an inarticulate figure that he's practically nothing more than a tripod. He carries the narrator's eye with him and only minimally interferes with the working of that eye. That's part of the genius of the book, and it's one of the reasons why McCarthy comes in for so much criticism, because the position of his narrative eye is so unskewered by a legitimate personality coming from that perspective, that one equates the voice of the narrator with the voice of McCarthy. It's an extremely unsophisticated way to read, but popular ways of reading permeate our criticism, and we are mistaken if we think that our criticism is immune from being colored by our popular sensibilities. As you know, my position is that a book gives away nothing about an author, except, perhaps, that he's an adequate or better than adequate craftsman—or not. I never read a novel to see what an author believes, and, frankly, I couldn't care less. The novel, for me, is a blueprint, a way to construct the bare bones of the edifice, but I'll paint it with my own colors, tile it with my own tiles, lay down my own carpeting, and hang my own art and bric-a-brac on the walls.

JOSYPH: Does *Blood Meridian* have cinematic potential?

WALLACH: *Blood Meridian* is *spectacularly* visual. Descriptive passages probably occupy forty or fifty percent of its total bulk. If you were to weigh up, as Judge Holden is weighed up on the stock scales at Chihuahua, the nouns and the adjectives on the one hand and the verbs on the other, the verbs would be outweighed by three or four to one. There is far greater economy of verb usage than of adjectival or substantive usage. The diagesis functions almost like a filmstrip that passes these vignettes before our eyes so that we *see* motion when in fact there may be none. It's meant to be a series of still scenes seen in sequence, much the way a filmstrip operates. That, too, is part of the charm of the subheadings at the beginning of each chapter. They are meant to enhance the impression that the entire text is a sequence of frozen vignettes that, when passed before our eyes—like one of those flipbook flicks we used to make when we were kids—the illusion of forward movement occurs. I think that's why so many of the predereates are *they rode on*. They are a kind of ligamentary coda of forward movement to offset the stasis of the descriptive passages. That the movement here is so smooth and seamless is, of course, a function of the superb cadences in the narrative. I think the emphasis on the visual, the *seen*, is part of what gives the book its cinematic force. Which, incidentally, is ironic considering how many critics have described the language of *Blood Meridian* as neo-Biblical, when the Biblical abjuration is to *speak* the world into being, to *talk* it into existence, and *Blood Meridian* is so visual by contrast.

JOSYPH: What is the potential in the book for drama? It's not a travelogue. Can it be done?

WALLACH: O I don't think the book can be filmed. I think you can make a film called *Blood Meridian*, and I think you can make the diagesis—the action, the storyline, the sequence of episodes—you can film those, but I don't think you could ever film the book. I think when people go to see the film of a book, that's what they think they're going to see, and they're not going to see anything like it. It's so difficult to replicate the references and effects of language in the cinema. It *is* a different language. The closest I've seen to it, and I think this was probably more by coincidence than design, was the doubling of the scenes of the factory smokestacks and the woods in *The Gardener's Son*: the reflections of the woods and the smokestacks in the water as a visual replication of McCarthy's synchronic referential system of doubling and doubling and doubling up his metaphors and symbols.

There are great episodes and stories in *Blood Meridian*. You can film those. But a film would benefit greatly by avoiding attempts to simulate language effects in the book. Music can, perhaps, provide cadences in place of that ligamentary prederate that I mentioned. But there is a fairly consistent tone in much of *Blood Meridian*, and you can't have too much of that because you're going to be depending on real-time chronometry to present the impression of action in the film, and not the ruminations of the imagination which can be spurred by the turn of a phrase.

JOSYPH: How would the Kid function in a film, given that he's essentially inarticulate?

WALLACH: You could make the Kid articulate, take a third person perspective, bring the lens back, and the Kid becomes a figure among other figures. If this happens there are two possibilities. You could make the Kid sympathetic and make his survival the emotional fulcrum of the film, or you could make him so *un*sympathetic that our desire for his destruction becomes the emotional fulcrum. Or, you can do something radical and pose the camera from his point of view—try to place the lens inside the empty consciousness of the Kid and dispense with the Kid as a physical figure. I would *not* try to film the Kid as he seems to be in the book. I would let cinematic considerations dictate his personality.

JOSYPH: How would you make Glanton bearable—or wouldn't you? You would at least need to make him possible. In *My Confession* there's the suggestion that Glanton is an unhappy and vengeful man because of what happened to his wife.

WALLACH: It would be easy to say that Glanton was either consumed by revenge—because one story says that his family was murdered by Indians—or that he simply came uncottered upstairs and was a suggestible psychotic being manipulated by the very canny Holden. Every screenwriter, every director, has his own reading and he will write and film for that reading. Out of all the characters in *Blood Meridian*, Glanton is the easiest to caricature. How do you direct a performer to represent Glanton—how do you *display* him? I don't know. I just hope that they won't default to the psychotic interpretation. Glanton is an unfortunate cultural product of an unfortunate juncture in history. Oversimplifying him would make it difficult for that character to resonate into our present political circumstances, where the kind of virulent racism that Glanton represents is *far* from gone, despite the utopian suggestion, for example, of anti-setasides and anti-affirmative action types who would like us to believe that we now live in a colorblind society and prosthetic attempts to remedy that incipient racism are now anachronistic. For me, it would play as an extraordinarily lazy piece of screenwriting, a shrinking back from opportunities for complexity, for representing the ways in which different motivations intersect in us, and to flesh out the matter of spiritual tragedy. It would make it too easy for an audience to read Glanton as a puppet animated by vengeance. Vengeance has a way of cleansing other moral considerations from the scene. "O well, they killed his wife—they deserved what they got." It's the excuse that we use to justify the monstrousness of Hiroshima and Nagasaki: "They had it coming." I wouldn't want to see our reflexes to think in that perilous and morally abdicative way reinforced by a film of one of my favorite books.

JOSYPH: *Blood Meridian* appeared in 1985. Akira Kurosawa died in 1998. You had a decade to visit Kurosawa-san and bring him a copy of the novel with a translator to read it to him. What do you think he would have done with it if he had tackled it?

WALLACH: He would have made a samurai epic that would have dwarfed *Ran*. And he might have gone after the fascistic jingoism that carried the militarists to power in Japan and brought us all to Hiroshima eventually—the even darker side, if you will, of Kurosawa's *No Regrets for Our Youth*. The Judge's rhetoric works quite well for that purpose. I suspect that Kurosawa might have used the 17th century massacre of Japanese Christians by the rising shogunate as the backstory, and depicted Glanton and his gang as a bunch of mercenary samurai hired to slaughter Christians. He might, for example, have used the "Christian Masada," Shimabara Castle in western Kyushu, in place of Lincoln's Ferry. With the Judge he would have had a field day—

found some especially hulking Sumo to play the part and given him a face like a *netsuke* or a forest sprite to infer some malignant supernatural intervention. The drawback, of course, is that if he had done this, some Hollywood hack would have produced a remake.

JOSYPH: What about Kurosawa's lifelong interest in the spiritual development, or awakening, of a character? Wouldn't doing that with the Kid pervert the novel? Crying over a dead old crone because he's lonesome, or telling the Judge he's full of shit, doesn't quite qualify as satori. What would Kurosawa-san do with this challenge—sit with sake in a *ryokan* and write his own *Blood Meridian*, or would he make the Judge into a kind of hero? If he is the hero of the book, should he not be celebrated in a film of the novel? Setting up a counterforce to find within it the elements of virtue and hope—that's someone else's novel, is it not?

WALLACH: Why should Kurosawa-san kowtow to McCarthy? McCarthy certainly took his liberties with Chamberlain, no? The emperor [Kurosawa] buys the narrative—or, to be more precise, the rights to the diegesis. After that, it's his show. Once you've turned a pack of horsethieves, defrocked acolytes, career criminals, army deserters, Tasmanian sheepherders, Indians, former Texas Rangers, and sundry other Wild West types into samurai, shoguns, Buddhist monks, Shinto beadles, bureaucrats, and Christianized peasants, why should you be hesitant to extrapolate the Kid's marginal evolution into something more profound? I wouldn't expect such a film to inhabit an American, or even a Judeo-Christian, ethos at all, and "spiritual development" just doesn't mean the same thing in a Buddhist-Shinto *weltanschauung*. One moves from saving one's soul in the Western tradition to the Buddhist realization that the "soul" is at worst a dead weight and at best an illusion altogether. What would the Judge say to the Kid in Fort Griffin? "Drink up, drink up. Tonight thy transmigrating monad may be required of thee." Right. It won't be *Blood Meridian* anymore. But in dealing with the Judge, I can't imagine that Kurosawa would miss an opportunity to tailor-make a great movie villain to his own specifications. His version of *Blood Meridian* would be *a Kurosawa film*, with all the accretions—market, mythic, and charismatic—that that eponymous genre-in-itself connotes. Much better that way, too. I can't recall any critics dismissing *Ran* or *Throne of Blood* as failed Shakespeare. If they didn't like the films, they regarded them as failed Kurosawa.

JOSYPH: How did you discover the novel?
WALLACH: I was in Australia in 1992, in conversation with a friend who is an Australian critic. We were discussing who they thought our best

writers were, and he mentioned McCarthy. I was thrown. I thought he meant Mary McCarthy. I said I didn't think she was all that good. He was shocked that I didn't know who Cormac McCarthy was. At this time McCarthy was out of print in the United States. *All the Pretty Horses* was something of a whisper on the horizon. But he was quite in print, in paperback, in Australia. So I picked a copy of *Blood Meridian* off the wire rack of a newsstand in the drugstore of the Adelaide Railroad Station and I read it overnight on the Ghan, a wonderful train that runs from Adelaide to Alice Springs. I sat up with it all night. I was flabbergasted. I finished the book as a bloodred sun was coming up in the east. Boy... it was an experience.

JOSYPH: Why, exactly?

WALLACH: Well, for one thing it was delirious to see the mythology of the heroic cowboy overturned. It was gratifying to see the barbarism and cruelty of Euro-American genocide against Native American populations so fearlessly and unblinkingly depicted. As horrible as the scenes were, it was tonic to see that someone was doing it so brilliantly and not ameliorating the moral sentence upon the act. I found that startling. And it was remarkable that I should be reading this book in Australia on the eve of the first Australian law that granted integrity of territorial ownership back to its own aboriginal people. That occurred the week that I discovered *Blood Meridian* in Australia, and so, from my perspective, there was irony in that. And of course the *gorgeous* language—the cadences, the rhythmicity of it, and the remarkable *words*. Words are *wonderful* things! Words are like uncut, unpolished stones, still very beautiful before you apply the lapidary art to them, and McCarthy seemed to have gone on his hands and knees on a beach strewn with the most spectacular words and picked them off and buffed them with his denim shirt and put them in his pocket and taken them home and worked them perfectly into the foil of his narrative.

JOSYPH: What does it say about American culture that *Blood Meridian* was out of print for so long?

WALLACH: The idealistic response is that *Blood Meridian* was out of print because it told such uncomfortable truths about ourselves that we refused to acknowledge its existence—but I don't think that's really the case. I think it was McCarthy's publisher refusing to invest a great deal of money and effort in marketing his books, especially given his own refusal to cooperate in that marketing. Albert Erskine was an editor of great integrity and foresight, having handled Faulkner and other major writers, but McCarthy emerged on the scene at about the time that Erskine's and people of his caliber's input in publishing was shrinking, while the authority and clout of the bean-counters and legal departments were on the ascendancy. The quality of the text was having less and less to do with the marketing effort that went into a book than the assessment of its commercial viability. That McCarthy fathered a *light* manuscript, *All the Pretty Horses*—light deceptively, perhaps, but a more commercial formula than his previous books—and that at that point he came out of privacy to do an interview with the *New York Times*, is not coincidental to the fact that *All the Pretty Horses* is the book that took off.

JOSYPH: Where does *Blood Meridian* stand in relation to the Border Trilogy?

WALLACH: If *Blood Meridian* had not existed, it would have been necessary for the Border Trilogy to have invented it. *Blood Meridian* is the *prima materia* for the Border Trilogy. It is the wound, it's the disease which the healing process of the Border Trilogy is meant to ameliorate—not to cure, for it's a wound that will heal with a scar certainly. The emergence of heroicism and decency—even if fatuous at times, and despite its lapses, which are human, after all—creates a balanced symmetrical whole with *Blood Meridian*. *Blood Meridian* is the dark side of the force that is the Border Trilogy.

JOSYPH: Is there anything in the Kid of John Grady, or of *The Gardener's Son*'s Bobby McEvoy?

WALLACH: Bobby McEvoy has a tremendous moral idealism, and I think it is the utter failure of that idealism to make a difference in the life that he leads and the lives and circumstances that surround him, that most infuriates him, and I think that his rage is a rage of impotence, and the loss of his leg is symbolic of the fact that he is maimed by things as they are, given his idealistic nature. He seems to think the fact that his mother doesn't belong at the mill is somehow going to take her corpse hundreds of miles to home, back to where they came from. He seems to think the fact that his family is utterly poor, and limited by the servitude of milltown life, will have no bearing on their ability to move this corpse. And the failure, ultimately, of his father to do anything with the corpse—except to burn it—highlights the difference and the distance between Bobby's idealism and the real world. That, of course, is something you see in John Grady's insistence on marrying Magdalena to save her in *Cities of the Plain*—to *reconstitute* Magdalena. Given the fact that his mother, in his mind, behaved whoreishly in the scene at the Menger Hotel, where he sees her on the arm of her lover, not even registered under her "own name"—which, of course, is his father's name, not hers—she's a Grady—I think in some ways John Grady is trying to resurrect his dead mother, or put the image of his mother the whore to rest, much as Bobby is trying to lay his mother to rest. So I think there are substantial resonances and connections between them.

The Kid is comparable to John Grady Cole in that if the Kid is not willfully attempting to emerge as a fuller human being, he is at least ambling toward it. As you mentioned, at the end of *Blood Meridian* he attempts to comfort the old woman before he realizes she's been dead for quite some time. You can read that as a metaphor for a *self* that is dead and *has* been dead for quite some time, and *cannot* be rediscovered or resurrected faultlessly and cathartically when all of the reflexes have been so thoroughly beaten down, suppressed, brutalized. That's also represented by the Bible the Kid carries but which, because he is illiterate, he cannot read. It's the code for a self the keys to which have never been learned. John Grady Cole is almost the opposite. He begins in that fullness of selfhood that he cannot read in other ways, cannot adapt, cannot *translate*, if you will, into the new realities. Yet there is a self there, a self to be sacrificed. At the time of the Kid's destruction there is nobody there to destroy.

JOSYPH: To stay with *The Gardener's Son*: I wonder whether you think that the world of McCarthy's novels is in any way clarified by elements that are more accessible in the film?

WALLACH: I tend to think of *The Gardener's Son* as an ancillary work in McCarthy's canon. I think that he was self-consciously trying *not* to write a novel when he wrote it, just as he was self-consciously trying *not* to write a novel when he wrote *The Stonemason*. I think in that gesture he fails. Because *The Gardener's Son* is a film, it's more of a curiosity to me than anything else. Auteur theory would make McCarthy the least important of the major contributors to the film. Richard Pearce, the director, would be the real author of *The Gardener's Son*, with McCarthy as one of the elements that Pearce put in place for the realization of his film. And I'm willing to think of it as Pearce's film before I think of it as McCarthy's, and find within it little McCarthean touches. The graphic shots of the surgeon laying out his instruments for the amputation of Bobby's leg. The carrying of the bloody limb downstairs, and the look on Nan Martin's—Mrs. Gregg's—face when she comes down after the amputation. The black humor of Brad Dourif plunging the knife into his wooden leg while he sits cutting slices of apple in the cart. And then of course that marvelous touch of having the same doctor who had saved his life a few years earlier appear out of the shadows after his execution to turn this now dead body, this suspended pile of garbage, as if it were just a sack of laundry, to check the pulse and look at his watch and then call the executioners to bring in the coffin. I read these more as Richard Pearce admiring things about McCarthy and trying to replicate them in cinematic language than as the language of McCarthy himself.

JOSYPH: It's no secret that you are fond of Judge Holden. You quote him at length from memory. You've written about him. You refer to him often. Why is he such an extraordinary figure to appear in 1980s literature? Why do you connect with him so strongly?

WALLACH: I don't think that I'm fond of Judge Holden *per se*. I'm certainly not fond of the *igmus fatuous* of a real Judge Holden. But I am in awe of McCarthy's artifice in creating and animating that being. I am wary of my own tendency as an academic to worship or admire too much the intellectual qualities of the Judge, at the cost of overlooking his monstrosity on the human and empathetic level. So the Judge is an object lesson about how I synthesize, attribute, and act upon my own values. I can't think of another lesson so vividly put in all of American literature *for its time*. I think that Ahab certainly comes close in *Moby-Dick*. But Judge Holden is a thoroughly unique and remarkable character. He is also the focus of much of the book's self-mockery. He's something of a caricature. He lapses into slapstick from time to time, as if to dissipate his own self-importance. I'm thinking in particular of the scene where the rioting Yuma Indians break into his room at Lincoln's Ferry, where he has been engaged in probably abominable sexual abuses of young Indian girls, and he's standing there naked holding a Howitzer under his arm with a cigar held to the fuse. His physical strength has become a kind of cartoon. The Indians tumbling backwards out of the room with Holden's Howitzer pointed at them creates a Chaplinesque dissipation of tension and malevolence which I think is deliberate. Only a creature of Holden's magnitude could be posed to generate comedy of that quality.

JOSYPH: You've spoken about neoteny and Holden.

WALLACH: Neoteny is the retention into adulthood of juvenile characteristics. Homo sapiens are neotenous. As you can see, I am far less hairful than an ape. Whereas all other hominids attain greater coverance of body hair as they attain greater maturity, we remain as hairless as newborn apes. Neoteny accommodates in hominids greater brain growth. And of course despite his bulk, despite his weight, despite his strength, the Judge's intellect is the most exaggerated feature of his personality. That goes along with his perpetual babyhood, if you will. Also, the Judge gratifies himself immediately. When he sees something he wants, he takes it. The self-indulgence with which he kills and manipulates others to kill—the young men and women whom he apparently rapes and murders brutally—his unbounded, uncontrolled sexual gratifications—are the sorts of libidinal excesses that a child might indulge in. He's disruptive. He's mischievous. His subversion of Reverend Green's sermon is the kind of thing a spoiled child would do. And he's never been disciplined. He talks constantly about fathers and sons, and yet clearly he has never himself been fathered.

JOSYPH: Is it an exaggeration to say that if the Kid, the Judge, and Glanton are the three central characters in the novel, the landscape—nature itself—would be the fourth?

WALLACH: This idea of nature as a character is hyperbole at best, sententious at worst. In McCarthy's fiction nature isn't motivated, doesn't think or suffer, learns nothing by its actions, and comes to no realization as a consummation of the narrative. Even if McCarthy populated his desert with talking rocks and tree people as in *The Lord of the Rings*, such entities would no longer be natural at all. The concepts of *setting* and *description* work well enough for me. Our language often personalizes inert objects—the sun "beat down" on the riders; nature is "hostile"—but we recognize this as a simple trope and as readers we aren't necessarily led into a pathetic fallacy over it. Only professional critics can take us *there*.

JOSYPH: How important, then, is *geography* in *Blood Meridian*? How, for example, does it try the Glanton gang, and does the Judge manage those trials differently than the others?

WALLACH: Certainly you cannot imagine the narrative of *Blood Meridian* taking place anywhere else. You have the conjunction—fortuitous only in the sense that it meets our ideal requirements for the literary venture—of corrupt, vicious, racist governments; the immediate, ethically disjunctive aftermath of a major war where the reflexive violence of former combatants may be harvested for other purposes; widely differing cultures at cross-purposes; and enough unclaimed resources and land to stimulate even the most latent acquisitive instincts. And, of course, an arid, hostile and highly variable landscape suitable for staging a range of dramatic set pieces. Try to picture an urban version of this story. No good. You can only push so many mules off a roof in Manhattan before someone notices. The great plains? Forget it. The Sioux Nations would have responded to the Glantons in a forceful and organized way, unlike their less well organized Southwestern counterparts. Australia? The landscape is every bit as arid and hostile, and there *were* efforts by settlers to exterminate aboriginals, but they never had official sanction, and the landscape is pretty much invariable. For the same reason, the sea wouldn't work either, despite the many allusions in *Blood Meridian* to *Moby-Dick*.

During the "trials," as you put it, the Judge generally disappears into the gang's experience. Even in the great gunpowder-making episode that casts the Judge as leader and innovator, he is still working cooperatively with the other gang members to save them and himself. One glaring exception is, of course, the Howitzer at Lincoln's Ferry. As I have suggested, it's an absurd moment, and I suspect that McCarthy was amenable to violating his own rule for the Judge's behavior in crises because the episode was just too good to edit out!

JOSYPH: Is there a sense in which the Judge is super-natural—or is that just another boast?

WALLACH: The Judge is not so much supernatural as uncanny. There's a rational explanation for everything he does that seems inexplicable at first. As for the Judge's ability to be in exactly the right place at the right time, or seemingly to transport from one spot to another with miraculous speed—as in the move from Reverend Green's tent to the bar in Nacogdoches—McCarthy is careful to craft another way of looking at it. After the Kid and the teamster slash their way through the tent, they stand on the porch of the saloon and watch it collapse. McCarthy doesn't tell us how long they stand there, how long it takes for the tent to implode. So, how long did it take the Judge to get into the bar? We don't really know. By stating that the Judge was "already" in the saloon, we are left with the impression of unnatural dispatch, but he has subverted that impression in the passage directly before it. And it's the Judge himself who claims that he will never die, not the authoritative voice of the narrator.

JOSYPH: What about the notion of the Judge *representing* a political or philosophical point of view, even if it isn't McCarthy's? The subject is constantly under discussion. Where do you weigh in on the question of what the Judge might *represent* if we were to treat him as if he has a coherent philosophy? As you know, I don't believe that he does. For me he is a wonderful bullshitter who loves to talk and can use his linguistic abilities to do and to get what he pleases.

WALLACH: I don't disagree at all. The Judge is the ultimate degeneration of the trickster figure. He represents all of our worst impulses, and the tendency to rationalize away their moral significance in favor of the sheer pleasure of self-indulgence. His verbal pyrotechnics are nothing if not precisely this. The Judge's physical bulk, however much it alludes to, say, the White Whale of *Moby-Dick* or the folk myth that Satan sank of his own weight into Hell, is also a symbol of gluttony in the widest sense—getting what you want merely because you want it—and his intelligence is harnessed to the goal of doing so, however it is necessary to achieve it.

JOSYPH: Is there a rational explanation for the fact that the Judge does not appear to have aged? Could it be that he maintains his youth by eating the flesh, or sucking the blood, of his favorites? Could it be that, like Dorian Gray, there is some other version of the Judge—an anti-Judge, if you will—who is absorbing the wear and tear that appears not to show?

WALLACH: No, that's just McCarthy being coy again. He doesn't say that the Judge *is* little changed or none at all, he says that he *seems* little changed or none at all. This is consistent with the uncanny sensibility he creates around Holden.

JOSYPH: The Judge lives forever in the novel—but will it be read a hundred years from now, the way we might still read *Moby-Dick* or *Les Miserables*? One prominent admirer and critic of McCarthy speculated recently that McCarthy's star might be waning. You've stated that the novel was an antiquated artifact when it first appeared, partly because its language is archaic and its style is opposite the fashion for minimalism. Will it be *more* so fifty or a hundred years from now? Could it fall into the status of an interesting curiosity about which readers will wonder why you and Harold Bloom have placed it among your all-time favorites?

WALLACH: No, I think it's the real thing. Anyone who thinks McCarthy is waning at the moment needs to have his analytical prowess sent in for a tune-up. What *is* happening is that McCarthy is spawning a crop of imitators in film and television as well as in literature. Oddly enough, the deliberate archaisms of the novel (which interject a wonderful element of parody) will be *less* of an issue in a hundred years. Someone will read it alongside *Moby-Dick* or any other text produced during that period in America, and its style will no longer seem out of place because it will no longer be a *contemporary* novel. Then again, at the rate that language skills are deteriorating in this culture, I wonder how many people will be left in a hundred years who will be capable of reading it in the first place.

JOSYPH: Some of what you've said reminds me of a review by Caryn James when *Blood Meridian* was published. "This latest book is his [McCarthy's] most important," she wrote in the *Times*, where she has written about books, television, film, and theatre for many years, "for it puts in perspective the Faulknerean language and unprovoked violence running through the previous works, which were often viewed as exercises in style or studies of evil. *Blood Meridian* makes it clear that all along Mr. McCarthy has asked us to witness evil not in order to understand it but to affirm its inexplicable reality; his elaborate language invents a world hinged between the real and the surreal, jolting us out of complacency" (James '85). I get the sense that you would agree.

WALLACH: With much of it, yes. Although I would ask when an "exercise in style" becomes style itself; when a "study of evil" becomes a story about it. There's an inference there that a study or an exercise is a failure of art. That leaves us to ponder which of the novels preceding *Blood Meridian* she might be referring to. I draw a blank. I don't think, for example, that

Child of God was a study of anything, evil included, nor is it an exercise in style any more or less than any other work of literary art. It is *surely* no failure.

JOSYPH: After quoting the Judge's line "Here are the dead fathers," James wrote: "The kid and the judge are our own dead fathers, whom Mc-Carthy resurrects for us to witness. He distances us not only from the historical past, not only from our cowboy-and-Indian images of it, but also from revisionist theories that make white men the villains and Indians the victims. All men are unremittingly bloodthirsty here, poised at a peak of violence, the 'meridian' from which their civilization will quickly fall" (James '85).

WALLACH: Too slick. How do you classify the motives of a native people who are viewed as commodities on every level? Grab their land, their food supply, their *scalps*—their *bodies*, for God's sake. Is it viciousness to resist that? How vicious would Native Americans have been if they had been approached as a legitimate nation and engaged in commerce—not unlike, say, Canada—well, wait, no—no good, we initially tried to *invade* Canada. Well, then, Mexico—no—forget that as well. Cuba? Hmmm... all right, let's try another angle. There were conflicts among Native Americans long before Europeans arrived, but there were also nations, alliances, commerce—all the traffic of culture. Certainly there was nothing north of the Aztec cannibal empire that remotely challenged the European genocide against our native population. They learned a lot of what they knew from our illustrious ancestors. In that great Comanche attack, the Indians are wearing western garb: top hats, wedding veils, dinner jackets. They have become our own darker selves. If there's a point to be made about native viciousness, the infectiousness of the European brand ought to be stressed.

JOSYPH: James is displeased with the ending and the epilogue. For her they amount to a "stylistically dazzling but facile conclusion." I can't see you admitting the word *facile* into *any* critique of *Blood Meridian*. "The judge's enigmatic dance and the long ordeal of the novel's violence demand more than this easy ambiguity," she wrote. "There are, of course, no answers to the life-and-death issues Mr. McCarthy raises, but there are more rigorous, coherent ways to frame the questions" (James '85).

WALLACH: If *I* wanted to be facile, I might say that ambiguity is the spice of life. But I don't want to be facile. Criticizing the ambiguity of the Judge's behavior at the end of the novel is itself the most facile thing about the review. The Judge is, among other things, a very icon of ambiguity. I have said that he's a figure of textuality, a figure of what Derrida called *dissemination*, the force that is generated by the inherent ambiguity in language—the property of language to mean multiplicity. The Judge toys with language like a kitten with a half-killed rat. Moreover, the questions *Who is he? What is he?* are the open ends that give the novel its force. Take away that axial ambiguity and you've got what is basically a Stephen King western. To have an ambiguous ending is completely consistent with the strengths that James has been praising all along. Trying to cap the irony of this work at the very end would be a colossal exercise in texticide. McCarthy's much too smart to do that. He played with that kind of closure in an early draft of the novel, wherein the Judge at the bar in Fort Griffin effectively admits to the Kid that he's some kind of immortal being—inferentially, the Devil himself. By the second draft, McCarthy had written it out. Thank Buddha for that, or I don't think we'd be talking about this book—unless you were interviewing me for *Famous Monsters of Filmland.*

JOSYPH: You appear to take it personally that an entire population was wiped off the map. Does reading *Blood Meridian* stir that ire or resentment more than it soothes it by the fact of being written?

WALLACH: A novel, whatever comforts it brings, is not like a broad spectrum antibiotic, and there are many things it isn't meant to do. I was already aware of how this proud civilization of ours floats on a sea of immolated native blood, so there wasn't much disengaged ire to stimulate. There certainly wasn't much about the novel to soothe it. What it does soothe—perhaps—are any fears I might have had that my culture had exhausted its capacity to produce great literary artists. You might say those fears were just the product of having read too much Spengler and Yeats at an impressionable age. The problem is, of course, that McCarthy read them too. There's still great value for me in knowing that this novel exposes, for those who *aren't* as aware of it, what has gone into the founding and maintenance of the Republic. For them, as well as for me, the soothing, such as it is, is forward-looking more than it is retrospective. It might be naive of me, but I am convinced that there are readers who are alerted by *Blood Meridian* that Judge Holden's rhetoric lives and breathes vigorously within our contemporary political discourse. "He says that he will never die" (335). He's right. There are I don't know how many hecatombs of Vietnamese civilians we incinerated—for their own good, of course—who could attest to that.

JOSYPH: You were instrumental in publishing John Sepich's *Notes on Blood Meridian* in conjunction with the first McCarthy conference, which you organized with Wade Hall at Bellarmine in Louisville. I recall meeting John at your house, and at some point John gave me a signed version of *Notes* that was bound in a slice of offwhite file folder with "Notes'" handwritten on the cover. How did you find out what Sepich was doing, and how did the first edition come to be published?

WALLACH: If I'm not mistaken, I was referred to Sepich by Tom Young Jr., who wrote the first doctoral dissertation on McCarthy.[3] I found his dissertation, looked him up in Austin and called him. This was back in 1992 when I had just returned from Australia and passed along my copy of *Blood Meridian* to you. Young gave me John's number and I called him that night in Durham, South Carolina. John sent me a pile of his short essays on *Blood Meridian* in the "pen club" format in which he had been circulating them among a small network of cognoscenti. When my friend Jay McGowan, who was president of Bellarmine College, asked me a few months later if I could think of a topic for a conference there, he accepted the idea of a Cormac McCarthy conference under Wade Hall's urging. I called John and suggested we compile his unrelated essays into a book. Jay was amenable to inventing the Bellarmine College Press, of which *Notes* was the sole publication.

JOSYPH: What has the book meant for the understanding of *Blood Meridian*?

WALLACH: Only 1200 copies were published. With so few copies extant, it's hard to say how much influence it had. I'm sure copies got passed around quite a bit. The rarity of the original *Notes* might have contributed to the impression that *Blood Meridian* was a cult novel beloved primarily of strange folks like us, but it also alerted people to the fact that this novel was complex enough to warrant a book-length study, and to the fact that the Glanton gang did exist, and that much of the content of the novel was historical, so to speak. It helped readers to get a handle on how McCarthy worked from his source material.

JOSYPH: What about the excitement for you to encounter this guy who was devoting a second life to the novel, and who was talking to McCarthy, following up on his sometimes sibylline hints—*Well, what law books would a judge have had to read?*—and having to rummage around in Coke to find an answer, like Woodward and Bernstein after meeting with Deep Throat in the D.C. garage?

WALLACH: I like John very much, and we shared some hearty slow-motion laughs during the project, but after the initial *frisson* of discovering his existence, and aside from my interest in the information he had discovered, the publishing of *Notes* was very much a blue-collar process, one percent inspiration and ninety-nine percent perspiration. The excitement, for me, originally came from getting my hands on a copy of Tom Young Jr.'s dissertation and finding out that Glanton and the boys were historical figures. Because Tom got on with his life and didn't follow up on his research by publishing it, John became the pioneer figure by default, which is in no way to minimize the value of what John accomplished. Hardly anyone acknowledges Tom's work except as a footnote or curiosity, which is too bad.

JOSYPH: Do you recall the special energy surrounding that first Mc-Carthy conference?

WALLACH: I recall sitting at the opposite end of a horseshoe of seats from Richard Marius at the readings from McCarthy that you performed with Raymond Todd, and watching him laugh so hard at the dumping of Leonard's father into the Tennessee River that he cried out one of his contact lenses. One of the things about that period that I remember best was that soon after I gave you my aboriginal copy of *Blood Meridian* to read for the first time, you called me in Northport to talk about the novel. When I said that I was on my way to the airport, I distinctly remember you exclaiming: "Well now wait a minute—you can't just drop something like *this* on me and run off to Florida!" I also recall that in the early stages of setting up the Bellarmine conference, you called me about what became "Blood Music" to express some concern that it might not be suitable for an academic conference, and I exhorted you to "just be yourself." Which you certainly were!

JOSYPH: Where does *Blood Meridian* stand for you in the McCarthy cannon?

WALLACH: I think it's his finest work. As a made object, as a balance of complexities and an artifact of language, I think it's sublime. In my own personal pantheon I rank it among the top five. It's in there with *One Hundred Years of Solitude, The Vivisector, Dr. Faustus*, and *Invisible Man*.

JOSYPH: For me, books that are favorites become allies, supporting me psychically on a day-to-day basis, or in times of need—which is often. They resonate continually—are somehow freshly applicable to new experience. Many of one's allies change over the years, but some of them remain—they are, in a sense, true, they hold up, they keep on meaning something—in fact they might mean *more* as time passes. There is also someone who adds to these books while I am away from them, because I keep finding new things under the same covers. How has *Blood Meridian* held up for you?

WALLACH: Taking *Blood Meridian* to heart is like having a recidivist criminal brother who loves you anyway and often proves useful, like the mob-connected Jerry Orbach in Woody Allen's *Crimes and Misdemeanors*. I often use *Blood Meridian* to take down books that I don't like—*Cold Mountain*, for example, or any of the other McCarthy clones, like William Gay's *The Long Home*. *Blood Meridian* has saved me from reading more than a few pages of each, but of course there have been many others. This is a roundabout way of saying that *Blood Meridian* sets a standard. Once you have read it, the number of works upon which you can no longer justify wasting your time multiplies exponentially. It becomes, in a sense, your bodyguard, and one cannot be too grateful for that.

JOSYPH: Why do you teach *Blood Meridian*?

WALLACH: I teach it to make my students uncomfortable. I teach it so that my students' reflexes for moral self-delusion may be shaken up a little bit. I teach it to upset them. I teach it to rattle their world.

NOTES

1. In Richard Ellmann's *Ulysses on the Liffey*, he says: "...the whole of *Ulysses* is a triumphant anachronism" (10).

2. When Rick says: "For Holden there are no references other than Holden—I mean, Chamberlain," it reminds me of a talk by William Goetzmann, editor of the deluxe edition of Chamberlain's *My Confession*, in which he said that there were only two sources for the Judge: *My Confession*, and *Blood Meridian*. Then he corrected himself. "Well," he said, almost reluctantly, "*Blood Meridian* is *fiction*."

3. Thomas D. Young Jr.'s dissertation is *Cormac McCarthy and the Geology of Being*.

III

THE STONEMASON

A stony business altogether.

—Dickens

· 7 ·

Older Professions:
The Fourth Wall of *The Stonemason*

THE STAGE

$\mathscr{T}$hat Cormac McCarthy's first published play, *The Stonemason*, is a failure places him more securely in the tradition of great novelists. Although the art of the play is distinct from and, in some respects, opposed to that of the novel, rarely does a first rate novelist resist the lure of the stage. And yet the yield is seldom successful. At one time novelists went to the theatre to make a killing, as if that were all it were good for, and most of them found it a slippery business indeed. A few cheerful speculators, such as Mark Twain, have turned a theatrical profit, but most of these successes are adaptations or ephemera that have not enriched the dramatic literature. When novelists collaborate, blame is bifurcated but is seldom less deserved. Many years have passed since I read *The Frozen Deep*, by Charles Dickens *and* Wilkie Collins, before the New York chapter of the Charles Dickens Fellowship. I am still living it down. Robert Louis Stevenson, while collaborating with W. E. Henley, wrote to his father: "The theatre is the gold-mine; and on that I must keep an eye" (3), but when the several bad plays they wrote together were not hits, they returned to the less glittering rewards of literature, concerning which disparity Stevenson's first biographer, Graham Balfour, in a polite understatement, wrote: "They had never affected to disregard the fact that in this country the prizes of the dramatist are out of all proportion to the payment of the man of letters" (3). With the lucrative lure of the screen providing ample distraction to novelists, the stage has been diminished as a solution for cash flow, but in the widening world of the workshop, which, by definition, calls for work that is flawed or incomplete, there is often more support to help a prose writer *develop* a first play than to commission a working playwright to create one. Unfortunately, the material hasn't improved because no one is more likely to develop a good play than to write one. Even works that are cast in dramatic form without the intention of performance, while they might prove interesting—Flaubert's *La Tentation de Saint Antoine*, Hardy's *The Dynasts*, Faulkner's *Requiem for a Nun*—seldom rank among an author's best (with the exception of the Nighttown chapter of *Ulysses*, which is delightful to *hear*, even when it is read by a single adept).

This is to say nothing against novelists. Most plays are bad. "Sir," says Voltaire's Candide to an abbé, "how many plays have you in France?" The abbé says: "Five or six thousand." "That's a lot," says Candide. "And how many good ones are there?" "Fifteen or sixteen," the abbé replies, to which Candide's companion, Martin, says: "That's a lot" (73). It is a lot. Few countries that do not have Shakespeare in them can boast that many for all of their centuries combined. Walt Whitman saw his share of shows at the Park and Bowery theatres in Downtown Manhattan, and he celebrated them as delightful entertainments; but in his most serious moods he was not much kinder about plays than I am.[1] "I should say it deserves to be treated with the same gravity," he wrote about theatre in 1871, "and on a par with the questions of ornamental confectionery at public dinners, or the arrangement of curtains and hangings in a ballroom—nor more, nor less" (58). Even God, Faulkner said, "dramatic though he be, has no sense for theatre."[2] The wonder is that authors of great novels are so blithe to enter a specialized forum in which they have no training at all.

This is partly because it appears to be a cinch to write for the stage, a view best stated by Alexandre Dumas *père*: "If you locked me in my bedroom with five women, pens, paper, ink and a play to be written, by the end of an hour I'd have written the five acts and had the five women" (Goncourt 58). Assuming that he puts the pen down, divides his duties in half, and portions himself equally, Dumas would have six minutes for each of the acts inferred. The novelist Henri Muger told the Brothers Goncourt that it was "just too stupid to slave away at writing books for which nobody thanked you and which brought nothing in, and that he was going to go on writing for the stage and make money the easy way" (57). Why not? Set people talking at cross-purposes, which *is* easy, and there you have the start of dramatic form. Talk, for most writers, perpetuates itself. Disencumbered of description, pens move swiftly. But writing theatrical dialogue can bring out the worst in even the best of writers. The more glib it is, even the more profound, the farther it tends to stray from theatrical action. Gertrude Stein cautioned the young Hemingway that remarks are not literature. They are not theatre either, but neither is literature. Theatre attains to literature only by being uniquely itself. Plays determined to make a point—*The Stonemason* is one of these—increase the odds against them for, as James Thurber said, between a good cause and a good play are a thousand miles of desert few writers can cross alive (202).

But the promise of the stage is a promise of blood to blood for which there is no substitute. When I once called theatre *the word made flesh*, Arthur Miller complimented me on my use of the biblical phrase, for, he said, it was the same for him. Despite the proliferation of bombs and baubles to chasten us, the last century was not able to stop James Joyce, Joseph Conrad, E. M. Forster, D. H. Lawrence, Ernest Hemingway, F. Scott Fitzgerald, John Dos Passos, John Galsworthy, Thomas Wolfe, Henry Miller, Somerset Maugham, Graham Greene, Vladamir Nabokov, William Styron, James Baldwin, Jack Kerouac, Saul Bellow, and other good novelists from proving that they, too, can write an unimpressive play. *The Stonemason* is a kind of anti-play, the *anti* deriving less from daring the rules of theatre than from holding the play above them. This will not work. It never has.[3]

Set in Louisville in 1971, *The Stonemason* centers around Ben Telfair, one of a family of black stonemasons, who loses his granddad and mentor, Papaw, to old age; his father, Big Ben, to suicide; his nephew, Soldier, to heroin; and he is estranged from his sister, Carlotta, for lying to her in trying to keep her son from breaking her heart. Ben, who despises every hour spent away from his grandfather, is brought to see the need for greater charity to all and that a family, like a freestone house, can only be built on what is true. Because its theme of personal, familial, and professional integrity is so overtly, even ponderously *stated*, the play is a useful text for the schoolroom and an aid to McCarthy studies, for when a lecturer comments upon, and substitutes for, dramatic action, as in the case of Ben Telfair, there is no mistaking the message. After a work of such studied and relentless moralizing, with lines like "The structure of the world is such as to favor the prosperity of men" (10), McCarthy can never again be charged with nihilism, although a case can be made, and probably will, for a schizoid variety that needs, now and then, to escape in the disguise of its opposite. Sadly, although it contains a couple of well-written scenes, some highfalutin language and an ethical idea, *The Stonemason*—along with *Cities of the Plain* and *The Road*, and a more recent play, *The Sunset Limited*—is one of McCarthy's weakest offerings to date.

McCarthy's one produced screenplay, *The Gardener's Son*, is not a great story and it is not great writing. Some of its ambiguities lead more to confusion than to mystery. Its class-consciousness seems surprisingly amateur. The last third of the film cries out for McCarthy to have written a great scene between the father and the son—the gardener and the son of the title—and the fact that it doesn't materialize leaves an unfortunate weakness toward the end of the drama, a weakness of which Brad Dourif, who played the title role, was conscious at the time.[4] Jerry Hardin, who played the boy's father, shared with me some of his dissents with the director over how the emotional arc of the story should have been shaped, dissents about which Hardin, two decades later, still felt quite strongly. And yet in speaking to the cast I was aware of how keenly they appreciated working on an artful and serious piece of writing, and *The Gardener's Son* is certainly sympathetic to the screen, enabling Richard Pearce, a first-feature director with a highly constrictive budget, to craft a film of intelligence and integrity—in other words, better than most of the crap that was made at the time. Though dramatically disappointing, it is nonetheless compellingly photographed by Fred Murphy (who would later shoot John Huston's *The Dead*, win an Oscar for *Hoosiers*, and direct second unit for *All the Pretty Horses*), and it is remarkably well acted with scenes that are strikingly memorable, such as Kevin Conway's attempted seduction of Anne O'Sullivan; Brad Dourif and Ned Beatty drinking together in a doggery; and Jerry Hardin burning his wife's coffin in a yard. And so there are certainly levels on which the film can be said to work, and it is clear from Pearce's memories of working with McCarthy, and those of the cast and the crew, that McCarthy took an active, enthusiastic part in the project.[5] The screen and the stage are, however, vastly different worlds. A look at *The Stonemason* chiefly in terms of its stagecraft can clarify, at least, the manner in which McCarthy has joined the long list of novelists who have tried the dramatic form and failed to meet its elusive demands. As for the why of this failure, I suggest that it happened because McCarthy did not care to meet those demands.

It is instructive to look at McCarthy's stage directions. Pleading a longwinded case for twin Bens—one to interact or to sit in silence while the second addresses the audience—McCarthy cautions: "Above all we must resist the temptation to see the drama as something being presented by the speaker at his lectern, for to do so is to defraud the drama of its right autonomy. One could say that the play is an artifact of history to which the audience is made privy, yet if the speaker at his podium apostrophizes the figures in that history it is only as they reside in his memory" (6). From this alone it will be obvious to any prospective players that McCarthy does not know, or care, where he is, for this is no way to speak to plain professionals of the theatre, and it savors of the authorial bloat—portentous tones, pretentious syntax—that is ruinous to *The Crossing* and, as we shall see, to Ben's monologues. Presumably as a pepcall to the cast, McCarthy makes the bizarre mistake of quoting the German astronomer-mathematician Carl Frederich Gauss (after whom the gauss, a magnetic unit, was named): "Go forward and faith will come to you" (6). Who does McCarthy think he is talking to? It is certainly not Gauss's nor any one else's exhortation to something called faith that I, as an actor, need to have in order to go before an audience. What I need is a relaxed instrument, burning objectives, refined character work, reliable personal parallels, energetic blocking, a talented cast that is tightly interconnected, a director who won't ruin me, and a very good play. Most of all it is the producer who needs more than faith to mount *The Stonemason*. He needs a bloody fortune, the world's widest stage, and a team of weightlifters.

Even more encumbered than stage-left, which contains only a podium, a telephone booth, the interior of a church, and the porch and the kitchen of a small frame house... or centerstage, which, for the first four acts, is freighted with only a frontroom, a livingroom, and a kitchen with a long table, a sink, a refrigerator, a working range and a woodburning stove... the stage-right of *The Stonemason* is one of the most oppressed in theatrical history, for it has to accomodate: 1) Ben's basement study, 2) a country farmhouse *with a real stone wall*, 3) a neighbor, Mrs. Raymond's house, 4) Carlotta's bedroom, 5) a parkbench and a streetlamp, 6) a backyard with picnic tables, chairs, lanterns and bunting, 7) Papaw's bedroom, 8) Big Ben's and Mama's bedroom and bathroom, and 9) the family cemetery—with a stone farmhouse in the background! Offered a desert of empty stage with tracks of sun burning above it, this novelist who is known for his starkly beautiful landscapes has called for clutter. By Act Five even McCarthy seems to have wearied of moving around so much Louisville, for he forgets to tell us where to unload a cheap hotel and the diningroom and the kitchen of the farmhouse. A dog must be cast who can pick up his cuelines; an actor who can pass for a hundred has to be able—and willing—to do a nude scene; wind has to blow through the picnic and the cemetery; the kitchen stove needs a working fire; a breakfast is prepared—onstage—so swiftly that the Telfairs would have to digest raw sausages and eggs with unpercolated coffee; pigeons have to coo, streets must be busy, and there are footsteps, doorslams, and traffic noises throughout. There is no theatrical sound more false than that of automotive traffic: it is impossible to suggest a running car convincingly, as any production of *Death of a Salesman*, with its climactic "There is the sound of a car starting and moving away at full speed" (129), will demonstrate. Or does McCarthy, who wants real stone walls to materialize and disappear, expect actual trucks to be driven backstage, flocks of pigeons installed in the flies, and gusts of wind and snow to be tunneled into the theatre?

Theatrical faith has not come to McCarthy. His persistent call for novelistic detail suggests a lack of trust in the enterprise of theatre, which is, as I have said, the word made flesh while *suggesting* a world around it. Many of Shakespeare's plays are busier with locations than five of *The Stonemason* but, as stated by the Chorus in *The Life of King Henry the Fifth*, Shakespeare's plea is from the heart of the player's contract: "And let us, ciphers to this great account/On your imaginary forces work" (17–18).

A closer look at McCarthy's fear of "defrauding the drama of its right autonomy" shows a deeper fault of stagecraft. To distinguish between the drama and the lecturing Ben Telfair is to attempt to place him *outside* of the play, which is logically and practically impossible, and this misunderstanding drains the play of impact, for no measure of highblown caution—even if it were read, chorus-like, aloud—will keep the audience from integrating, or trying to integrate, the figure of Ben 1 with the action of Ben 2; or, alternately, from willing him off the stage. McCarthy's stated purpose in doubling Ben Telfair—to place the events "in a completed past" (5)—misses the fundamental fact that in theatre, no matter what you do, *everything* is happening in the present because the audience is sitting in front of it. It also misses the fact that the goal of good performance is the illusion of *the first time*. Whatever else a scene is saying, it must be saying *now*. In trying to place his drama in a completed past, McCarthy is a host who wants his dinner guests to not taste the food they are eating. In fact, from the outset McCarthy disobeys his own dictum. "Above all," he says, "we must resist the temptation to see the drama as something being presented by the speaker at his lectern" (6), but no sooner has Ben 1 begun to speak than his double appears writing in a notebook. When Ben 1 introduces his grandfather, Ben 2 looks toward the kitchen and there is Papaw, who has entered to fix tea, after which Ben 1 says: "He's come into the kitchen to fix his tea" (7). With Ben 1's mention of the house they are building together, there it is with the two of them chipping away. As Ben 1 speaks of reading in Papaw's Bible, his double does exactly that. This is puzzling from an author who wants his action not to be "robbed of its right autonomy." These and other instances of action mirroring word create the static sense of an illustrated lecture, worsened by the mistake of staging bits of funeral service after two of the deaths in the family. These stilted illustrations, far from vitalizing the play, suggest amateur docudrama. It is incorrect to call them cinematic: short, ineffective scenes are out of place in any drama.

The twin Bens, as managed by McCarthy, are infelicitous, but there is nothing unworkable in the notion of a monologist. If anything, though, Ben needs to be worked *into* the action. In his most defeating choice, McCarthy has set him squarely behind a podium or lectern, which, with Ben behind it, is tantamount to a pulpit. This is effectively the real stone wall of *The Stonemason*, and it prompts speculation that it cuts off Ben because it cuts off McCarthy the prose writer, the novelist, from the theatrical situation surrounding and threatening him. As long as he has that pulpit to stand behind, McCarthy can, in a sense, novelize a little, and the novelist can sermonize a lot, a tendency apparent in McCarthy's recent work. Ben 1 has the cadence, the vocabulary, the tone, and the Hemingway *and*s of McCarthy's prose, but it is McCarthy at his worst, and the property I can best call bullying, which has increasingly hurt that prose, is largely what has shaped Ben's persona. The central character of a play should not resemble his author's pompous stage directions. McCarthy, like Faulkner, has striven for a style that is numinous—that is to say, an utterance of hallowed ground, inspiring us with wonder and with dread by association with deity. It works magnificently in *Blood Meridian*.[6] Here and in the latter three sections of *The Crossing* it has put him into a bad way. Earthly entertainers such as playwrights and novelists ought to be leery of the numinous. One day an author is sitting behind his desk, next day he is standing behind a pulpit.

The fourth wall of a play is imaginary. If it is set up at all it is to help a cast to reach beyond the footlights by making its own world more tangible and compelling. Between the audience and the interpersonal conflicts of *The Stonemason*, McCarthy has set a fourth wall of words. Ben the sermonizer so monopolizes the stage that he keeps the action off it; or, to put it another way, Ben's inactivity *is* the action. Rather than drawing us into the scenes of the play, he bullies us about them in order to sanctify his and his grandfather's participation. If Ben is a sourpuss, a blowhard and a bore, he is so, I believe, because he is fashioned to be the mouthpiece of McCarthy's prose voice at its most misguided and misplaced.

In the drug-driven Soldier's defense, I am sure that if I were raised with an adult addicted to speaking, or even thinking, in these terms: "I stood with my job-book beneath my arm in which were logged the hours and the days and the years and wherein was ledgered down each sack of mortar and each perch of stone and I stood alone in that whitened forecourt beyond which waited the God of all being and I stood in the full folly of my own righteousness and I took the book from under my arm and I thumbed through it a final time as if to reassure myself and when I did I saw that the pages were yellowed and crumbling and the ink faded and the accounts no longer clear and suddenly I thought to myself fool fool do you not see what will be asked of you?" (112), I should have been driven to shooting dope before I was ten, and how could I blame Big Ben for putting a bullet through his head? Ben, who views professors and books as dangerous, refers to his own escape from teaching with palpable gratitude—"Were it not for him [Papaw] I'd have become a teacher. I nearly did. I nearly did" (11)—messages that, along with his swipes at other professions, are not likely to lure his wayward nephew off the streets. If this is what Ben is like in the lecture hall, I would rather see him piling up stones.

To this activity, Ben attaches a near psychotic measure of mystification, superstition, and exclusionism, in all of which he is proudly both belligerent and didactic. He is not the first man to make a religion out of his job but he is one of the most obnoxious. Ben's teleology for the profession—"God has laid the stones in the earth for men to use and he has laid them in their bedding planes to show the mason how his own work must go" (10)—is positively medieval. Not content to puff it up with "the warp of the world," "the thumb of God" (9–10), and the plumb bob "pointing to a blackness unknown and unknowable both in truth and in principle where God and matter are locked in a collaboration that is silent nowhere in the universe" (67), Ben will have it the first and last of professions, the one that "can teach you reverence of God and tolerance of your neighbor and love of your family" (64–65), but which itself cannot be learned. And since "to a man who's never laid a stone there's nothing you can tell him. Even the truth would be wrong" (66), and since Ben is not likely to clam up, the audience is, of course, justified in walking out on McCarthy's play. Why waste our time, or Ben's?

The simplistic Socialism that informs *The Gardener's Son* is here in full force. "All trades have their origins in the domestic," Ben says, "and their corruption in the state" (65). In an absurd misreading of history and religion, Ben scorns hewn stone buildings as "priestridden stonecraft" requiring "nothing but time and slavery for their completion," he praises the Semitic God as a God of the common man and the Old Testament as "a handbook for revolutionaries" because it will have no slavery, and he believes the thought of a laborer is likelier to be tempered with humanity and tolerance (65). Standing at Speakers Corner in Hyde Park recently, assailed by old gents of Labor on one side, zealous religionaries on the other—both sides equally sincere, equally off their rockers—I was reminded of Ben 1. The Marxist mission—consigning to a fabulous upper class everybody to whom you wish to feel superior—is fully realized in Ben, for whom it is not merely teachers, archeologists, historians, lawyers, psychologists, and priests who have known no honest work, but everyone else in the world who does not lay freestone. Ben tells us: "When the last gimcrack has swallowed up its last pale creator [the mason] will be out there, preferring the sun, trying the temper of his trowel" (32), but Ben is in for a surprise when, after the last day, he discovers that it is not only masons, but gardeners, bathing-belles, sailors, poets, publishers, mountain-climbers, surfers, dictators, gigolos, and recipients of MacArthur grants who are out there tanning under the sun. That the Bible of which he and his grandfather are so enamored was proposed by a paleface Puritan, translated by forty-seven paleface scholars who stole its best lines from a paleface genius who went to the stake for his vocabulary, patronized by a paleface king who dissolved his paleface Parliament, and cranked out on one of the king's gimcracks called a printing press, does not trouble Ben's sanctimony.

Reading the play together with half a dozen do-it-yourselfers such as *The Art of the Stonemason* by Ian Cramb, *Practical Stonemasonry Made Easy* by Stephen Kennedy, and *The Forgotten Art of Building a Stone Wall* by Curtis Fields, one would expect that, in the light of Ben's philosophy, these down-to-earth guides would appear rather simplistic. In fact, they situate Ben even farther over the mountain, for their healthy, welcoming lack of pretension is a breath of fresh air. Of course they are not literature, but *The Stonemason* is literature that makes itself immensely unappealing when its author, despite the play's compassionate message, sends another message, equally plain, in the way that he cannot resist, through the autolithic Ben, looking down on the world of weakness, a curious strain that, although perceptible in *All the Pretty Horses* and *No Country* and, intentionally, the essence of *Blood Meridian*, seems here to have run out of control and to have wrecked his enterprise. This emerges most strangely when we are furnished with the detail that Ben's grandmother loved reading books. That is all we need to know, but that, in *The Stonemason*, could never be enough. She could recite, we are told, all hundred pages of Sir Walter Scott's *The Lady of the Lake*. So much the worse for her. As often as I have read this section of the play, my reaction is the same: *Come off it, Ben—come off it, McCarthy—can't you leave the old bird alone?*

It is a stretch, but an interesting one, to compare the figure of Ben Telfair with Trollope's description of Roger Scatcherd, the stonemason in *Dr. Thorne*, bearing in mind that Scatcherd has little in common with Ben Telfair excepting his occupation, at which he is sensational, and the fact that he is a vigorous, if unselfconscious, democrat (in the anti-Tory sense), and has a sister engaged to be married to a man who, like Carlotta's ironically named Mason Ferguson, is sober, industrious, and respectable:

> He [Scatcherd] was known for the best stone-mason in the four counties, and as the man who could, on occasions, drink the most alcohol in a given time in the same localities. As a workman, indeed, he had higher repute even than this: he was not only a good and very quick stone-mason, but he had also a capacity of turning other men into good stone-masons: he had a gift of knowing what a man could and should do; and, by degrees, he taught himself what five, and ten, and twenty—latterly, what a thousand or two thousand men might accomplish among them: this, also, he did with very little aid from pen and paper, with which he was not, and never became, very conversant. He had also other gifts and other propensities. He could talk in a manner dangerous to himself and others; he could persuade without knowing that he did so; and being himself an extreme demagogue, in those noisy times just prior to the Reform Bill, he created a hubbub in Barchester of which he himself had had no previous conception. (17)

The reader who knows Trollope can see, of course, that he is smiling, and expects us to smile, when he tells us that Scatcherd can do the work of thousands. The tone of *The Stonemason* invites no such play. When Scatcherd's sister Mary is seduced by Dr. Throne's brother Henry, Scatcherd falls against him with his fists and a big stick, slaying Henry with such a blow that Scatcherd is accused of having attacked him with a stone or a mason's hammer, an accusation we could bring against Ben—and McCarthy—when they fall against us. Scatcherd, with Dr. Thorne paying for his defense to save him "from undue punishment" (19), is given six months for manslaughter. Ben, who, hopefully, will find his own defenders, has been put away for longer, for although he has been published, he has never been performed as written, the worst sentence for a character of the stage.[7] But not, in McCarthy's case, a reformative one. After Scatcherd becomes a railway magnate and a baronet, he tells Dr. Thorne on his deathbed: "I'm worth three hundred thousand pounds; and I'd give it all to be able to go to work tomorrow with a hod and mortar, and have a fellow clap his hand upon my shoulder, and say: 'Well, Roger, shall us here have that 'ere other half-pint this morning?' (112)" Who could Ben have around him, clapping him warmly on the shoulder, excepting, perhaps, his own double?

Trollope, in his genius, enables one to hear Scatcherd's gravelled heart beating: the mason's affection for his old life is palpable. Ben, by comparison, may as well despise his craft. It would be no shock to find him secretly ashamed of it. Michelangelo, they say, had the feel for stone in his blood because he suckled at the breast of a stonemason's wife. He certainly had it in his urinary tract, and Ben, who was nursed the same way, seems to have got it into his spleen. Ben is so sullen, so truculent over *the trade* that no joy of stone is communicated, nothing such as we find, for example, in Herman Hesse's *Siddhartha* when, in one of its finer passages, Siddhartha tells his old chum Govinda:

> This stone is stone; it is also animal, God and Buddha.... I love it just because it is a stone.... I see value and meaning in each one of its fine markings and cavities, in the yellow, in the gray, in the hardness and the sound of it when I knock it, in the dryness or dampness of its surface. There are stones that feel like oil or soap, that look like leaves or sand, and each one is different and worships Om in its own way; each one is Brahmin. At the same time it is very much stone... and that is just what pleases me and seems wonderful and worthy of worship. (117)

When, in Jacob Walter's *Diary of a Napoleonic Foot Soldier*, Walter, a mason and stonecutter, steals a moment away from the blood of battle to look at the fortifications at Torgau, his simple admiration of "the beautiful jointing of the stones" (35), and of casements "on the other side of the Elbe... which were all, even the roofwork, built of beautifully hewn stone" (36), is more moving in its appreciation of ashlar than anything that is said of freestone in *The Stonemason*. Ben cannot even refer to Papaw's affection for stone—"He speaks of sap in the stone. And fire" (10)—without defensively adding: "Of course he's right. You can smell it in the broken rock" (10).

If this defensiveness is merely a character trait in Ben, then it is Ben who wrote the Border Trilogy. If McCarthy is a master of writing about men at their tasks, he is either not good at, or not as concerned with, inspiring real love for them in the reader, for his descriptions of work are often *assertions* of work, and often they push too hard, savoring more of the dare than of the lure, as if he would rather pick a fight. When I am in Paris, I, who love cities of stone more than any man alive, and am made mad by a fever of stone, of which I cannot have my fill and am driven to walk amid the stone until I am flung down, senseless, in a terrible stone seizure, cannot, at such times, bear to think about Ben. Ben will make you want never to hear of stone again and could drive a man to write an ode in praise of Portland cement. One might even question his workmanship. At hewn stone he is, of course, an *obermensch*, laying seven hundred eighty-two at a time and, like John Grady in *All the Pretty Horses*, drawing galleries of adorers (as his grandmother must have done with *Lady of the Lake*); but if Ben applies the rule of "one over two, two over one" with characteristic constriction, his stonework could be as dull as he is. The lack of predictable order is part of the beauty of old stone. It is also part of the wonder of households. From all that I have observed, every kind of myth and mendacity contributes to the building and endurance of family structures, many of which hold together not like one-over-two, two-over-one stone, but like a windblasted spider's web, a thread here, a thread there, and yet, somehow, surviving.

Without Ben 1, *The Stonemason* is less a play than a series of conversations too short on conflictive tension to raise a spark. Plays need pressing objectives, hard obstacles, and willful resolutions being worked out between interesting characters. McCarthy, in whose novels men and women have the most tenacious wills in current fiction, has here not *played* out his themes but has *proclaimed* them, making them overly transparent and, at the same time, insufficiently bodied forth in dramatic event. We are told too much, shown too little. The fine first scene introducing the Telfairs shows McCarthy adroitly establishing situations with crisp crosstalk and humor, but the promise is unfulfilled. In a house full of flammable materials, nothing combusts. And it is almost the only time, prior to *Cities of the Plain*, that McCarthy lets his characters be cute, or glib, such as when Maven asks Ben: "Are you sicklied over with the pale cast?"

(122) or when Carlotta says to Ben: "You know, I don't think I could bring myself to actually shoot you. But poison's not out of the question" (88).[8] The boy Soldier, whose lawless living precipitates the crisis of the play, is, along with his gang friend Jeffrey, that rare thing in McCarthy: a nonentity of a character, less important for being out of place in Ben's house than for being out of place in McCarthy's. One acknowledges Soldier's plight, but one does not feel for it. Carlotta will never forgive Ben's lies, Ben will never forgive himself—but what is all the fuss about? Have we missed something? Drama. The *its* of the play don't happen. In an embarrassing exchange, Jeffrey, in sneakers and jeans, tells Ben: "History done swallowed you up except you don't know it." When Ben asks him: "If history swallows everybody up who do you think is running the world?" Jeffrey answers: "It look to you like somebody *runnin* it?" (74–75) Someone is certainly running them. Made to service a plot that is made to service a thesis, Soldier, Jeffrey, and most of the population are as stifled as the marionettes of G. B. Shaw, whose socio-political demonstrations would not permit even a rustic to cross the stage without making his contribution to the argument.

The scene in which Papaw recounts the senseless murder of Uncle Selman while withholding the killer's name is effective use of monologue within dialogue, and it hints at one of the many powerful dramas that might have been. In fact this short scene alone is worth the price of admission, worth more than a year of theatre bundled together. It is especially tantalizing that in Ben's query to Papaw—"What was the man's name?" (52)—there is the kernel of another kind of play, and in its repetition—"What was his name?"—and Papaw's response—"I guess I'd rather not say it" (53)—that play begins to generate itself to such a degree that if McCarthy, at his best, had proceeded from the focus of this scene in both directions, backward to the beginning, forward to the finale, erasing as he went, he could not have failed to bring off a winner. As it stands, all that is tangibly developed—and not compellingly—is Ben 1's relationship to himself. At play's end, taking the blame for the ills of his family, Ben says: "I lost my way" (111). So has McCarthy. It is not too late for Ben. It is for the play. It is a mistake to equate the error of Ben with the error of Ben's ways and to excuse it as intentional. If McCarthy has lost his way, it is because he has lost his balance. Less a character than a McCarthy sound-off, Ben is kept from being dramatically interesting, or interesting at all, because he is kept from being Ben.[9] At his worst, McCarthy, like Hemingway, wants to prove too much of what he knows, and the burden of proof is on his characters. Right autonomy is the last thing McCarthy wishes to give them. But unless he can let his players play, a playwright does not have a drama.

Before the first stone walls rose up around caves such as those in the Aran Islands, one of McCarthy's ancestors acted out a scene in which was circumscribed the war of the rough winds against his people. It went poorly, so he set about refining it for a century or two before he formed it into something that would play. Ben is wrong in telling us that masonry is man's first gift and oldest craft. Theatre is made of older professions whose secrets are just as long, as hard, and as necessary to master.

THE DREAM

Ben has annoying views on many things, including evil, which he sees as "not selective but only opportunistic" (97), and he is taken with a metaphysical construct, God, which or who amounts to a kind of cosmological handyman and ineffectual Mister Clean of the soul: kindly, authoritative, unavailing—fatherly. This makes sense in a play full of fathers but it does not make much more than that.

Ben's God is a *he* until turning into an *it* when Ben says: "I know nothing of God. But I know that something knows. Something knows or else that old man could not know. Something knows and will tell you. It will tell you when you stop pretending that you know" (97). For a man who knows nothing of God, Ben has certainly got God busy, collaborating with matter... putting to hand whatever a man can invent... laying stones in bedding planes... making laws to show the true mason how to build... shaping men in his own image... favoring the common man and disapproving hewn stones and slavery and presiding in a court of ultimate justice. Even God's thumb is occupied pressing keystones in place. God is nearly as busy as the stagehands needed for *The Stonemason*. Probably through a proofreader's lapse, the *he*-God becomes a *He*-God only when Ben dreams God.

In this self-styled "cautionary" (112) dream, Ben goes to see God. He brings the job-book of his life but it's a mess, and Ben imagines old God stooping to ask him: "Where are the others?" (112) There is no less bloat in the dream-Ben than in the waking, for he envisions God gazing into his soul "beyond bone or flesh to its uttermost nativity in stone and star and in the unformed magma at the core of creation" (112), a passage suggesting that Ben should *not* be worried about his book, for if God is looking through him at the stones and the stars and the unformed magma he is not likely to notice the poor condition of Ben's assignment, and if there is any blaming to do, God will probably blame the magma and whatever is beyond that, presumably

Himself. For Ben, however, this is a terrible question, as if he, not God, were responsible for "the others," despite the fact that "He whom the firmament itself has not power to puzzle" (112) is put in charge of an awful lot. We aren't told whether the dream-God does, in fact, ask this question: this is only what the dream-Ben *imagines* he will be asked. We never go in to God at all. It is thus an anxiety dream about anxiety itself, a dream about a man who is standing around worrying; the ultimate, end-of-the-line *called into the office*. Ironically, we learn that the question is thought to be terrible by the Ben who dreamt the dream but we do not know the reaction of the Ben who is *in* the dream, the Ben who has imagined God's question while awaiting judgment. Even in the dream Ben is *anticipating* a God and what God will say and do to him, but he does not *see* this God and this God says nothing and the room next door, for all we know, could be empty. He sees God only as a figure of his anxiety, a function of his fear about the worth of his lousy book. God does not come to Ben in a dream, *Ben* comes to Ben in a dream, and this dream-Ben is worried into God. In his dream, as in his sermons, Ben's God is God *talk*.

Why is Ben's interpretation of his dream so literal? Ben is an educated man. Unlike Papaw, who knows nothing of psychology, Ben knows at least enough psychology to trash it and to say that it knows nothing of Papaw (whatever that means); and yet he appears to have taken the Ben in the dream to represent himself, the job-book in the dream to represent his job-book, the God in the dream to represent God, and the *others* in the dream to represent—others. In fact there *is* no symbolic representation in the dream: things are what they are and not other things. McCarthy, one of fiction's great searchers and researchers, appears not to have looked at his own dreams or anyone else's, for this is simply not the way that dreams operate. McCarthy is great with many things but he is not great with dreams. It is hard, for example, to say which is duller, the so-called dream with which the Border Trilogy drags toward conclusion, or the windbag deposing it. When Ben asserts that "I had this dream but I did not heed it. And so I lost my way" (113), it is not because Ben has misinterpreted the dream—he has not really interpreted it at all—but because he did not do what it allegedly told him to do.

What should he have done?

We need to determine what he has lost. According to Ben, he has lost his way, although this business of the *lost way* is one of the flaws of the play, for the plaint is more imposed upon than rising out of the action. If Ben dreams a dream in which he worries that God will ask him about *the others* and then he *loses his way* for not heeding its message that "we cannot save ourselves unless we save all ourselves" (113), Ben, then, is lost because he did not save *the others*.

Who *are* these others?

His father shoots himself. What could Ben have done to save him? Ben might have gotten closer to his father if, instead of submerging himself in the gravity of his work, he had submitted to "that true bend of gravity which is the world's pain" (111); but the father-son relationship, even the lack of such a relationship, is sketched too sparsely to mean much at all, and there is little to suggest that an improvement in relations might have spared Big Ben his suicide. The play in which Big Ben shoots himself is barely the same as the play in which his son mourns the loss, and even that regret is poorly managed. There can hardly be a clumsier, less evocative line than: "Why could he not see the worth of that which he had put aside and the poverty of all he hungered for?" (111).

Ben's nephew overdoses. So what? He is presented as a thoughtless punk. What could Ben have done, under the bend of the world's pain, to save *him*? When we discover that Soldier's name is also Ben, the boy's position as an *other*, one of Ben's selves to be saved, is underscored, but not persuasively, for Soldier is doomed from the moment he enters the play.

More than any McCarthy character prior to John Grady Cole, even more than Suttree, Ben has concerned himself with *the others*. Are we meant to believe that for all his praise of stone, praise of Papaw, praise of God, praise of spirit, praise of the Bible, praise of his grandmother, praise, in fact, of everything he loves, nothing and no one taught him, in advance of this wonderful dream, to love his neighbor as himself? He must have heard it. And if there is nobody and nothing in his life that could help him, either before or after the dream, to fasten to his *way* (however he may define it), why, then, are all these things, or any of them, praiseworthy? What good are they to him? What is the use of the message itself?

McCarthy has asked too much of Ben. He wants Ben to be a fundamentally good man and he wants us to feel for his imperfections. He also wants him to talk stone, mason, Bible, God, and he tries to superimpose an appreciation of *lostness* that does not make sense either in light of what he has told us (too much), or in light of what we have seen (too little). With regard to his family, Ben, for all his self-mortification, has not done a damn thing wrong, or very little. He may, for instance, have lied to his sister, may have paid off her son, but it does not *feel* wrong: what feels wrong is the manner in which he regrets it, telling us, in effect, *this is my tragedy*. What was he supposed to have done? Carlotta's break with Ben, meant to underscore Ben's Big Mistake, seems severe, and it works against the effect McCarthy is straining for. It is thus more puzzling than affecting for Ben to be lost of not saving all *the others*, and it is questionable to claim that philosophically the themes of *The Stonemason* are, at least, played out better than its action.

The Stonemason shares a fault with *Cities of the Plain* in the divergence between McCarthy's bent for rendering his characters in (or at) their perfections, and his ability to put these men in trouble. If Ben's alleged downfall—"I had this dream but I did not heed it. And so I lost my way" (115)—is simply not credible, it is even less credible that John Grady Cole, with all his boy's book abilities, imagines for one moment that his heart-of-gold whore can enter a taxi, *a Mexican taxi in Mexico, alone*, and be driven, without accost, away from her Mexican pimp, her Mexican cathouse, and all her Mexican johns, over the Mexico border into John Grady's brilliant loving arms. With all that McCarthy has asked me to believe about John Grady Cole over the course of two novels (not to mention all the collective wisdom, skill, and strength of character at the ranch, including his friend Billy, another boy's book hero), he cannot also ask me to believe of John Grady *this is the best he can do*. I can only believe that this halfassed scheme for springing his beloved is a lapse on McCarthy's part. The cause of trouble for John Grady, like the cause of trouble for Ben, is insufficiently imagined, with the result that it is wholly unconvincing.

As for Ben's dream, Ben has, in fact, misinterpreted it, but I believe he has done so because McCarthy has done so. As I have suggested, the message in the dream—"Where are the others?"—does not derive from a dream-God, it derives from a dream—Ben's anxiety attack, an attack so upsetting to both the dreamed Ben and the dreamer that the dream is never concluded (or that is its conclusion). The message is judged as a glimpse into God's expectations. But to take its significations literally (and to maintain its cautionary status), the message of the dream is that to worry about justifying yourself through your work will make you fear even worse accusations. In other words, let your book speak for itself and do not go to answer questions about it. Regardless of who calls you in.

THE STONE

When I am in Paris...

Now that I *am* in Paris, my apartment looks out on the quiet Passage des Abbesses. As this is Montmartre, which does not let you forget it is a mountain, the cobbled flagstone *passage* culminates in forty-eight steep stone steps. Half a minute up the street, the Place Emile Gudeau—where young Picasso, in the shitstinking dump they called the Bateau Lavoir, formerly known as the Trapper's House, stumbled through very bad French while inventing a new tongue only two men could speak—is made all of stone, as are most of the walks and ancient edifices of Montmartre. Nearby, the little Cemetiere de St. Vincent encloses me in stone and reminds me that the mortals among us are fated to rest with stone over their heads. When I stumble in the streets because, carousing in circles daily, I have walked myself stupid, it is stone I am falling upon and breaking my back over. When I kneel to tie a lace I kneel on stone. When I lean against a wall to make a notation for my novel or to ink a small sketch, it is stone—as in the beautifully blackened northern fortifications—that supports me. Down at the Ile St. Louis or the Ile de la Cité, pausing against the parapets of the Pont au Change or the Pont Louis Philippe to scan the city with a monocular, I rest my case on stone. When I walk down stone steps to reconnoiter the Seine while forgetting, for an hour, Cocteau's remark (made in 1963) that "Paris has become an automobile garage" (76), it is quais and bridges of freestone, burrstone, limestone, tombstone, Bastilles-stone, *true*stone, over which I run my hungry hands and do whatever is legal to do with stone, including occasional yanks and turns of those big rusty rings, used for mooring the Seine barges, that look like remnants of antic creatures trapped and memorialized in stone when the quais were first laid. When, during his walks along these quais, the autobiographer-pornographer Restif de la Bretonne impulsively carved into *les pierre* perambulatory reflections and the date of his passage here, he was carving them into this Pierre as well. When Dickens walked off his insomnia in the streets of London, he touched the rough stone of Newgate and thought of its sleeping prisoners. I touch the rough stone of Paris and marvel how it awakens the sleeping prisoner of myself. Crossing the oldest of Paris bridges, the Pont Neuf, from which entire sections of Paris-blacked *parapet, corniche, console, claveaux,* and *mascaron* are being removed for reconditioning, I reach over the barricades and swipe a few pebbles of crushed white stone from one of the huge blocks and I rub the powder into my scalp for a more direct form of influence. I would prefer the black stuff but that is rather silly because I, all of us in the city, are, in effect, the black stuff, for that is what we do to the stone we live by. In that old popular scrapbook, a devil who is renowned enough to be called *the* devil asks a very young rabbi to make the stones bread. This is because the devil is not a poet, at least he wasn't in those days, or he would have been out eating the stones without the aid of his enemy. Henry Thoreau, dear man, would embrace the shrub oak—"a match found for me at last" (Journal 146)—and thus his life was simplified. Stone complicates me and I am devoted to it.

For this it rewards me.

A few nights ago, leaning out the window with my dinner in hand, observing the Montmartoise in the *passage,* I saw, by the spill of a streetlamp, a slender man in a dark coat standing over a man in a beige jacket who was lying with his back on the pavingstones and appeared to be in trouble. Short words passed, then a shining silver object appeared. *Don't let it be a revolver*, I thought. It was, and its barrel went up to the temple of the unfortunate on the ground. In the novel I was writing, the old curé of St. Eustache importunes a loaded revolver against the head of an armless giant, prompting my narrator, Matisse, to say: "Have you ever seen it? It will make your eyeballs fold over themselves." I was wondering whether to cry bloody murder or to order the *guardien* to call the police but, writers being writers even in panic, I corrected the phrase to *coil around* themselves, which does not make any more sense but which is truer to the sensation. I was grateful to the stones of Paris for giving me the perception, but I was sorry I had not seen this when I was writing about *Blood Meridian*. Well. It testifies as much against the world in which we live as it does for the achievement of that novel that it follows a reader everywhere. As for saving the man's life, I hesitated a moment because the gunman behaved strangely. The exchange of words continued and he fidgeted over the best way of raising his weapon to its purpose, repeating the gesture of drawing it out of his coat with barely discernible variations. Incredibly, his antagonist appeared to be helping him out. And they call the French rude! I began to detect signs of my own profession. When a third party sprang out of the dark with further suggestions, it was clear that the people of Paris, a city of cinevores, a city mad for film, were making one of their own on the cobbled *passages* of Montmartre.

This morning I mustered early. Having returned from my gallerist in Heidelberg, I was eager, as after any absence from Paris, to dive back deeply into the streets. Without taking the time either to shave or to shower off my journey, I somnambulated Montmartre to observe it about its morning ablutions, its incomparable bakery business, its runty little canine constitutionals... I genuflected before its conventual plainsong... and I descended into the heart of Paris, carrying *The Stonemason*.

I was a man with a mission.

But in Paris it is a mistake to go directly to one's object, for Paris is only knowable by diligent divagation, cunctation, circumambulation, and for me the first of any business in Paris is the business of Paris itself. Only the other day I digressed, in the heat of urgent business, in order to follow a man in the street. My mark was Michel Roethel, proprietor of the Librairie Jules Verne and a Jules Verne authority, but it was not out of tribute to one of the heroes of my youth that I tailed this man like a criminal across rue la Grange, down rue Favarre and rue Dante, to number 63 in the cobbled rue Galande, a *brasserie* called The Navigator, where he sat in the last booth with a very well-dressed crony and joked heartily with his beautiful waitress... nor was it be-cause he had thrown me out of his shop during my first encounter with Paris and had answered, when I asked him whether he spoke any English: "Why should I?" so that I swore to return whenever I could say, in bad French: "So you can thank my country for saving you from having to speak German"... no, I tailed Monsieur Roethel solely because he is the essence of a man who *needs* tailing, because Paris that day would be sadly incomplete without a tail on Monsieur Roethel and apparently I am the dick for the job... and so, without question, without rancor, even without interest, I follow him, consoling myself for delaying actual business with the reflection that if I decide to murder a man a la Roskolnikov or *Compulsion*, for the sake of the deed itself, this will be the beginning... and it is because such digressiveness is necessary in Paris that I have had to digress, and must continue to do so, here.

So in rue Montorguil I bought a cake for Pére Bénéteau, the kind curé of St. Eustache who was helping me to the curé in my novel, some of which is set in his monster church in the *quartier* of Les Halles where my Matisse, born the same year as Papaw, has one of his worst adventures... and I purchased exquisite *papier à la main* on which to paint Racine's house, which, since Paris plaques can lie as well as Paris men and the house that reads **ICI MOURUT (HERE DIED) RACINE** is not Racine's at all, can only be found in my pictures... and I wrote for a couple of hours on the Ile St. Louis while the sun settled slowly over the buttressed behind of Notre Dame. Finally, with McCarthy's play burning a hole in my hand and sinking a small stone in my heart, I sauntered along rue St. André des Arts to the Boulevard St. Germain where, at the intersection of rue Bonaparte, I sat on steps opposite the church of St. Germain-des-Prés, which is actually the ruins of an abbey whose mysterious faithful stone I have tried to suggest in hundreds of paintings, paintings that have always, thankfully, failed because its stone cannot be rendered in oil pastel. One would have to be painting in stone, with which I would end up building a St. Germain-des-Prés in New York, a contradiction in terms. After a dreamlike session—it lasted nearly two hours—in which I papered the stone floor of one of the chapels of St. Germain with some of my paintings of that church, the curé, shaking my hand warmly as the members of his board clucked like hens over the pictures, told me that he was moved to see someone else sharing his obsession with "my tower."

I have brought *The Stonemason* in order to read it directly in front of this great tower; to read it, so to speak, under the gaze of this glorious building and within its sphere of influence, which has exerted itself since the 11th century. As an approach to criticism this is tomfoolery, but I am not a critic, only a reader in the extreme and an irrational guilty American who is driven to inexplicable acts of worship and is hoping this dislocation will transform, or, at least, temper his bilious view of a very great poet's play. It was only as I viewed *The Gardener's Son* in slow motion—literally one frame at a time—

that it began to disclose some of its higher contrasts. This is a way, if you will, of slowing the play down. After reading the play in typescript in 1994, I endeavored, one could say, to slow the play for myself considerably by offering to direct it in the city in which it is set—Louisville—but that production was not to be. To be friend to a man's work calls for constancy the way an Elizabethan understood it. Perhaps I am here in the Place St. Germain-des-Prés only to say: *I am constant*. If this evening only a few stone statues will hear me, that is sufficient.

About rue Bonaparte, Henry Miller, during the days of *Black Spring*, wrote to his friend Alfred Perlès: "Anything said away from this street is a lie" (Aller Retour 77). If this is a fact, as I am certain it must be—any city that cruises its transvestites on a street called rue des Martyrs, and will tolerate, for window dressing, a string of stuffed rats, and can get away with publishing an *unabridged* graphic novel of *As I Lay Dying*, must have a street of truth, and if anybody can find it, Miller can—then everything I have said about *The Stonemason* must carry its weight here or it cannot be taken seriously. With any luck what I have written will fall to pieces and I can sweep out the wreckage before any of it is published. We know from Thomas Merton that one of the Desert Fathers—a Christian hermit of the 4th century—carried a stone in his mouth for three years in order to cultivate silence... permission enough for me to carry *The Stonemason* in mine for much the same purpose.

Sitting on the steps of the *hôtel* at number 8, which houses the trunk-maker Louis Vuitton and is one door down from the Café des Deu Magots, whose expensive *terrace* is packed and buzzing, I read aloud, slowly, the part of Papaw, using my softest Southern inflections, watching the words spirit off to the stone, savoring them as they home their way back down my throat. Not surprisingly, Papaw, even in the evening shadows of St. Germain-des-Prés, holds up beautifully. He is a sturdy old man. He is far from out of place. The streets do not disdain him. The Paris night protects him. The tower understands him. His recit moves me, not because of its anecdote: because of its nobility, *because of the way it is written*. Perhaps, too, despite the distances between us, because we are Americans together. Tears form. An American in Paris is sobbing over McCarthy. When I turn to the tiresome Ben Telfair, Ben proves as irksome a pest in Paris as he is in Louisville or Manhattan. What worse can be said of a man? When the prose of an author is so overindulged, it can hurt the rest of his work because it can poison the reader's ear. I do not want to be hearing the voice of Ben behind the novels. After less than half a page, I am compelled to close the book.

I am beginning to feel the cold.

But as this is slow motion, I sit beneath the blue, red, and white striped awning of the café Le Bonaparte, one of the several in which Jean Paul Sartre, whose window on the *place* was five flights directly above my head, used to set up house at the height of his powers, and I order a *thé à la Menthe*. The last table on the left, adjacent the little booth of a *crêperie*, is very good for sketching one corner of the church and for catching the heat of a coalburning *brazier*, a fine French system that, without alleviating the cold, offers a countersensation with which the chill evening air can coexist, an encouraging combination for a novelist in Paris. One sips the hot tea... one scribbles... one watches the promenade... one shivers... one calculates the tip... one appreciates the coal... one eavesdrops and misinterprets the gibberish... one wearies of being the foreigner forever... one regrets that half of Paris wants to become an American gangster... one shakes one's head over the myth of the Revolution... one is reduced to an imbecile by the entrancing columns of crêpe smoke rising in the booth... one wonders why, with everybody drinking all the time, no one is ever drunk... one delects in the sensation of being a time bandit, stealing away with pockets, valises, rucksacks filled with every hour, every minute that has not been fastened down or imprisoned in the machine... one thinks about the list of great novels about cities—too few, too few—and one does not care whether McCarthy will write "another" *Suttree*—or *anything* that holds a candle to it—for one *Suttree* is Knoxville enough and novel enough to last a man a lifetime... one hums the little four-note tune—*Bonjour, Monsieur!*—that becomes your familiar from the first day here as announcing, defining, celebrating the nation and the city even more than the *Marseillaise*... one is impressed by the beret above the blouse above the skirt above the stockings above the heels above the stone above the ruins of an outpost of old dying Rome... one postulates the sound of French love... one plots to steal Pére Bénéteau from his monster church and into a quick matinee of *The Naked Spur* with Jimmy Stewart... one wishes that McCarthy had drafted Billy Parham into the army, into the war, into the Allied invasion via Normandy and into the city of Paris where he would marry a beautiful starcrossed Algerian with a brother who leads Billy into adventure until he dies in front of my table and escapes the demeaning subjugations of sequel and epilogue... one is acutely aware that this is eternity, that you will never not be here, even without the whistle of a train to tell you so... one prays to Descartes' ashes, which reside across the street, for a sentence for one's novel or a thought about *The Stonemason* as good as anything in the *Meditations*... one calls for a *couteau* to cut the pages of an unread copy of *Corot* circa 1902 that, if one is lucky, ought to yield at least a sentence, not a bad return for a hundred francs given the high cost of sentences in Paris... one is fortified, welcomed home, exculpated, humiliated and put in one's place by the remains of St. Germain-des-Prés... and, with conversation for cover, again one voices *The Stonemason*. Here in Le Bonaparte, at the center of Miller's street, Papaw shines. "A man that's killed by a fool that aint never had the first thought in his head it aint no different from if a rock fell on him" (50). Yes a failure of a play, but one in which McCarthy has planted a marvelous miniature. (Where is Miller for me to read it to him?) But this is as far as I can go with *The Stonemason*. Ben is booted out of the café.

If old Sartre were over my head now instead of under my feet, he would embrace Ben's blockheaded folderol, as would his Communist comrades reading *L'Humanité* and smoking over their second drinks in the fashionable cafés surrounding me. But I am forgetting about Ben's godtalk. Would that not ruin the romance? It ruins me. It ruins philosophy. It nevertheless puzzles me that critics who want to generate philosophy out of McCarthy character, landscape, image and event have been slow to turn their attention to a philosophy—an attempt at it—delivered to them, *preached* at them, directly. With respect to *The Merchant of Venice*, James Shapiro, in his interesting book *Shakespeare and the Jews*, writes simply: "Plays, unlike sermons, are not reducible to one lesson or another" (121). But McCarthy *has* brought a man into the pulpit to sermonize—or something like it. For God's sake, McCarthyites—what are you waiting for? Perhaps we all prefer what is hidden to what is plain because it allows us to shape it into something we admire. "Be devout under trees/At midnight on the ground," wrote Kerouac, and so I shall (MCB 123). But kneeling is not the only position in which to praise a writer. Nothing wrong with tough love in literature. "In reading," wrote Proust, "friendship is suddenly brought back to its first purity. With books, no amiability" (55).

A few tables down, two Polish men are talking international business. At least for them it is. In the course of this amazing conversation, which is conducted all in English, one of them—called Roman—says: "I go for a walk and I establish a certain argumentation. Actually, it turn out to be worse than I thought. This was a nostalgia to argue."

A nostalgia to argue... Yes, Roman, perhaps it was for me too... but can we not at least concede that there are some works of art that do not know their own form or destiny?

That a writer might believe, as Hemingway did, that he has fashioned a beautiful novel about loving and dying in Venice—"If it isn't good," he told Charles Scribner about *Across the River and Into the Trees*, "you can hang me by the neck until dead" (667)—when he has, instead, rendered a superlative sportsman's sketch about duckhunting in Venice appended by forty-four chapters of flapdoodle?

That there are firstrate characters who, because their authors cannot give them more than a page or two of adequate world to act in, are fated to exist only as fragments, and for a novel or a play to be attached to these fragments constitutes a case of mistaken identity?

That some plays exist only for one small story to be told in them, told by a character who is lacking sufficient story of his own?

That *The Stonemason* is not a failed play about a family, it is a good short story about a very old murder told from grandfather to grandson flanked and oppressed by superfluities?

That with writers of highest worth it is sometimes their abject failures that compel us to return to them and to give them another chance, a lifetime of chances, if for no other reason than a reluctance to be so sorely disappointed, a refusal to accept that they could fall so very far beneath the rules *they* have created and the standard *they* have set... or a suspicion that the time was out of joint and that we must have been blind to something... or the hope, irrational but not unfounded, that the work, over time, will have rearranged and disdisgraced itself?

That if a disaster does, in fact, drive us to a type of anserine desperation, that is something to thank it for, as I am thankful to *The Stonemason* for bringing me here tonight... or for parking me under a tree along the Neckar River, on which a Heidelberger calypso boat is playing a slow "Perfidia," forcing me to ponder the play in the dark and to marvel, in drunkish dream-fatigue, how some strains of art, like some strains of music, come closer as they float away from us, up river, and to capture a streak of light from one of those big yellow German phone booths the better to scratch out a couple of ideas... or for leading me to the Campo San Vidal, the site of *The Stonemason's Yard*, Canaletto's masterpiece, by the Academia Bridge along the Venetian Grand Canal, where I sketch piledrivers, the original heroes of Venice, for a picture of my own, and where I contemplate McCarthy with my legs dangling over the *fundamenta*, and where I smooth one of my faces over the dark cool stone within the Church of San Vidal, stone you can see being cut for that structure when you look at the Canaletto, stone that would never have grazed my cheek were I not so disappointed in *The Stonemason*... or for helping me to nose my way, with no map and no working knowledge of El Paso, to the house of which I have painted a hundred pictures, and to nudge me across the front yard, abandoned now to political handbills and soda bottles, to crouch under a low tree and to kneel in front of a few yards of freestone wall, a modest little wall that I had not noticed before, a wall with a rusty pipe and an open bag of trash behind it, a wall such as a man might make in his spare time just to keep his hand in, a wall McCarthy built while constructing one of the sturdiest reputations in America, and to put down my pen, my glasses and my paper and to lean my brow against it, not to tribute the man, the work, the wall, or this play that has led me to it, but to ask myself what the hell do I do now that I'm here, and to answer that by easing myself down from the pressures of life and to feel myself kneeling on McCarthy's old land and to realize *this is the point of reading*, to be brought to a place you wouldn't have thought mattered, to touch something you never expected to find, to kneel in dirt you are happy to have beneath you, to follow an indefensible impulse as if your life depended on it, to dream the world back that insists on dreaming you, to make an ass of yourself and to get yourself arrested or chased off or shot in the head or healed for being a trespasser on property not your own.

Next morning in Montmartre, I find myself watching the City of Paris stonemasons who, in their bright red and white-striped outfits, are repaving the narrow blocklong rue St. Rustique, a street at least as old as Villon and the highest in Paris... a street named for Rusticus, one of the priests who, executed with St. Denis by the Emperor Diocletian, gave Montmartre one of its several derivations, *Mons Martyrum*... a street where Van Gogh took a studio... a street you can find in Utrillo much the way it is this morning... a street that offers an obscured and, because of that, the best view of Sacre Coeur... a street where I have set one of the scenes in my novel. What was wrong with the old rue St. Rustique? What is a stone that is no longer street-worthy? Worn down? What am *I* if not that, and what am I doing here if not to replace myself? But an old Paris street is, of course, more important than a man. If it is worn by the Dutchman, should we not leave it alone?

To defend a cobbled street it is helpful to have groveled or rejoiced in it, at least to have raised or have needed to raise a man from the dead in it, especially if that man is you. A mender of roads is one of the revolutionary heroes, or rabid dogs, of *A Tale of Two Cities*, but if you happen to be a mob a revolution is not necessary: an uprising will do. In the spring of 1968, the students of Paris defended and appreciated the streets around the Sorbonne by hurling, over barricades of burning Renaults, twelve thousand square yards of pavingstones to answer the *batons*, tear gas, and concussion grenades of President de Gaulle's CRS. Of course it ended in defeat and deportation, but it taught that spiteful son of a bitch de Gaulle that, when it came to the streets of Paris, for which the man cared nothing, heads could be broken in both directions. Alas, it is too late for any apologist for the old stone of rue St. Rustique. As this is not a city of waste, doubtless it will reappear (already a small chunk has made its way into my pocket). Is it too late for me to be an apologist for *The Stonemason*?

I watch these masons for an hour, playing the part of a man who is not self-conscious about it, eventually *becoming* that man, for Paris permits the idler, the loiterer, even the loafer, the do-nothing—Paris permits *me*. One of these workers, a black man, barrows stones from a site in front of the oldest church in Paris, St. Pierre de Montmartre, whose arches knew a century when cement was made with the blood of a bull, and he dumps the stone, in rather a rude tumble, in front of a kneeling comrade who will select the stone with the most suitable shape, chisel off a chip or two, have a smoke, watch the girls, consult with one of his bosses, and pound it into place with that characteristic sharp stone-chink over dull thumping of earth. Because of its weight, its density, its powers of resistance, I am conscious of a rudeness inherent in the treatment of stone, as much as in my treatment of *The Stonemason*. These hardworking men, however skilled, are laborers to me, not artists. I prefer to preserve that term for something other, and I would begrudge it even to Papaw, despite all that Ben would have us believe about his work, which, in the world of stone, is doubtless in the higher altitudes. And this morning I would begrudge it to myself. When a man sails through the stone commotion with a large stretched canvas, I take it as a cue to return to work.

Passing the indefatigable schlock painters setting up their shitty little pictures in Place de Tertre, I can acknowledge that rocks, words, and masters of both are old things together, but I am unhappy with the notion, as applied to *The Stonemason*, that the art of laying stone is analogous to the art of literature. Nothing is analogous to literature; or, if it is, the analogy is less apt to enlighten than to confuse. "Isn't as if we're talking about *journalism*," I think... I am also thinking that, while the work of the mason is, indeed, intended to last, often it is intended to be ignored. Stonework is not only for buildings: stone is a smoothness to walk upon, that is, *to be forgotten*, to be injured and insulted, to be wheeled, bounced, bled, drooled, pissed, puked, spat, shat, sleeted and spunked upon. The Phrygian hearth-gods that Aeneas carries away from Troy appear to him in a moonlit dream, saying: "You must prepare great walls for a great race" (71), evidence for me that the gods are a pack of dolts, for the cities of all the greatest of races are built without walls. Even the beautiful fortifications with which I am so infatuated inspire only contempt in Rabelais' Panurge who, after telling Pantagruel "an old cow with one fart could knock down more than a dozen yards of them" (300), proposes building them properly with the vaginas of Frenchwomen which, he claims, are cheaper than stone, more resistant to blows than metal, and perfectly disposed to rain pox upon the enemy. Henry Miller, who went to school under Rabelais and who adored his master, did, in fact—in *Tropic of Cancer*—build his own Paris with the vaginas of Frenchwomen, using *cunt* upon *cunt* like stone upon stone and producing a city of Paris that's as well fortified and will last as long as any. One of the Clowns digging graves in Elsinore asks his partner: "What is he that builds stronger than either the mason, the shipwright, or the carpenter?" (5.1.41–42) He elicits this answer: "The gallowsmaker, for that frame outlives a thousand tenants" (5.1.43–44), but the response he is fishing for is *gravemaker*, for "the houses he makes lasts till doomsday" (5.1.59–60). In *Child of God* the fool of a smith who dresses

Lester's rusty axhead imposes a lesson upon him, volunteering, flame-by-flame, the secrets of his trade without imagining that Lester is only there to get the ax, so that when, after three packed pages of instruction, Lester is asked whether he reckons he can do it, Lester cannot imagine what the smith is talking about and can only say: "Do what" (74). For all of Ben Telfair's talk of secrecy, I am afraid that he is fated for a premature dotage of such smith-like prattle, to which a Thoreauvian will say: "I love better to see stones in place" (312), or: "The world is but outdoors,—and we duck behind a panel" (211), taking the wind out of Ben's view of building with stone, or building with anything.

But this morning what disturbs me is not the unbearable pride of Ben... this morning it is my own pride that irks me... as in the attempt at fine writing in my piece on *Blood Meridian* and its cautionary stance, as if a caution from me is worth half a damn to Cormac McCarthy or the world ("Up yours," I say to the essay, *aloud*)... or in the way my "Older Professions" has to go to such lengths to make a few simple points... as if the author of *Child of God* and *Suttree* doesn't deserve to have us lying, at least a little, or forgetting, perhaps a lot, about his play... as if we oughtn't to say that McCarthy had *gotten a little carried away*, or that Ben, who has lost a great deal, was having a bad day and, in that condition, ought not to have come to the theatre... as if the first planned production of the play having been canceled after its author, who should have been black, had been accused of being white, were not reason enough to stage it, perhaps employing an all-white cast in blackface so that McCarthy, who went from being politically useful when he was black to being politically undesirable when he was not, will not be charged again with subjecting black performers to racial stereotypes...[10] as if I oughtn't to play the part of Ben myself and in the transubstantiation by which Ben 1 and 2 become my own Ben 3, see him justified, for *as* Ben (as McCarthy), I, Ben (I, McCarthy), will make you, audience, believe and I will leave you entertained, for that is the player's promise...

When, in Dublin's Talbut Place, Stephen Deadelus walked past Baird the stonecutter, "the spirit of Ibsen would blow through him like a keen wind" (176). When I walk past *The Stonemason* this morning, a spirit of shame blows through me. I come away from rue St. Rustique sick of myself, profoundly, and disgruntled with my work. For the remainder of the day I try to recover and redeem myself in fiction and in paint, where the fine French paper will admit of no notion, no argument or complaint.

Before day's end, the City of Paris stonemasons have departed. Rue St. Rustique has been restored for another century of dogs to squat upon it, motorscooters to park in it, lovers to press in its darkness, geniuses to howl in its light, saxophones to swank down it, pilgrims to verify it, foreign exchange brats to laugh past it, long-aproned waiters to carry trays through it, veterans to limp across it, novels to be imagined in it, sisters of mercy to die on it, and, on it too, for unlisted, distempered, five-way fractured sons of bastards like myself to wonder about poets, about the uses and abuses of criticism, about lifelong failure, about trying to write one word truly, about stone and *The Stonemason*.

NOTES

1. See Whitman's "Old Actors, Singers, Shows, &c."

2. This Faulkner quotation, which I have not been able to trace, is taken from *A Sound Portrait of William Faulkner*, part 8 of National Public Radio's *A Question of Place* series, 1980.

Regarding the dearth of quality in theatre, there is this exchange between two players in the BBC production of Robert Graves' *I, Claudius*:

"The theatre isn't what it was."

"No. And I'll tell you something else. It never was what it was."

3. In her *Paris Review* interview, Lillian Hellman said: "There shouldn't be any difference between writing for the theatre and writing for anything else. Only that one has to know the theatre. Know it. To publish a novel or a poem one doesn't have to know print types or the publishing world. But to do a play, no matter how much one wishes to stay away from it, one has to know the theatre" (137).

4. "If he had had a really good resolving third act," Brad Dourif told me, "he'd have had a movie. It was close." For an interesting comparison to *The Gardener's Son*, see Bertrand Tavernier's first feature film, *L'Horloger de Saint-Paul*, released here as *The Clockmaker of St. Paul*, a compelling adaptation of Georges Simenon's 1955 novel *L'Horloger d'Everton*. This 1973 film, which transposes the story from upstate New York to Lyons, France—Tavernier's hometown—features Philippe Noiret as Michel Descombes, a man whose son, Bernard (Sylvain Rougerie), has shot a workman in the factory where his girlfriend is employed. Despite great gaps in their relationship, father and son have an important scene together at the end of the story.

5. Pearce has written about working with McCarthy in his foreword to the printed edition of *The Gardener's Son*. In a press release for the film, Pearce talks about McCarthy's reaction to his proposal that he write a screenplay about the incident.

> McCarthy agreed, and he and I went down to South Carolina, rented a couple of motel rooms and went to work.... As a documentary person working with a fiction writer, I was the more compulsive of the two. I compiled background material in every form I could—census records, trial records, letters from old company and state archives. I wanted McCarthy to have all this, knowing we could throw it all out once we had assimilated it and built our own dramatic fiction story. But McCarthy became as fascinated as I was

with the documentary material. Our research came up with elements that we never could have imagined. (3)

McCarthy told me that, aside from the decision to shoot the film in 16 millimeter color instead of 35 millimeter black and white, he was pretty satisfied with how it worked out.

6. In an excellent compilation of interviews with Gore Vidal called *Views from a Window*, Vidal expresses a distaste for the numinous in terms that would please any reader who does not agree with me that it works in *Blood Meridian*. His comments are worth quoting in full:

> I deeply dislike the writers of Romances (Melville, Hawthorne, Faulkner), despite their great gifts. The windy obscurity of so much American literature derives from the windy obscurities of so much of the beautiful but often opaque King James version of the Bible. Our Serious Solemn Writers are the result of a religious tradition whose central dogmas (the trinity, for instance) make no sense at all. Therefore, in order to make sense of the nonsensical, a vague windy periphrastic style is all to the good. Serious Solemn Folk (most Americans) feel positively sanctified by rolling, roiling sentences that contain perfect confusions posing as mysteries. Just like a good sermon. Currently, the University-novel is the embodiment of the quack religio-style. Written in what I call Near English, these books can only be understood by diagrams on blackboards, helped out by commentaries as clumsy as the texts examined. But then clarity has never been admired in the great republic, possibly because everybody has always been busy conning everyone else—usually in the style of the evangelicals (rabbis, too—and their spin-offs the mental therapists), who peddle the incredible in a language that will only yield its meaning if you have Faith—or tenure. (80)

7. In 2002, a revised version of *The Stonemason* was performed in Chicago. In it, only the character of Ben was retained. See "A *Stonemason* Evening," by Edwin T. Arnold.

In May 2006, McCarthy's two-man play, *The Sunset Limited*, was produced by the Steppenwolf Theatre Company in Chicago, and that fall I saw it at the 59E59 Theater in Manhattan. It was directed by Sheldon Patinkin, with Freeman Coffey and Austin Pendleton playing two men, Black and White, who argue about religion sitting at a kitchen table after Black rescues White from an attempted suicide and takes him home to his tenement. Despite antagonizing differences between Black and White, the play is fairly static and will suffer miserably if the performances are not well focused and kept in motion at as swift a pace as possible. The show that I saw did little to disguise the play's weaknesses, for it was under-rehearsed (e.g., Coffey did not know his lines) and under-directed (e.g., Pendleton, a veteran New York actor with great abilities, was at loose ends). The published version of the play carries the subtitle *A Novel in Dramatic Form*, which could be taken to mean that McCarthy initially considered the situation as a novel, but it can also be taken as acknowledgment that he is not truly a man of the theatre. *The Sunset Limited* is a rare instance of insufficient research in McCarthy. Two examples: Manhattan's Bellevue Hospital is on 27th Street, but in Black's tenement, which is within walking distance of the 155th Street subway, White refers to Bellevue as "up." It is also disturbing to a New

York ear to hear the New York subway repeatedly referred to as a commuter train, which it is not.

At the CAPITAL Centre of the University of Warwick in Coventry, England, director Tom Cornford was invited, by Nick Monk, to mount a staged reading of *The Sunset Limited* as part of an international Cormac McCarthy conference. With only a few hours of rehearsal, and with the performers—Michael Gould as White, Wale Ojo as Black—having to read from their scripts, Tom's version was more vital, intense, and clear than Patinkin's rather sleepy rendering. When I asked Tom about directing *The Stonemason*, he said: "I'd love to, but I'd need a fairly long leash. I'm drawn to it because it takes a documentary-realist story and moulds and blurs it to explore its mysteries. Papaw, Big Ben, and Ben almost become a part of each other, not reliably distinct selves. Their stories and natures are twined. I was watching *The Godfather II* last night, which does a similar thing. The significant difference, though, is that Coppola has the confidence to do it with very simple montage. He dissolves from young Vito to middle-aged Michael and back again, and he juxtaposes the revelation of Fredo's betrayal with Batista's resignation and the ensuing disorder. McCarthy's staging, on the other hand, seems clumsy. I see what he means in his note about placing the events in 'a completed past' (5) and allowing the drama 'its right autonomy' (6), but his double-Ben isn't the best way of achieving that—there is a more elegant solution, although I'd need to try out a few options before I could say what it is. But I think his novelist's eye for actions and images that capture larger stories serves him very well." Tom's reaction to McCarthy's stage directions was more discriminating than mine. "I *love* the 'wall of actual stone' (9)," Tom told me. "Next to that, the lectern and the podium and all the other scenic stuff in the stage directions sound like clutter to me. But I think the action in *The Stonemason* is eloquent and economical." When I asked him to compare *The Stonemason* to *The Sunset Limited*, he said that he hears a lot of echoes: "Black has a good deal of Papaw in him," Tom said. "Ben has learned from him that 'True stone masonry is not held together by cement but by gravity. That is to say, by the warp of the world. By the stuff of creation itself' (9–10). If Black were on a building site, he'd be saying that. He'd have been similar to Soldier as a kid. He must have gone through Big Ben's despair. And he has Ben's evangelical urge. Ultimately, he's most like Ben in that Ben feels that he, too, has lived the lives of his family, and he has the demanding, god-like example of his grandfather to live up to."

My conversation with Tom, "Believing in *The Sunset Limited*: A Talk with Tom Cornford on Directing McCarthy," appears in a forthcoming anthology, edited by Nick Monk and Rick Wallach, tentatively titled *The Road Ahead: Interdisciplinary and Intertextual Approaches to Cormac McCarthy*. For another perspective on the play, see "Cormac McCarthy's *The Sunset Limited*: Dialogue of Life and Death: A Review of the Chicago Production," by Dianne C. Luce.

8. As I suggest in "Suttree Sutured," Suttree's stay at Knoxville General contains conversation that is comparably cute.

9. With few exceptions, most notably Judge Holden in *Blood Meridian*, McCarthy sound-offs ruin McCarthy's work and represent his greatest weakness as a writer: the inability to resist putting the journal of his readings and ruminations into the mouths of his characters. His unpublished screenplay, *Whales and Men*, which contains numerous

Ben-like passages that do to whales what *The Stonemason* does to stone, is so suffused with sounding off that it is hard to imagine how McCarthy could have envisioned it as a film. The sounding off of Sheriff Ed Tom Bell in *No Country for Old Men* is one of the novel's least attractive properties, and its evaporation in the film by the Coen Brothers clears the way for Tommy Lee Jones to say all that we need to hear from him.

10. See Edwin T. Arnold's "Cormac McCarthy's *The Stonemason*: The Unmaking of a Play."

IV

THE GARDENER'S SON

...and of the tribe of Cormac...

—Joyce

• 8 •

Getting the Voices Right:
A Conversation with Robert Morgan
about *The Gardener's Son*

For a film called Acting McCarthy: The Making of Richard Pearce's The Gardener's Son, *I asked novelist and poet Robert Morgan to speak with me, on camera, about* The Gardener's Son. *Based on the murder of James Gregg by Robert McEvoy in the mill town of Graniteville, South Carolina, in 1876, the picture was co-produced by Richard Pearce and Michael Hausman on a budget of $200,000, which was provided by Public Television station KCET's Visions series. Fashioned from an original screenplay by Cormac McCarthy, shot in color by cinematographer Fred Murphy on 16mm film, using locations chiefly in North Carolina,* The Gardener's Son *was director Richard Pearce's first full-length feature. The film, which aired on January 6, 1977, was favorably reviewed by John O'Connor in the* New York Times, *who called it "a haunting production" and praised its "almost poetic vividness;" by Alan Kriegsman in the* Washington Post, *who said that it "abounds in privileged moments," and features performances that "lend the drama an almost Aeschylean depth;" and by Tom Allen in the* Village Voice, *who called it "the most provocative unknown American movie of 1976" and rated its ironies "on a par with* The Battle of Algiers." *As I have suggested, it was superbly well cast and is some of the best work by all of its participants.[1] McCarthy himself appears briefly (and silently) as a tophatted investor who is shown around the mill by James Gregg, who is beautifully played by Kevin Conway. The film has never enjoyed a theatrical release.*

My conversation with Bob Morgan took place in a small room at the Gramercy Park Hotel in Manhattan on February 12, 2000, when Morgan was in New York to meet with the publishers of his novel Gap Creek, *which had recently been chosen for the Oprah Book Club. Speaking about Algonquin, which published the book in hardcover, Morgan said: "Before this, the most copies they had sold of a book was 150,000. The day Oprah made the announcement, they had orders for 650,000 copies overnight."*

JOSYPH: You are one of the few people I know who saw *The Gardener's Son* when it aired in 1977.

MORGAN: Purely by accident. I turned on the television to PBS. This film was already in progress. It grabbed my attention because of the voices, the accents. I realized: "My goodness, here's something from National Public Television where they really have the accents right and the dialect is right on the money." I remember the foreman in the cotton mill who says to the kid: "If I'm not mistaken you'll find a broom in there." My goodness—who has done this! So I kept watching, glued to the show.

I've never forgotten, after over twenty-two years, Ned Beatty coming to the door of that old tavern. He's told the mother is dead, and he says: "I didn't know that. C'mon in, honey, and get ye a drink. I'm mighty sorry t'hear that." That was so perfect. I was enthralled. Watched the whole thing. Very sad, very dark story. Credits came on, said it was directed by Richard Pearce, script by Cormac McCarthy. I, of course, knew about McCarthy, but I had never read him.

It was a very important thing for me to see that film because it showed me what you could do with the voices of that region. The cotton mills of upper South Carolina mostly employed poor whites from the mountains. Many of my family members had worked in those cotton mills. My mother worked in a cotton mill when I was young. She supported us. So I was quite taken to see the anger in the character of the boy. It was a breath of fresh air to see that kind of realism. Particularly in terms of the voices, and the way in which those cotton mill workers were at such a disadvantage, but were, in a way, happy to be working there, to be making wages. They had come down from the mountains, having sold and abandoned their farms.

I did not start writing fiction immediately after that, but within the next four years I did, and I believe that's one of the things that inspired me to start telling stories about Appalachia, about the mountains where I had grown up.

JOSYPH: Prior to that, had you not thought of using your native land as material?

MORGAN: I had published several short stories and they were all set in the area, but then I published only poetry for about fifteen years. The important thing for me in going back to fiction was learning to use voices. I had not done that in my earlier stories very much. It was a process of learning to let my characters tell their own stories, reveal themselves in the way they talk. The genius of Cormac McCarthy is partly in his ability to get the voices right. In all of his fiction and in the screenplay he has an amazing ear. That was a kind of revelation to me, to see that that's where so much of the life of the characters was, in the voices. This is certainly true in all of his books, especially in the Appalachian novels.

JOSYPH: Brad Dourif told me that he enjoyed watching McCarthy's delight in local speech patterns during the filming around Glencoe, North Carolina. "I guess there's something about the way characters use language," Brad told me. "You know, Dickens always defined his characters so well with language. And I'm just remembering what a kick it was. We were out looking at locations, and this old guy was showing us around and he'd say: 'Well, y'know, th'other day… went over, got in m'car, so t'speak… turned on the engine, so t'speak…' And I remember McCarthy's *delight* at that. He was describing it to somebody, saying: 'My God—this guy was talking about things that'd really happened, but he'd always say *so to speak* as if it were a metaphor, as if it didn't happen!' There it is. There's the writer. How the way this guy used the language was telling you so much about him. So easy to do, so easy to write—but so clear."

Does one have to *cultivate* that kind of an ear?

MORGAN: I think you have to teach yourself to do that. Often the people who have the greatest trouble writing dialogue and dialect accurately are the people who have spoken it themselves. Because they do it, they are not aware of how to write it down. It can be an advantage to come in from the outside and consciously study it, listen to it. It probably begins for any writer, including Cormac McCarthy, with an ability to listen. My experience is that writers are often better listeners than talkers. Other people may talk better about fiction than its writers, but almost all the good writers I know listen and watch people.[2]

They say Faulkner used to sit on the square in Oxford and listen to people tell stories. People often ask me: "How can you write so accurately about women? You're a man." My answer is, I have known a lot of women and listen to them talk. I used to listen to them as they strung beans or peeled peaches. I am sure McCarthy worked that way. I have heard that he used to hang around a country store in Tennessee and talk to trappers, construction workers.

But *it is a made thing*, that's the answer to your question. It doesn't come naturally. Nothing about writing is natural. But if you work *really hard* at storytelling, at language, you can make it seem *perfectly* natural, as though it happened spontaneously. The best art does seem to be virtually spontaneous. I tell my students that you do not take a story from real life and transcribe it to the page, you *create* a sense of reality, one detail, one sentence, one image at a time.

JOSYPH: In a lot of fiction that tries to capture a region, or a class or a category of person, the writer assumes that once he gets the language the way that he heard it, that's the prize, that's literature. But it has to attain a level of poetry, doesn't it? Often that's missing. It isn't missing in your books. It isn't missing in *The Gardener's Son*. McCarthy is a poet, is he not?

MORGAN: He certainly is. His writing, his dialogue, is so compact. If you look at a page of *The Gardener's Son*, or *Child of God*, it's amazing to see the poetic energy there, the way he's caught the flavor of speech but *compressed* it. If you transcribed a conversation among people like that and printed it, it wouldn't be very interesting. McCarthy's writing is art. It is a made thing. He has caught those tropes, those expressions, and put them into a very compact form.

I believe a lot of people writing about poor people, people in Appalachia, may approach it with an agenda instead of trying to get inside the characters and let them tell their own story. I believe that if you write from someone's point of view, let's say Lester Ballard in *Child of God*, it can only be done if you really try to see the world as he sees it. This is the great thing that McCarthy learned, perhaps, from writers like Dostoevsky. That you take characters who may be repellent to a lot of people, and who would be considered criminals or insane, but as a writer you try to get inside those characters and tell their story from their point of view, and that makes it live. It's very different from having an agenda, where you are going to show the world what poverty is like, or what the criminally insane are like. It's the difference between fiction and non-fiction, perhaps. The fiction writer is not writing an argument. You want to show real people.

JOSYPH: Were there elements of place that rang true to you in the film?

MORGAN: The scene that I remember most vividly is the tavern scene. That was just astonishingly real to me. You have a tavern that was really just a shack, a barn, with these men sitting around passing a jug of moonshine and slicing off a bit of potato as a chaser. Also, the house where the mother is lying in state was particularly well done. I think the script mentions black cloths hung over the mirrors. That was a particularly good detail. But beyond the detail, the tone of the piece, the realism, the hardness of it impressed me. This was not a romanticization of cotton mill life, and it was not an essay. Here was a filmmaker, a writer, and actors who were willing to look at poor people as they were.

JOSYPH: James Cagney used to have an expression, "dropping the goodies," for some actorial touch that, even if he were playing the bad guy, would charm the audience, warm them up to him. Most of the performances in this film don't attempt that. Certainly Dourif's doesn't. Were your sympathies with the kid? He *is* a murderer.

MORGAN: I certainly sympathized with him. Because you know that had he had a good lawyer, and if he had had money, he might have been convicted but he probably would not have been hanged.

The story is about moral ambiguity to a great extent. You don't know, finally, why he is so angry.[3] It may have been almost an accident. In modern times it would have been judged differently—he was unbalanced, he was an-gry, it happened spur-of-the-moment, it was not premeditated, it would have been Murder Two instead of Murder One—so you have to be sympathetic to a character like that.

One of the great things about the story is that it's not a story of moral judgment. You do feel Gregg, the mill owner, taking advantage of people. He's propositioning his women employees. I know that happened all the time. I've been told stories about that. McEvoy certainly knows that the owner does that, so that even if Gregg didn't proposition his sister, McEvoy knows he *might* have. It was considered more or less a right of the cotton mill owner.

I guess my greatest sympathy is for the sister, the female characters. I really wish more of the script had been kept in the movie. Some of the great-est writing McCarthy has ever done, probably, is in the later scene where the sister is in the hospital in Columbia, that monologue where she keeps circling back to the horse called Captain, who they sold and who she sees in the streets of Greenville later.[4] *That* was a *very* telling detail, that the horse had a name, that they remembered the name of the horse, that the horse was important. The loss of that horse symbolized the loss of their farm and their identity as a rural people. They had moved to the cotton mill and they had lost their horse. The loyalty of the horse, the fact that the horse recognizes them years later on the streets of Bringle, that's a wonderful detail.

I think McCarthy thought his way very deeply into that story.

JOSYPH: It's also poignant that the horse is named Captain. It's a boss's name—"Cap'n"—plus Gregg is "Captain Gregg"—but here it means something different.

MORGAN: Yes, it's her memory of the farm, which is probably viewed as a kind of Eden lost. It certainly was *not* when they were living there. But living in a cotton mill town with all the problems they've had—the father's alcoholism, the son's murder conviction, the mother's death—she certainly looks back to that mountain farm as a much better place and time, and the horse is symbolic of that.

Horses are so close to the people in rural life. You work with a horse. That's why it fascinates me so much. I worked with horses when I was young. The horse has a *name*, it's not just *a horse*. It's Captain.

JOSYPH: In Graniteville I spoke to a girl who was working in a con-venience store just outside of town. She said: "What d'you want to go *there* for?" I told her we were doing some research. She said: "Well I *live* there. You don't want to go *there*." I told her that we needed a place to stay. She said: "There's *nowhere* you can stay in Graniteville." She just didn't want me to *go* there. Being there of your own volition was crazy to her. I had to be warned off, chased away. I saw her point. It's still a mill town... still a company town to a degree that the cops pulled up and came over, a pair of them, and tried to prevent my pointing a video camera at the mill—which I did anyway and I can tell you, those smokestacks are *smoking*... there are "cardboard" company houses, uniform, depressing, all in a row... and the stench is, at times, overwhelming. In the cemetery on the outskirts of town, where James Gregg is buried and where you can still hear the mill and you can still smell it, clearly, I thought: "Having been here, I could see where a guy would commit a murder just to get *out*."[5]

MORGAN: They paid *very* low wages before the year of the minimum wage. My mother, on her first job, made nine dollars a week. She was the only person in her family employed. This was 1931, when she graduated from high school. In the 19th century they paid even less. The same people who had owned the plantations, after the Civil War, in the Reconstruction period, built cotton mills. They had lost the slave labor and they replaced it with the poor whites of the Piedmont and the mountains. They could pay them almost nothing, because these are people who were not used to a cash economy. They had practiced subsistence farming. They were attracted to the cotton mills because, hey, they were making wages, they could live in town and buy things. But it was a pretty bad system.

Yes, I could see where somebody would be so angry. But the brilliance of the film is partly that it's never explained. McCarthy is a writer who doesn't *explain* his characters. They do what they do and you can interpret that however you want. I think that's part of the fascination of his stories. They're not stories of moral judgment, they're about people.

JOSYPH: It would be nice to have the film reshown. Nan Martin (Mrs. Gregg) said to me: "I have always been puzzled about *The Gardener's Son*. Did they think so little of it that they just put it off in a dusty warehouse? This is Americana. This is *pure* Americana. It is *almost* a documentary. We shot it in a town where the mill was still there, where the looms were still set up. I was wearing a bustle that came from somebody's attic, I had a parasol from the 1800s. And you think this wouldn't intrigue people? You think there's much more interest in Jane Austin? No!" Kevin Conway (James Gregg) said: "Just the fact that it's an early work of someone who has evolved into one of the great American writers—that's important in and of itself, right? There aren't that many Cormac McCarthys writing in America where you can just say well, we're not going to show it. The beauty of film—the only reason to *do* film—is that it's going to be around for a while. You can preserve special moments in our cultural history. There's no point preserving them if you're not going to show them."

How would you answer someone who says: "Why bother with this one? It's an old film, it's about a very small region of the country, it's the 19th century, it's not *like* that any more, it's a murder by an unknown guy no one cared about then and no one cares about now. It's important to you, Bob Morgan, because it influenced you, but does it have a lick of importance beyond that?"

MORGAN: My first answer is the artistic quality of it. Works of art are important not only because of the subject, but because of the way they are made. It is so brilliantly written, directed, and acted, that it should be brought back. But it's also about a very important issue and a very important time in history. I believe that fiction and film are the main ways people know about history, and to know who you are you have to know something about history. I think there would be a real audience for this movie, because we are, now, looking more into our roots than we have in the recent past. If you want to know something about this country, you have to know what happened in the 19th century and the early 20th century.

Often the best stories are set way off in places nobody's ever been, about incidents they've never heard of, and this is a particularly interesting story because it's about one of the great transition periods in American history. Most viewers of films and television know more about the Civil War than they know about the period just after it, when the upper South, the Piedmont South, was in a *terrible* period of poverty. I've heard stories in my family about this period. There just wasn't *anything*. There was no way to make a living. The land had been devastated. That was one reason why these people went down to live in the cotton mill towns and were enticed to work for wages, because everybody was having such a hard time. So I would say it's important for people to know about this period and these kinds of people.

What makes a story accessible to a general audience is the artistry. We like stories that are real, that are detailed, that are local. Oddly enough, what would make a story set in an exotic place accessible is the specificity. Paradoxically, it's that local color, that local detail, that makes it accessible to any audience. Instead of *stripping that away* to make it accessible, you do exactly the opposite: you get the dialect right, you get the details right, and that makes it understandable to somebody in Russia or Japan, or to somebody a hundred years later.[6]

JOSYPH: You gave a talk in which you referred to something that you, certainly, achieve in your own work. You said that it's in the detail that a story achieves a cosmic element. You said: "The greatest writers evoke a sense of the poise and scale of eternity in their work."[7] That's a fascinating phrase, *the poise and scale of eternity.*

MORGAN: I believe that's one of the things that makes a writer a poet. To bring into play a very local story, in the foreground you have a character, you have a very angry young man, McEvoy, in South Carolina, who inadvertently—or with a plan, we're not sure—commits a murder. It's an engaging story, partly because the detail is so specific to the time and place, so it seems real, we get involved in it. But *the effect* of a story such as that, one that is really well done, is that it seems universal, it seems to fit the way we view humanity, history.

It's a tragedy. Cormac McCarthy is a tragic writer. When you pull back from a story like that, you feel that it fits into the larger world and into the larger human condition. It isn't *just* a local story. Viewed from a distance, it seems even more tragic, these individuals caught up in the great processes of history, economics. And it's that combination of double vision that's one of the marks of a great writer. They see the local *this* story, but you also feel it connects to the larger patterns of nature and history.

In some ways, McCarthy is a great naturalistic writer. You can feel the forces of nature as well as of the personalities of the characters. You see this in a novel such as *Child of God*. You see it particularly in *Suttree*. The story's all about the city, but at the end, as Suttree is leaving the city, you expand to the countryside and then to a mythic sense of nature and destiny.

JOSYPH: Where would you rank McCarthy among American writers, particularly those of the 20th century?

MORGAN: My sense is that some of the writers of the last half of the 20th century and the beginning of the 21st are as good as the great writers of the earlier 20th century. In the future, writers like Cormac McCarthy, Tim O'Brien, Louise Erdrich, Lee Smith, Doris Betts, Reynolds Price, Alice Walker, will be seen as great writers the way Faulkner, Hemingway, and Fitzgerald are. Academia has canonized certain modernist writers, talked and talked about them so long that we think of them as deities, and nobody can ever be that great. I suspect that that is just a myth created by academia, as I suspect modernism is a myth created by academia.

In the longer context, you can see that Cormac McCarthy links up with Melville and Dostoevsky and it has very little to do with modernism, it has to do with these great tragic stories, with the drama and power of them. Perhaps some of the great modernists are not as good as the great contemporary novelists. It would be hard to find a writer about war better than Tim O'Brien, for instance, even considering Tolstoy and Stendhal and the writers about World War II. Of course we don't know how these people will be ranked because we don't know what the tastes of the future will be, but I suspect that McCarthy will be thought of as one of the great American writers a hundred years from now.

JOSYPH: I used to say to academics: "I don't acknowledge post-modernism because I don't acknowledge modernism. There are things in Laurence Sterne that are every bit as postmodern as Pynchon!"

MORGAN: *(Laughs)* Absolutely. All the elements of fiction seem to have been present at the beginning, in the 18th century. Nothing has happened that's entirely different from what Sterne, Richardson, Fielding, and Defoe did at the very beginning. The great dramas, the historical epics, the ironies, the experimental tongue-in-cheek writing in Sterne, the comedy of Fielding—it was all there at the very beginning.

JOSYPH: Can you think of other films about the South that have struck you with comparable force to *The Gardener's Son*?

MORGAN: So many films about the South have been romanticized. One of the most realistic films that I have seen recently is *Sling Blade*, by Billy Bob Thornton. That seemed to hit that note of the real. The voices have that sense of discovery. A character says: "Are you going to carry me over?" Meaning, am I going to ride with you. Hollywood *can* get the South right, but it rarely does. In television and film they usually rely on stereotypes. The first major American movie was about the Civil War, and the most famous movie of all time is about the Civil War, so around the world that's the audience's view of the South. What you get in *The Gardener's Son* is the smaller picture. You get down to the finer details, and it has a realism and a toughness that's very special. I would like to see more films like that.

JOSYPH: To get such fine performances, it does seem to help, doesn't it, to have good writing? In talking about McCarthy, Anne O'Sullivan (Martha) told me: "You wanted to rise to the occasion because it had so much texture and depth, and you wanted to be as good as you could be to do it."

MORGAN: It's a lot easier to be a really good actor if you have really good lines to say and a really good character. I'll never forget that when he was given a lifetime achievement award, Cary Grant thanked the writers, and he named half a dozen.

JOSYPH: Billy Bob Thornton directed *All the Pretty Horses*.

MORGAN: He has a wonderful sense of characterization through voice, both as an actor and as a writer. I noticed this in *The Apostle*. He's the man who tries to run the preacher off. That just seemed *absolutely* right. That anger—he got that anger right, and the fear of religion, of the spirit—and the way he changes on camera. *That* was an awfully good movie, also. But both as a writer and as an actor, Thornton has such a feeling for the complexity of characters who are poor, or are not well educated. He doesn't think of them as simple. He sees their complexity.

JOSYPH: *Sling Blade* has something in common with *The Gardener's Son* in that there are no easy answers there, either. Even in the way that it is lit, you get the sense that parts of Karl will remain dark to the viewer and, perhaps, to anyone who knows him.

MORGAN: Well, the good writer and the good actor will find the character often through the paradoxes, the contradictions that will make him or her most real. Nobody is either all good or all bad. The challenge is to include those contradictions and yet, at the same time, to give the character an overall unity, and I think Thornton is one of the best at doing that.

JOSYPH: In my own work, I have allies who support me by what they do. I look at them and say: "Someone else is aiming at the same sort of thing." I couldn't get by without the touchstone of knowing that they've done it, or are doing it. Is there any sense in which McCarthy has been an ally to you?

MORGAN: Yes. He is one of the writers who showed me the possibilities of working with the region, with characters who are at the fringe of society, as it were. I believe it was easier to get back to fiction writing after having discovered his work, encountering the power of the language, the way in which he will look at the world in its contradictions and pain. He is one of several writers I rely on for a sense of encouragement and of possibility.

My first writing teacher was the novelist Guy Owen, who planted seeds I'm sure he never realized, talking about dialect, learning the terms local people used, that sort of thing. Owen was a great influence on me. Not at the time. Later. And certainly Cormac McCarthy. Lee Smith, another writer about Appalachia. Fred Chappel was one of my teachers. I've learned a lot from Fred. He's been very encouraging over the years. A short story that has meant a lot to me over the years is Alice Walker's "Every Day Use," which is about a family of farm women in Georgia. The older woman brags about how she can kill a hog all by herself. *(Laughs)* She can run the place all by herself! That has a wonderful realism and toughness to it.

It is easier to write knowing that there are writers like Cormac McCarthy who are successful, that great writing is not something of the past, but also of the present.

JOSYPH: What will you do when they come to you and say: "It's not enough that *Gap Creek* is a novel, we're going to film it—will you do the screenplay?"

MORGAN: I would like to have a shot at it. Screenwriting is very different from fiction writing. I believe literary people don't realize how hard it is to adapt something for film. It seems easy, perhaps, because it's not about writing but about visualization and drama. I think it would be a great challenge. I would like to try it. I love movies. I had never seen a movie in a theatre until I went off to college. I grew up in the country and my parents wouldn't let us go to see movies, but when I moved off to college I just went wild going to see movies and loved them. I believe that film has had a lot of impact on fiction writing. We have learned a lot from film, particularly about pacing and compression. So I would be thrilled if somebody made a film of one of my books, and yes, I would enjoy at least trying to write a script.

JOSYPH: I won't ask whether you'd feel a loss of power being stripped of your prose. As a poet you work very sparsely, don't you?

MORGAN: I believe film and poetry do have a lot in common, and film and the short story. But I'm in awe of film and its power. It's different from language. Often the hardest novels to adapt are the best written, the novels that live in their language, in the narration, in their descriptions. That's very hard to adapt. It may be easier to adapt novels that are not that great.[8] The way you tell a story in film is somewhat different. I tell my students that film is, oddly enough, more a medium of *reaction*. To know what something means, the camera turns to the face of the actor, and we know, by their expression, if it's moving or mysterious. Since you don't have that actor or the camera in fiction writing, you have to show what happens and the reader responds to that. Paradoxically, film is more the medium of reaction, and fiction the medium of action. You tell the reader *what happens* and you don't have to explain what it means.

JOSYPH: Your face is very congenial to the camera. Have you done any acting?

MORGAN: No. I sort of wish I had. I believe fiction writing is very similar to acting. The great pleasure of writing fiction is that you don't have to be yourself. You can get into your characters. You can forget your own troubles for a while and think of the troubles of your character Julie, or Jimmy, or Hank. I feel there's something very close to acting in writing. I often wish I had tried acting, but I never did.

JOSYPH: When they film *Gap Creek* they'll probably find a part for you.

MORGAN: *(Laughs)* I can be the old guy!

JOSYPH: James Dickey tells the story of playing the sheriff in *Deliverance*: "Well, they just had a costume that fit me..." But when you look at *the size* of Dickey... *(Laughter)*

When we make our own dramatic films, we might have to put you to work.

MORGAN: Okay. That's a deal.

NOTES

1. In *The Gardener's Son*, Kevin Conway plays James Gregg, who is shot in the office of his mill by Robert McEvoy, played by Brad Dourif. Robert's father, Patrick, a gardener at the mill, is played by Jerry Hardin; his mother is played by Penny Allen; his sister, Martha, from whom Gregg tries to buy sexual favors, is played by Anne O'Sullivan. Nan Martin plays James Gregg's mother, and Ned Beatty plays Pinky, a good ole boy with whom Robert takes a drink in a doggery when he returns to Graniteville to see that his mother is *not* buried there. Paul Benjamin plays the attorney hired to defend Robert, who is hanged at the end of the film. My documentary about *The Gardener's Son* was never completed, but its participants recalled the shoot so vividly, and spoke so fondly and intelligently about the screenplay and about their contribution to the project, that I have contemplated turning the documentary into a book.

2. The conscientiousness with which a serious actor approaches a character's accent is typified by Nan Martin's approach to Mrs. Gregg. "Everybody thinks there's a Southern accent," Nan told me. "Couldn't be more wrong. *(Demonstrating each variation)* Mississippi is one thing—it's slower. Georgia is quite patrician—Georgians were gentlemen farmers from England, thank you very much. The dirt poor in North Carolina... when you ask directions... you cain't understand where they're tellin you to go an turn t'the right—I mean it's just all atwisted around. Louisiana is sort of a nasal thing. Then, of course, in Texas it's all flat, it's drawn in. There are *all kinds* of variations of Southern accents. When I got down to North Carolina, my ears and my antennae went up like you wouldn't believe. Everything was fried. In the morning you had fried pone, you had fried eggs, you had fried fritters—lunch was friend, dinner was friend! Well—I listened to the waitresses... and you begin to get it by osmosis. The patrician quality is something that's innate. You have to say *I own this*. There is a moment when I turn to a little girl in the McEvoy family, when I come into the house and they ask me to sit down in this little dirt farmer's house, and I sit *(demonstrates royal bearing)* like I was at the queen's ball... and this little girl is sitting on my left and I say: 'What is *your* name?' There is an accent there, but it is not the dirt poor—it's once removed."

By all accounts, on the set of *The Gardener's Son* McCarthy was as good a talker as listener. "He's very good at talking to people," Brad Dourif told me. "He's very respectful of people, he's wonderful at bringing people out, he gets a real kick out of people—*and he's funny as all getout!*" Cinematographer Fred Murphy said: "Cormac would show up and, in my memory, he would give these marvelous speeches and tell these marvelous stories. We used to eat in this Chinese restaurant in Burlington, a small, industrial-to-bacco city, middle of the state. We ate there at least once a week. The whole crew would often eat there, all of us at one giant table. Cormac would stand up, on occasion, and tell a marvelous joke that would go on for ten minutes. He was *the* single best shaggydog storyteller ever. He would hold us all spellbound telling us some story about when he was working as a siding salesman or *some* kind of salesman—stories of driving through the south, selling things." Brad Dourif said that McCarthy would fabricate dreams that would feature the quirks of each member of the crew. "And it was *hilarious*."

A different but equally flattering view of McCarthy's presence was expressed to me by Anne O'Sullivan. "If I had been older I would have talked to him a lot," Anne told me. "I was a little shy. But he had a *beautiful* presence. He's an enigmatic person and has a quiet reserve that's *very* attractive. A kind of peaceful sweetness about him too. His ego was not evident. He was one of those writers that you want on the set. I know several writers like that, that you want in the room because they don't say too much but when they do say something, it has meaning. Once in a while, McCarthy would explain something, and he was always to the point. He didn't babble on. Everything he said was pertinent and helpful, and that's the kind of writer you want around."

3. In the press release for *The Gardener's Son*, Pearce addresses the issue of Robert McEvoy's motivation.

> The problem for me as a director in this film was that McCarthy and I choose to portray a character who was acting without any clear motive as such, at least in traditional dramatic terms.... And that was what was fascinating about the story itself, the reason it has survived and is still told to this day in the town where it happened.... What I did was to try and create an emotional framework, a structure of motivation within which Robert McEvoy's peculiar kind of rage would feel accurate and true but still remain unexplained. (4)

4. The shooting script and the script published by Ecco Press contain a framing device—a contemporary scene preceding, and another succeeding, the historical narrative—which is not in the finished film. Cinematographer Fred Murphy is fairly certain that this frame was shot, and Anne O'Sullivan vaguely recalls seeing it. "I was an old lady who never married," she told me. "It was a real woman of that age, it wasn't me in makeup. It informed how I played the character, because it made me think: 'This is somebody who takes something in, and each day it lives in her.'"

5. In the press release for *The Gardener's Son*, Pearce says: "I found out the town not only exists but is still a company town today with a remarkable number of descendants of the original thousand or so textile workers who came to live there when it was built in the 1840s.... Their descendants still tell Robert McEvoy's story—stories, I should say, because there are now at least eight or nine different versions" (3).

6. In the press release for *The Gardener's Son*, Pearce says: "McCarthy and I had from the beginning a kind of tacit assumption about the power of the basic story as a kind of 19th century legend. The problem was to place it within its specific social and historical context and let it sort of unravel without killing the mystery at its center" (4).

7. The text of Morgan's talk can be found as "Cormac McCarthy: The Novel Raised from the Dead," in Volume 1 of *Sacred Violence: A Reader's Companion to Cormac McCarthy* (revised edition). The full sentence from which I have quoted is: "It has been said that the greatest writers evoke a sense of the poise and scale of eternity in their work, no matter how cluttered or twisted or violent the scene in the foreground" (12).

8. A similar view of adaptation was expressed to me by the film's line producer Michael Hausman, whose subsequent credits include Pearce's *Heartland, No Mercy*, and *Family Thing*; as well as *Amadeus, Ragtime, Silkwood, Things Change, Nobody's Fool, The People vs. Larry Flint, Man on the Moon, Gangs of New York, Brokeback*

Mountain, and *Recount*. "I have an axiom," he told me, "which may or may not be true. I have examples of pictures I've made myself that prove it either way. Good underlying material is not necessarily good for either the screenplay or the movie. *Ragtime*, for example. Wonderfully written book by Doctorow. A wonderful movie on its own that Miloš Forman directed and I helped produce. The complaint I got all the time: *it wasn't the book*. I don't know how to answer that. It *wasn't* the book. If you wanted the book it'd be much cheaper, you could photograph the pages, flip em, we could probably make it for twenty-five dollars. Sometimes good material can't ever be translated to film. There's too much meat on the bone, there's too much fleshing out. I'd rather have a lousy book with a good idea and get a good screenwriter, rather than a tremendously popular book. That's a producer's bank, the popular book. Producers want to have successful projects so if the picture goes bad, they can say: 'But it was a great book!' I would rather pay less for the book and make it into something."

V

ALL THE PRETTY HORSES

That was in my old light days, before these troubles came upon me.

—Stevenson

· 9 ·

Notes on Billy Bob Thornton's
All the Pretty Horses

1.

*Y*ou might conceive that the story is John Grady Cole's, but for Matt Damon, as an actor, a film is about what happens to everybody in it. The result—uncanny for the lead in a big-budget feature—is that at times you can almost not notice him in the frame. Henry Thomas has achieved the same effect. *I'm just a San Angelo saddlehand out to see the world because my buddy had a bug up his ass.* Like Julio Mechoso, who plays the Captain, Henry had wanted to be involved in filming the novel even before he was cast, and he referred to the book as his bible, which he, Matt, and Julio—along with Bruce Dern, who plays the Ozona judge—relied on for guidance in shaping their performances. These guys who were worried about letting the novel down delivered fine, understated, deeply *dedicated* performances. "On the set," Henry told me, "you wouldn't always see it in Matt's demeanor, but I knew from being around him for a month how important this was to him, and because *I* was worried about my performance, the dynamic became each of us pushing the other to greater heights. There were many moments when they said 'Cut' and I thought: 'My God, we've really *nailed* this scene,' and there wasn't any fear. As you probably know, that doesn't happen very often. It was happening every day on this."

The casting is criticized for being too old. Perhaps. But to question whether Matt's John Grady is sixteen presupposes that McCarthy's John Grady is sixteen. In fact, John Grady is more McCarthy than sixteen can handle. This is spelled out in ninety percent of what he does. Ages in good writing can't be literalized: they're an integral part of the poetry. A university actor can be old

161

enough for Hamlet, but is he old enough for *Hamlet?* Shakespeare knew the answer, for in roughly two months, Hamlet advances from being a student in Wittenberg to a mature man of thirty. If this leap is the error of a Jacobean copyist, it is a fortuitous one that the play itself appreciates—as did Richard Burbage, who played the prince in Shakespeare's Globe.

With an obsession of vitriol that hasn't abated, my pal Rick Wallach loves to slam *Pretty Horses* for precisely this fault, that the casting is *too old*, and he is chiefly thinking about John Grady Cole; but what Rick and like-minded critics have missed is that a John Grady Cole who is closer to sixteen would make it more obvious that this is *not* a story about a dispossessed Texas saddlehand, it's a story about—well, Superboy. Billy Bob was not unaware of this challenge. He told me that he liked Matt Damon for John Grady Cole because he could be as mature as he needed him to be, and also *a kid* when that was necessary. If, when Billy Wilder's *The Spirit of St. Louis* first hit the screen, its reception was untroubled by the fact that Jimmy Stewart was nearly twice Lindbergh's age when he made his historic flight, it was partly because Lindbergh's deed—and, by extension, Lindbergh himself—was impossible for twenty-five—or for any age.

This is not to say that it wouldn't be interesting to see an *All the Pretty Horses* with much younger leads. A younger Alejandra might carry the implication that John Grady penetrates her virginity, a suggestion that would color all the ensuing complications and would cast a different atmosphere around the protectionism of her father and her aunt. An even younger Jimmy Belvins would be interesting, and if the boy that John Grady knifes to death in prison is barely out of puberty, that would make a difference to the scene and its aftermath in the home of the kindly Ozona judge. As with any great novel, it is healthy to see Billy Bob's *All the Pretty Horses* as *a* version of the book, one of many that we could, might, should get to see. Unknown performers in a more or less handheld rendering of the story, directed by a Mexican, cut without music, could make for a fascinating comparison—and maybe a great film. As much as I appreciate *The Gardener's Son*, I have fantasized securing the rights to the project, not to direct McCarthy's thoughtful, highly shootable screenplay, but to really *adapt* it, having the freedom to embellish or invent wherever it might be interesting. When you know and admire a piece of material, you then have to trust your respect for its author and free yourself *to be a writer*. Devotees of the original—of course they will complain, but they will complain anyway.

Too old… If it pleases you, here: *Matt Damon is too old…* but you, then, must grant me that John Grady Cole is too old for himself.

One of Billy Bob's producers, Bruce Heller, told me that when Matt met McCarthy, he, Bruce, saw McCarthy as John Grady Cole grown up. As Matt is also Private Ryan, the actor who plays Ryan when he's an older man ought to look like McCarthy—*and he does*. Because of that connection, the film now reminds me of *Ulysses*. Proving that old Private Ryan is Cormac McCarthy is like proving that Hamlet's grandson is Shakespeare's grandfather. Stephen Dedalus uses algebra, I am using long division, dividing large quantities— McCarthy, his novel, the talent that made the film—by a very small factor: myself. But on this issue of who is too old, old enough or not to inhabit and embody a literary persona, the last word should be given to the kid in *West Side Story* who says: "You was *never* my age, none a ya!"

2.

I can see why Lucas Black's mother, Jan, wanted to secure, as a keepsake, the outsize Tom Mix hat that characterizes Jimmy Blevins. I told her: "You'd better get it fast." Who *wouldn't* want to steal it? Blevins is both an endearing imposture and a bona-fide badass punk. Big ridiculous hat on small earnest head accentuates that duality. What is perceived as costume design is often integral to an actor's character work. The hat demonstrates how every dimension of filmmaking can constitute a viable way of reading a good novel.

Even the wonderful absurdities of Martin Ritt's *The Long Hot Summer* say something about Faulkner, as would any cartoon executed by geniuses. Better a spirited distortion than an insipid exactitude. After the author writes a novel, let the novel write a novel. A silly scene in a bad film or a motherous hat in a failed film or an unforgettable line in a crazy film—say, Orson Welles in *The Long Hot Summer* saying: "I want Varners and more Varners to infest the countryside!"—are equally answers, reverberations, after-effects of the printed word. For me, *The Brothers Karamazov* confounds itself with *Come Blow Your Horn* because Lee J. Cobb played the father in both films. I envision Fyodor Pavlovich shouting: "Spite! Spite!" but it's a line from Neil Simon. In this way, *Come Blow Your Horn* has worked its way into Dostoevsky. As to whether it worked its way into the book or into the film, I would say that it worked its way into me, and with wonderful fake snow from Richard Brooks's Hollywood that, along with Father Cobb, Yul Brynner, Claire Bloom, William Shatner and Richard Basehart all bundled up in a Cinemascope Petersburg, made Dostoevsky's job a little easier: the Russian winter was there before the novel was handed to me, in private, by a Russian-born homeroom teacher who wanted me to read "The Grand Inquisitor." Even Josef Von Sternberg's *Crime and Punishment*, with Peter

Lorre as Roskolnikov, a film that Columbia double-billed with a comedy called *Oh My Nerves* and promoted with a poster that read **WHY DO YOU SAY A GIRL LIKE ME CAN'T REALLY LOVE A MAN?**... a film that neuters urban architecture, deletes nationality (no snow here—no weather at all), and strives to be set, as a title card tells you, "any place where human hearts respond to love and hate, pity and terror"—in other words, a film that removes the Russia and the Russian from Dostoevsky—cannot entirely exile the author from its moody Interzone of painted shadows. Even the poster's hint of Chicago gangsterism, Hollywood style—"Sure the police know what I am. But I'm in love... in love with a murderer"—is followed by a plaintive appeal—"and I can save his soul... just as he saved mine"—the likes of which would never have existed in Hollywood were it not for Dostoevsky, and were it not for Peter Lorre wanting to film the book. Despite its fabrications, oversimplifications, bloated orchestrations, crazy lines ("If they send me to Siberia, will you wait for me?") and hamstrung or underdirected performances (Peter Lorre lapses into a fugue state until it is time to strike his next attitude), the film manages, in its oddball way, to remind me of—and return me to—the novel.

Of course a film can give a novel a hard time. One example: For the best line in *Wuthering Heights* ("What do they know of heaven or hell, Cathy, who know nothing of life?") you *must* see the film because it isn't *in* the novel. Another example: It was decades before I gave up trying to extricate Ava Gardner from *The Sun Also Rises*. This occurred when I discovered that the mistake of casting Ms. Gardner in the film is equal to the mistake, made by Hemingway, in depicting Brett Ashley. Hemingway shows you what an irresponsible bitch she is to the men—all of the men—in her life, but he forgets to make her attractive, or to communicate her attractiveness; instead, he simply shows you that men are attracted to her, which is not the same thing. Were it not for the casting—the miscasting—of Ms. Gardner, I might not have noticed this flaw in a novel so near to perfection.

You never know what will open your eyes to a book. If, in Zen, it can be the whack of a stick or the croak of a frog in the moonlight that turns on the power, the voice of a large actor playing a Neil Simon father in Dostoevsky ought to qualify too. We all own our own readership. Mine's mad, but so's the world. If you serve me Dostoevsky and *Come Blow Your Horn* at the same famished age, *they will mingle*. Whatever its faults—there are many—a film as loaded with talent as *All the Pretty Horses* ought to be giving a few people interesting ways of reading the novel. Seeing the film *is* reading the novel, as was everything done to prepare it—even what was done to *talk* to me *about* that preparation. This is part of what reading is, it encompasses seeing films.

3.

One could make an entire film from any part of *All the Pretty Horses*—John Grady's hitch to San Antonio, his relationship to his father—but one cannot make a film from that *entire* novel because the novel *can't* be filmed. I would rather see a four-hour version, but that is because I'd like to see the film's heart beating at the pace Billy Bob intended for it, not because the novel will necessarily work better.[1]

It might. The boys' relationship to their horses—as to everyone else in the story—would be bodied forth better—unless, ironically, this entire issue of *the horse*—not Blevins' horse, I mean *the horse* as a sentient and sensuous creature of beauty, a trusty and trustful companion—was not one of Billy Bob's concerns, and he let *the horse*, if not the film, get away from him. In the two-hour version you get to see horses, but you never get to know one: no horse is a character, or has character, so that *All the Pretty Horses* says as much about horses as films about writers or painters have said about sentences or paint. When the boys cross the Rio Grande, the scene is so much about music—music that displays a lack of trust that the crossing, which is symbolic of so much in the story, can generate meaning enough to defend itself—that the horses—even the actors— are unnecessary. The fact that three wranglers rode for the crossing isn't a fault in itself, but it symbolizes the impersonality of the moment. If one can look at *Suttree* from a trolley's or a token's point of view, one can look at an adventure that is all about the horses from the horses' point of view. After all, they are crossing the border too. Alas, despite the whooping and waving of hats, the crossing in the film is neither about horses nor about men, it's about the composer, Marty Stuart, and second unit photography.

In a longer cut, at least little flaws could be corrected. When a line by the Ozona judge: "Can I ask you a personal question?" is followed by: "Would you mind showing us your wounds?" one thinks: "That is *not* a personal question." This is because the judge wants to know whether John Grady's shorts are clean enough to show in public, but that exchange has been cut. This saves a few seconds, but the price is incoherence. When Alejandra asks John Grady "Where will your home be?" there is a cut to the two of them on a bench, as if the question can stand on its own—which it can't, it needs to be answered, even if in silence, but this cut leaves little room for silence. The fact that nothing happens on the bench betokens a larger fault: the relationship between the young lovers is never developed—in fact, it doesn't happen.

Billy Bob's first film, *Sling Blade*, was edited for me to place my trust in practically every scene. I can't relax the same way here. To borrow a phrase from John Grady, everything feels fenced in n' sawed off. Some scenes cry out for closeups, while a number of potentially evocative two-shots—the

John Grady/Alfonsa chess game, for example—are discomposed into crosscut closeups that hurry things along, as if to reduce scenes to their essence. But in dramatic situations, pause is part of essence; so is the patience and the tension of a character preparing a parry, a lunge, an attack, an escape. We need to see that, and we need to see what's happening when *nothing* is happening. The problem here, of course, can be traced to a timeclock ticking toward a two-hour limit defined by a nasty piece of math: the length of a film divided into a day at the multiplex. The scenes with John Grady's father are among the joys of the novel, but they are reduced to plot points during the credits. Scenes shouldn't summarize themselves.

Treated as a whole, this story can afford to lose sequences, but it ought not to be losing its themes, of which there are more than most novels—fathers, homes, faithless women, friendship, honor, blood vs. oil and icewater—and if they aren't in play before they reach the Rio Grande, they won't mean much in Mexico. However, putting them in play creates more problems. The more that you care about the fate of Jimmy Belvins, the harder it is for you, as a filmgoer, to leave him behind and start a new life on the ranch in Mexico. The deeper you feel for the starcrosed lovers, the less sense it makes for you to drop the whole affair and set a new will toward retrieving some horses—especially if that is all they are for you, *some horses*. The closer you follow the novel, the harder it is to turn it into a film that is not a mini-series.

Kurosawa's *Hakuchi*, an adaptation of Dostoevsky's *The Idiot*, ran for four hours and twenty-five minutes. When the studio, Shochiku, complained about its length, a furious Kurosawa suggested that they cut it "lengthwise." After he reluctantly reduced it to three hours, adding intertitles and narration in an attempt to give it coherence, Shochiku removed another fourteen minutes without the director's participation. When Kurosawa returned to Shochiku forty years later, he searched in vain for the lost footage. The original has only been seen at the premiere. Was it better? As with *All the Pretty Horses*, the answer might be yes and no. The truncated *Hakuchi* is both frustrating and fascinating. Kurosawa's first cut might have been both more frustrating and more fascinating, and the same could be true of *All the Pretty Horses* at the length for which its director designed it.

4.

All the Pretty Horses is not a constant. Even a viewer who hasn't read the novel yet is reading it by watching the film: novels radiate numberless worlds around them. Those worlds belong to the novel—*are* the novel, even the world in which you say: "This is not *it*." You read novels everywhere. Reading *All the Pretty Horses*, you look at the dustjacket photo of McCarthy—rolled denim sleeves, folded arms resting on wood—you might do this dozens of times, *as a way of reading the book*, and you look at the text *as a way of reading the picture*. I once proposed a course that would take for its texts the photographs and portraits of writers, all images that we would never see were it not for the written word. You cannot print a writer's photograph without publishing his work because the picture *is* the edition. If Marion Ettlinger, who shot the author photo on *All the Pretty Horses*, weren't a publisher of sorts, you wouldn't look to see the novel in McCarthy's eyes. Do I exaggerate? A little—but not too much.

During a recent attempt to write about *Blood Meridian*, I found myself drawn into Mark Morrow's photograph of McCarthy at the Colony Motel on Kingston Pike, Knoxville, a picture that was taken in 1981 as part of a longterm project of Morrow's, *Images of the Southern Writer*, an ambitious undertaking that included photographs of Walker Percy, Eudora Welty, William Styron, Tennessee Williams, Robert Penn Warren, Shelby Foote, James Dickey, and Erskine Caldwell. In that book, which was published the same year as *Blood Meridian*, McCarthy is pictured behind the ticket window of the old Southern Railway Depot in Knoxville. "This is the window where you get a ticket with the destination left blank," McCarthy told Morrow (52), and of course *Blood Meridian* is, itself, a ticket with the destination left blank. It's an arresting photograph—perhaps too much for a dustjacket. As an experiment, I taped a cropped copy of this picture to the back of the dustjacket on my reading copy of *Blood Meridian*, which happens to be a first edition of the novel. The effect was so disorienting that I became nauseated, a reaction that I have when the universe appears unnaturally tampered with. As I hadn't played fair in copying the image onto plain paper and taping it onto a glossy dustjacket, I copied it onto high-gloss photo paper and taped it over the shot in the Colony Motel. Now the image appeared to belong to the dustjacket, but the effect was equally disturbing. Now McCarthy, smiling at the open window with black space behind him and a kind of brick wall, his striped shirt open to three buttons down, appeared to be peering out from the darkness of his own creation, as if he had climbed out, or climbed up, to gaze at us for a moment before descending again into the story. What is disturbing is that he is more looking at me than I am looking at him... looking at me trying to pierce the darkness behind him... bemused by the sight of a joker like me apprehending this impossible object, this seanachie séance he has chosen to call *Blood Meridian*.

Of course to Mark Morrow this would have to be falderall: McCarthy is looking at the young man with a camera. Yes, but that was then, this is now.

Today, the black behind McCarthy is no longer a room in an abandoned train station, it is the interior, or a passage to the interior, of something inscrutable, something that is, to this day, known only to the author. Susan Sontag identified art photography as "an enterprise of notation" (126), a good way of viewing either of Morrow's images: for me they are both—to borrow a phrase from John Sepich—notes on *Blood Meridian*. If it is true that Judge Holden is a devil, or *the* devil, or that there is, at least, a devil *in* Judge Holden, no need to look any farther than this image: there he is, a big-eared handsome devil with a Warren Beatty mouth but a devil nonetheless.

Perhaps many devils. According to railroad historians in Knoxville, McCarthy's ticket window in the Southern Depot is really a taxi window under the stair to the second floor, a window that you passed before exiting the depot into the parking lot under Depot Street. Wesley Morgan, the *Suttree* enthusiast you met in another chapter, has sent me photographs. It is closed, all its glass is gone, but there it is, and it is *not* where you bought your tickets, it's the place from which the taxi caller signaled your ride and organized the loading of your luggage from the baggage room. Ticket indeed! Imagine—fiction from a novelist! Was McCarthy misinformed? Was he misremembering? Was he playing pretend and didn't care what the window was for? Was he banking on the camera not knowing the difference? Here's what he was doing: he was setting up a shot, he was orchestrating a career. Around Concord, Thoreau used to plant arrowheads that he could "find" when walking with a visitor. The butterfly perched on Walt Whitman's finger in the famous photograph—Whitman's favorite, taken in 1877 by W. Curtis Taylor (of Phillips & Taylor, Philadelphia)—a butterfly Whitman liked to say that he had tamed, was in fact an Easter novelty made of cardboard on whose wings were printed lines from a hymn by John Mason Neale. However uninvolved McCarthy might have been in the sales of his books, it is silly to think that he wasn't at all engaged in creating his image. A writer cannot not be involved. Even Salinger has created an image of himself that is indelible, and confining his visage to a few photographs intensifies the few beyond measure. As Sontag said: "To live is to be photographed," and, as she smartly added: "to live is also to pose" (134). If you take a photographer to a railway station at which you are, for the moment, gainfully employed in striking a pose and telling a tale, that's publicity—and it's being a novelist.

Enterprise of notation... Imagine that McCarthy is presented with the Portuguese translation of *Suttree*, published by Relógio D'Água Editores on rua Sylvio Rebelo in Lisbon. McCarthy could look at the image on the cover, predictable, and say: "Not bad—at least they used the Tennessee, not the Charles, the Mississippi, or the Hudson." But he would probably not imagine what a complex *they* his novel had created… for his translator, Paulo Faria, was so deep in his love for the book, so fastidious in his monumental task, that he did a lot more than ply me with questions—as he did Wesley Morgan and as he did McCarthy. He also traveled to Knoxville to see the streets whereof McCarthy had written… Knoxville, where we walked the city together under Wesley's tutelage… where I found him a rusty old railroad spike that I shipped off to Lisbon as a household god… and where I took hundreds of photographs with *Suttree* in mind… one of which found its way to the cover of the novel when it appeared in Portugal.

5.

In a land that despises literacy, we can't *stop* reading. Wherever you go, whatever you do, you end up reading the Bible, or watching it read you. *There's* a novel that, once it answered for all its ridiculous adaptations, would then have to answer for the Western world! Frequently we find ourselves eating or walking or looking into the mirror or driving a car, or making a choice, even an insignificant one, and realize it is something we have read. This is more than a quotation: it is the film or the novel enacting itself in the flesh. Whenever I rode a bicycle as an adult, I was reading Alan Sillitoe's *Saturday Night and Sunday Morning*, not because the first thing that I did with my degree was to ride an old delivery boy's bike to an Aurora Plastics plant in Hempstead, Long Island, where I was a packer at the end of an assembly line; no, it was due to a few seconds of Albert Finney—very young, very handsome—bicycling to work in the Karel Reisz film of that novel. Those few seconds, which I saw as a teenager, brought me back into the novel more often than my own hard experience *or* the printed text of the story.

I asked Julio Mechoso what happens to the Captain. He said: "Remember Paulie in *The Godfather*? 'Aw Paulie, you won't see him no more.'" The perfect answer to my question entailed reading Mario Puzo through the fatso lens of Richard Castellano playing Clemenza for Francis Ford Coppola. I can't say "I don't know" without playing Jon Voight in *Deliverance* when the sheriff, who is James Dickey in the flesh, asks him about the number of life-jackets. "Sheriff, I don't know," he says. That reading of the line is the only way to express myself, so that every time you elicit that answer from me—"I don't know"—I am reading *Deliverance*—or it's reading me. When someone asked Bruce Dern's wife where she got something or other, she fell into the habit of saying: "At the gettin place," which is where Jimmy Blevins acquired his 32–20 Colt. When she did that, she was reading McCarthy; when Blevins said it, he was reading Faulkner, because Luster, in *The Sound and the Fury*, says the same thing.

6.

I remember Matt saying: "You're doing half your scenes with Billy Bob," telling me how Penélope Cruz was watching Billy Bob making faces at her when she says to John Grady: "You *are* in trouble." For directors, master illusionists working with people-props, the rule is: *whatever works*. Sometimes funny faces work, as do ludicrous suggestions, such as Billy Bob's: "Imagine yourself enveloped in Ernest Borgnine's rectal tissue." Critics can learn from this. If clowning and hyper-reality are justifiable tools for translating a novel into the language of film, might they not be useful in translating a novel into the language of criticism? All over, books are telling critics: "I know that you love me, but you never *say* it, and tonight I want you to dance with me." Books—which, like people, can't speak without reading, and often through films—are saying, Zorba-like, to critics everywhere: "I love you, Boss, but there's one thing you need: a little madness." Thousands of books are out there on the beach, snapping their fingers, waiting for critics to dance with them. Rabelais, Swift, Wilde, Joyce, Henry Miller are all people who danced with books and made masterworks that we might not even regard as criticism. When I conducted my tub talk about *Blood Meridian* with wet Rick Wallach in the Menger Hotel, one of McCarthy's masterworks was prodigiously admired while a man took a bubble-bath—and criticism was none the worse for the water. Cocteau thought it marvelous that we don't dissolve in our baths. The point is, we *don't*, and McCarthy doesn't either.

7.

Let's return to casting an actor who looks "too old" for his or her part. I have a complaint, but it's not a matter of too old, it's a matter of too clean. The movie is too scrubbed for me. It's partly to do with the makeup, which is sometimes painfully obvious; partly to do with the lighting, with indoor sunlight and outdoor moonlight looking, at times, like floodlight. Billy Bob's fine DP, Barry Markowitz, who shot *Sling Blade* and *The Apostle*, talked to me about pressure to "see their faces" better, and—surprisingly for a film by a director who begs him to *turn off* the lights—*All the Pretty Horses* is often overlit. But there is something else behind the disturbing *cleanness* of the film, a cleanness that gives some of the scenes a feel of playacting. The best examples of this are the scenes in the jail when John Grady and Rawlins meet Blevins again. They come across like a rehearsal, partly because no one is filthy enough, lousy enough, infected enough, weighted enough—*centripetal* enough. Clint Eastwood's *Unforgiven* is far from a favorite of mine, but Eastwood's and Morgan Freeman's characters are, at least, properly weighted with the vile and the rot of the Old West. Even the rain is convincing—hellsent, relentless—a Kurosawa rain, wet with more than water. Imagine the jailhouse reunion appearing in *Unforgiven* and you can visualize the difference. With the entrance of Julio Mechoso as the Captain, the film's *cleanness* is made more apparent precisely because Julio is working, consciously, *against* it. Julio's Captain could make it into *Unforgiven*, Matt's and Henry's performances could not.

For this we have to fault Billy Bob. About directing a big-budget Hollywood feature, Billy Bob told me: "It's not that hard." I found this encouraging. I still do. But perhaps there are times when it needs to be hard. When the first cut of *Husbands* was shown to employees and guests of Columbia, it was praised and enjoyed by everyone—with one exception: Cassavetes, who hated it and spent a year and a half re-cutting. "The film is too soft," Cassavetes said. "It's not tough enough. You've got to really feel these three men's pain. They have to pay a greater price. It can't *be* too hard" (242). A good mandate for filming McCarthy: it can't *be* too hard. Director Richard Pearce and the cast of *The Gardener's Son* seemed to have understood that.

From the interior monologues that he shared with me suggesting the Captain's train of thought; from his keen understanding of the Captain's situation based on repeated close readings of the novel, his studies in anthropology, his youth in Little Havana, and a job conducting interviews with Death Row inmates; and from his insistence upon finding his way in the eyes of the other actor, Julio Mechoso displayed a level of preparation that typified the actors in this film (excepting Lucas Black, who doesn't need to prepare)—but then Julio went beyond it. And yet how did he summarize his performance? "Billy caught me on a good day." Only if taken to mean that he was inspired will I accept that. Julio's performance is a deed descended from heaven— queer thing to say about a character who denies the presence of God in his workplace, but the incandescent divinity here derives from sheer actorial talent captured during peaks of inspiration. It also derives from a choice to make the Captain the filthiest entity in the film.

Given a choice between seeing the Second Coming and seeing Sean Penn's performance in *Hurlyburly*, I would take Sean Penn. The reason is: *it's the same.* Penn's character is a mess, the Captain is a slob and a killer, but the transcendental in art is not confined to its heroes. Julio, who filled with emotion when he told me how Billy fought to have him in the film—"Billy must have gone out on a freakin limb to hire me, brother"—has given it a life and a weight in two scenes, and with a glow that all men, even the Bad Guys, are born for. True believers who place God in the Bibles of racist courts, in the building of empires, at the heads of pious tables, in the rationale for war, in the corporate halls of Congress, might argue against seeing him in the face of a character actor who is playing a killer-Captain with bad teeth, many mistresses, and a talent for graft... but that is because only atheists and saints are permitted to see God everywhere.

Too scrubbed... Yes, damnit—everything is scrubbed! If this film were all a rehearsal, I would take a reading off the Captain and use that as the base level of vile before *descending from there*, so that the Captain, when we shoot again, will be positively rank but no one else will be quite so clean—in other words, quite so Hollywood. One reason I am sorry not to see more of Robert Patrick's Mr. Cole is that, in the tone of his voice alone, he is smoked-out, corrupted, dying—*beat*. But it's another case of the unscrubbed scrubbed out.

8.

The long shot of John Grady Cole sliding off his horse when he returns from Mexico to sit in American grass again—this brief moment is my favorite in the film. I was sold on it when the editor, Sally Menke, showed it to me in her small editing chamber in LA, and I admired it as much on the big screen. It makes me think of Hemingway's "The Big Two-Hearted River," not an easy thing to be reminded of. They are both short poems about war and its aftermath without mentioning war at all. In the way that Matt dismounts, and in his posture in the grass, there is the full weight of the story we have seen; a sense of all that he has lost, all that he has tried to salvage. In the novel, John Grady sits Redbo naked in the rain and he cries. Here, it isn't necessary to see him in tears: there is crying in the way that he is received into the ground. It is a brilliant improvisation around the themes in the novel that reinforces what I learned from the cast of *The Gardener's Son*: filmmaking is an outland of literary criticism. Matt Damon, Billy Bob, and Barry Markowitz are interpreting character as legitimately as a Harold Bloom anthology.

In digital editing systems such as Final Cut Pro, when you assemble sequences, you drag the cursor along a little patch of color, reducing a twenty minute clip to twenty seconds or less; but then you can re-expand it, because *the full twenty minutes is contained within that sliver*. If I could drag a cursor in both directions over this little scene, you wouldn't get the film that was released to the public, but you would get a movie, and it would be astonishing.

Perhaps I am touched by the scene's simplicity. Seeing it on Sally Menke's monitor in a nondescript cottage on a crummy little street in Los Angeles, I felt: *this is as much of the film as I need to see.* If you were making a four-hour cut, I would say: look at that scene, do it justice. My guess is that Billy Bob's longer cuts of the film are more contained within that scene—as they are in Robert Patrick's pause before telling his son that it's not his mother's fault, and "I ain't the same as I once was"—than they are within the two-hour version we have seen. If I had to have shown a single snippet to McCarthy, it would have been awkward, socially, to sit him down for twenty seconds of film, but that is what I would have preferred, or at least have fantasized. Had I needed to argue the case for a longer version, one that would have reduced the number of multiplex screenings while increasing the number of screenings a viewer would want to see, that scene would have been the foundation of my case.

9.

Notice the position and disposition of Bruce Dern's hands when John Grady comes to sit with him. Bruce Dern's hands tell all. They tell you that the Ozona judge is home, the judge is in his favorite chair, the judge loves this crazy boy, the judge is proud to be living in Texas, the judge has a chest full of stories, the judge will die doing his job, the judge is living forever now, the judge will sleep better tonight than he has in half a year.

From what I know of how Bruce Dern prepares for a role, I am sure that if he had brushed his teeth, he'd have brushed them as the judge. He would never have connected with Matt or anyone else on camera in a way that *wasn't* the judge. His art is to be wholly Bruce and wholly the part together. After Thomas Harris saw *Black Sunday*, he told the actor that he, the author of the novel, hadn't understood his own character until he saw Dern's performance. Miriam Colon, who plays the aunt in the film, said it well: "Authors don't know how much they revealed, or how big a possibility they opened for an inquisitive actor or actress to go into."

I wish you could have heard him speaking about the role. Let me give you a for-instance. Bear in mind that the West Texas town of Ozona, where the judge is sitting, is the only town within the 3,000 square miles of Crockett County, and its population then was under 4,000.

"What's important to me about the judge," the great Bruce Dern told me, "is that he's transgressing four generations. In 1949 you're dealing with a guy who is probably born in the late 1880s. So he's born into the world at the end. He's born into the world probably a year before they caught Geronimo.

He's growing up reading about Geronimo being in Florida. Harry Tracy being captured in western Washington. The Grey Fox, Bill Minor, going down in Washington, the Canadian border. The West is over. And yet in Southern Texas, particularly in Southwestern Texas, there is a sense of lawlessness that to this day they like to think still exists. Well, in 1949, as the Levittowns were going up and the interstates were being thought about and Route 66 was not just a place where you got your kicks—it was a thoroughfare—in the midst of all that was Edna Ferber's *Giant*, and there was a breed of men that still thought they had a link to the Old West. Well, in certain situations there *was*. And this judge is a throwback. He is a guy who has taken an early twentieth century education, parlayed it into sitting on a bench where we've gone through the end of the lawlessness, the end of the '30s gangsters, and come out of the great learning experience in America, which was the Second World War, the wakeup call. And at the end of that, there are still people insisting, well, you know, is it like it was? Is he Judge Roy Bean? No, he's not Roy Bean, but he's *read* about Roy Bean, trust me. Because *they all did*. And they *love* that about them."

"But what *he* lifts from it," Bruce Dern continued, "is that he's a country gentleman. He always has been, he always will be. He's rural. Cities bother him. He's in the country for a reason. And every now and then someone will come across his path who has an interesting story to tell, and in this case he hears one he's never heard before, and it's an ordeal. And *he gets it*. The judge is a guy *who gets it*. And as an audience, and as John Grady Cole, we thank God from our knees that there are still people left who are throwbacks to fairness, to integrity, to doing the right thing, who call it the way they see it, but, more chances than not, if you'll trust them, you'll find they may come down on your side—*if you'll tell them the truth*. That's why it's so important when John Grady says: 'I ain't a liar,' and I say to him twice that I know he's not a liar. That's the first time he realizes, *whew*, maybe just maybe he caught a lucky day.

"Although John Grady Cole comes out of the movie as the hero, *the judge makes him a hero*. Would John Grady Cole survive if he never came in front of the judge? Don't think so. He'd live. And he wouldn't spend a long time in prison. But he would've become jaded. By seeing that there was somebody out there who had the authority to give him a passing grade, he realizes he hasn't done anything wrong—he was just growing up. I say to him in the film: 'I think you appear to me to be one of those kinds of people that has a tendency to be a bit hard on themselves.' And then I say: 'My dad always said to me, don't chew on what's botherin ya. Let it go. And that's what *you* gotta do. You'll be all right.' And of course the judge knows *exactly* what he is doing."

"The thing that was so fabulous to me about *All the Pretty Horses* was the unfolding of the story," Bruce Dern said, "and the turns that it takes and who's watching who, you know? Somebody asked me: 'How would *you* sell *All the Pretty Horses* if you had to coin a phrase or do it in a sentence?' If they said: 'Well is it contemporary?' I would say: 'Absolutely.' If they said: 'Well, it's 1949, that's really *period*,' I would say: 'Yeah, the story takes place in 1949, but *the circumstances are no different today*.' And if they said: 'What d'you mean? It's about kids who want to be cowboys!' I'd say: 'Let me tell you something. The minute you cross that border at San Ucedro, you'd better have paper on you saying who you are, that what you're driving belongs to you, and somebody back here better know where you're going and how long you're supposed to be there.' If they said: 'Well what if I don't—what happens?' I'd say: 'Well, if you don't, *then will come a story*.' And that's *All the Pretty Horses*. They went, they dreamed, they took along somebody that didn't tell them the whole story, and *that's* got to be in the selling of *All the Pretty Horses*. They've got to make you know that *they are different folks there*, and when you cross that line, when you go across that river—you go down to San Diego and you go in even for just an afternoon—*they're different folks, even though it's two blocks away*—*it's another culture*. And that's the one thing that Billy did better than anything else in this movie. Of course that's also Cormac McCarthy, and Ted Tally too. In *All the Pretty Horses* there isn't a character on the other side of the border *who isn't right*. Their point of view is *totally* valid. Blevins *is* 'the other kind of boy.' Up here, maybe not. But *down there*? You do that... Now, did he kill all the people and steal all the horses? No. He shot one guy and he died. Was it *his* horse? Don't know. 'Is it *your* car?' 'Well, I, I—O Jeeze, I forgot the registration, excuse me.' 'Come on...' When Blevins is laying there with the shit kicked out of him in jail, he says: 'I went back to get my horse and I saw a son-of-a-bitch had my pistol in his belt!' And then Matt Damon's crouching down to him, and whispering— cause the jailer is right outside: 'You shot a *rurale*?' And Blevins says: 'I didn't mean for the son of a bitch to die.' Well, he *didn't*, but he wanted his horse back, you know? And he's also thirteen! I mean, shit—*it's just perfect writing*, What can you say? The guy writes. He's just a wonderful wonderful writer."

Of course this means that Bruce Dern is in the novel now. Once an author opens the door and invites the world in—which begins when he types his title—he cannot control the form or the degree of habitation. Some readers enter a novel and never entirely exit. I will never get out of *Gulliver's Travels*, *Tropic of Cancer*, *The Sun Also Rises*, *The Time Machine*, *Great Expectations*. It could be argued that half of the world that I don't see, I don't see because I am walking within those books; but it could also be argued that half of the world that I *do* see, I see because of them, and without them I would see nothing at all. The bootlegger Collins whom we meet in *Tropic of Cancer* is a touching evocation of this syndrome:

> I liked the way Collins moved against this background of literature contin-
> uously; it was like a millionaire who never stepped out of his Rolls Royce.
> There was no intermediate realm for him between reality and ideas. When
> we entered the whorehouse on the Quai Voltaire, after he had flung him-
> self on the divan and rung for girls and for drinks, he was still paddling up
> the river with Kurtz, and only when the girls had flopped on the bed beside
> him and stuffed his mouth with kisses did he cease his divagations. (203)

And of course you can't enter a novel without leaving something behind. It's especially true of screenwriters, directors, actors. Who that sees the film of *No Country for Old Men* will forget *those looks* on the face of Tommy Lee Jones, looks that tell you as much as any dialogue, looks of such concision and control they could only have graced an actor of his age and experience... who that sees *All the Pretty Horses* will eradicate entirely the image of Lucas Black being dragged to his death, or Henry Thomas and his shotup wallet, or Matt Damon turning on his horse to watch the girl, or Julio's: "God is not in this place"? Some will—but some won't.

It's a big responsibility toward an author for any actor or director undertaking a great story. When I adapted Bartleby and played the lawyer in it, every smallest prop, every physical action, every nuance of drama, every breath that I took on stage meant the world to me and to all of us—it would have killed us to get even a moment of it wrong. It is exactly this sense, on everybody's part, about entering McCarthy, knowing they were going to leave a part of themselves behind, that I cannot tribute enough. They wanted it to be the best of them. When Billy Bob said to McCarthy: "Sorry I fucked up your novel," that was his way of saying *It's greater than I am.* As with *The Gardener's Son*, McCarthy could not have been luckier in his tribunes. The fact that this film, shot in the Southwest, too often has an uncomfortable feel of Hollywood testifies to the fierce dominion of Hollywood and its power to ruin almost anything, for it is, after all, a Hollywood movie, few of which are any good at any length.

10.

A long final scene that was shot as a single take—the boys riding out for a final talk—it was Henry's favorite scene—Bruce Dern loved it too—and Billy, who said that it was pure John Ford—isn't even in the film. But I don't dislike the ending as it is. With that ranch in the middle of nowhere, and Rawlins feeding the chickens like Dega feeding the pigs at the end of *Papillon*, when John Grady says: "Thought you might like to have your horse back," the gift to Rawlins is a gift to the audience. Makes it a film about friendship, and putting *something* to rights.

After the premiere in Manhattan, I told Billy Bob that the ending is okay, you don't need to hear that John Grady is not going to work the oil rigs and that Rawlins is never going to split. You intuit that from what you see. Billy Bob answered that this was not the reason he had wanted the final scene. Which I knew, because he had told me that when a jet had ruined the take—you could see it in the sky during a very long shot of John Grady riding off—he realized that no, the jet was helping to make the point of the scene. Leave it in—it's perfect! Ted Tally told Mike Nichols: "You've got to let me have a long film here," and that's the way he wrote it. Billy Bob inserted more of the novel, then he added Billy Bob—keeping the jet, for example—which is what any author should ask of a good director. Whoever wanted *a short film* disrespected the artists who were paid to make the movie, effectively abrogating his respect for McCarthy. These are more than hired hands: you've a moral obligation to let them do their job. Artistic dedication is an account that you cannot draw upon carelessly without becoming a bad man. Can a film that is written, acted, and shot for complexity be cut for anything else? As Flaubert said, you can't change the blood of a work of art.

11.

There is a Kafka story of an orthodox rabbi who *must* make a trip. He cannot travel at sundown. There is a mountain separating him and his destination. He cannot delay the trip, he cannot travel at night. The morning of the trip, he looks out of his window: the mountain is gone. If I keep finding traces of the film described to me by its participants in the film that was released by Miramax, one morning the two-hour version will awaken to find itself transformed into a giant, delightfully unwieldy work of cinematic art.

A few weeks after the premier of *All the Pretty Horses*, I went to see it again, this time at the Stadium Cineplex in Farmingdale, Long Island. Throughout the screening I was distracted by a flickering sensation and by a dull look in many of the scenes, a look of low budget, not of forty-five million. I spoke to the manager, who walked me upstairs and introduced me to the projectionist, a quiet but congenial young man who showed me the great roll of the film itself as it sits in the projector. My complaints, he explained, had to do with the fact that the bulb needed changing. If a film does not do well in its opening weekend, it is moved, by orders from above, to a smaller theatre in the multiplex, and in those theatres—because the films there are less important—they use projectors on which the bulbs are changed less frequently. Sometimes, he explained, it hurts to do this, especially when a film deserves a better chance, but they had learned that to argue was a waste of their time. Thus after only a few days, this forty-five million dollar *All the Pretty Horses*—a film that was advertised with U2 music to disguise it as a love story for adolescents—had been condemned to a projector with a bulb that made it flicker like a cheap little oldtime movie.

And yet... given that, as film historian Dudley Andrew has said, "our new century has become definitively that of the computer screen, so that films are reduced to the scale of YouTube, where they exist as just one (tiny) window amid a stack of windows" (42)... and given that at least one generation exists that couldn't care less whether an anamorphic film like *All the Pretty Horses* is bannered before them on a Cinemascope screen or is housed in a notebook computer... it occurs to me that, in climbing those stairs to investigate a faulty projection, I was on a mission to defend an enterprise that had already seen its brightest day.

NOTE

1. In his November 2009 conversation with John Jurgensen of the *Wall Street Journal*, McCarthy sounded as if he had seen a much longer cut of *Horses*. "As it stands today," he said, "it could be cut and made into a pretty good movie. The director had the notion that he could put the entire book up on the screen. Well, you can't do that. You have to pick out the story that you want to tell and put that on the screen. And so he made this four-hour film and then he found that if he was actually going to get it released, he would have to cut it down to two hours." See "Hollywood's Favorite Cowboy," WSJ.com.

· *10* ·

Losing Home: A Conversation with
Ted Tally about *All the Pretty Horses*

*W*hile *I was shooting* Acting McCarthy: The Making of Billy Bob Thornton's *All the Pretty Horses*, *it was clear that the participants were grateful for the
intelligence and restraint with which Ted Tally's screenplay fit McCarthy's narrative into the time dictated by the conventions of cinema. Bruce Dern said: "Tally
lifted it." Julio Mechoso, sculpting the air with his hands, said: "Tally played with
Cormac. It's Cormac. He really respected him." The script was shot essentially as
written, although Billy Bob could not resist restoring some omissions. Julio said:
"You know one thing that really amazed me? I've been in how many films, and
it's the only one I didn't get the blue revision, the pink revision. It's just one script.
I was cast about three or four weeks before I went out there, and I wasn't getting
revisions, so I called them in Texas: 'Hey, I'm not getting revisions—what's going
on?' They said: 'We've got gold here. We're not going to touch it.' I said: 'God bless
you, brother, because I don't want you to touch it either.'"*

In discussing actor-director Tommy Lee Jones's intention to film Blood Meridian, *I said: "I wouldn't want to have to adapt that," and Tally responded: "I
wouldn't want to have to sell it to an audience at the multiplex!" Of* All the Pretty
Horses, *he said: "There's no doubt that it's McCarthy's friendliest book to an audience." At the time of this interview, the film was still being edited. In a subsequent
discussion, Tally expressed his disappointment that the film, which premiered in
December 2000, was not a popular success, but it was tempered by the wisdom of
experience. "These films tend to take on a life of their own," he said, and he gave the
example of an earlier film he had written that, despite a lukewarm reception upon
its release, is now highly regarded.*

*Born in Winston Salem, North Carolina, Tally attended Yale University
before moving to New York City, where he became an Obie Award winning playwright. He won an Oscar for his adaptation of* The Silence of the Lambs, *and*

his adaptation of All the Pretty Horses *won an award from the National Board of Review. Our initial conversation, Part One, took place on June 30, 2000, in Tally's small, comfortable office in the quiet town of New Hope, Pennsylvania. The Delaware River ran behind him as we spoke. A subsequent exchange, Part Two, took place in September 2008.*

PART 1

JOSYPH: I love that poster in the bathroom that juxtaposes your *Terra Nova* with *Front Page* and *Cyrano de Bergerac.*

TALLY: An odd trio of plays, yes. That was a great experience. That was the first time I went to Santa Fe. They had a festival of summer theatre there. That is actually a David Hockney poster. He donated it to the theatre and signed them to benefit its first season. I love it down there. I was so excited when I found out that a lot of *All the Pretty Horses* was going to be shot in that area. I thought: "O boy, someone's going to pay me to be in Santa Fe for a while!"

JOSYPH: The beauty down there is not like the postcards. It's an austere beauty. Arid. Sparse. It has to be earned.

TALLY: Right. It's like another world. The colors are so different. The light has such a different intensity. You go up into those hills and see the oranges and pinks and purples—

JOSYPH: And you're out in the middle of nowhere—there's absolutely nobody—and they'll say to you: "Yeah, but it's getting crowded around here," because there's one house a hundred miles away.

TALLY: *(Laughing)* Right, exactly. We were shooting one day at the Zia Pueblo, about forty-five minutes or an hour from Santa Fe, and I thought: "This is about as far as I've been from anywhere in the United States." You leave the main highway and you take a dirt road, on and on and on and on into this reservation, and you just don't see *anything.* Cactus and prairie dogs. It's *very* sparsely populated. Then you come up over a hill and you see the circus is in town: the meal trucks, the campers, the camera trucks out in the middle of nowhere. That's one of the great thrills of making movies, to see that traveling circus pop up somewhere.

JOSYPH: A film crew will turn any location into a studio. They'll take West End Avenue, or—

TALLY: Anywhere, anywhere, bossing around the people who live there, saying: "Could you move, please?" And people so meekly obey them— policemen, people who have every right to be there! "O, it's Hollywood, they're in charge—I'd better do what they say." It's hilarious. We're on this pueblo in New Mexico, and when it got to be four o'clock in the afternoon, if it was a cold day, the catering guy would come around with Styrofoam cups of hot chili and hand them out with a spoon in each one, and if it was a hot day it would be iced cappuccinos, handing them out like we were at Spago! Hollywood brings its whole world with it, especially on a fairly big budget movie like this one. So you get that childhood fantasy whack of: "We're out in the desert—we're making a Western—O boy!"—it's everything you've ever fantasized about when you were growing up—and you also don't have to give up your creature comforts. So, pretty good deal.

JOSYPH: Your plays are still being performed, and they're in print, but no one makes a living in theatre. To what degree is getting paid for what you do responsible for your second career as a screenwriter?

TALLY: It's great to get paid more money than you ever thought you would for writing. But when I was growing up I never imagined myself working in movies. That seemed to me like something that happened on another planet. I thought: "You have to live in California. How do you pay for the camera? Boy, you need all those technicians and lights and so on." It never occurred to me to *imagine*, in movies, in my head. I could do theatre in the town where I grew up, so I expressed creativity through being an actor or director, then I started writing plays. I went to drama school, I moved to New York, I had several plays done Off-Broadway, and my only ambition was to be a playwright. Movies sneaked up on me. I was a fan, but I couldn't picture writing them. The first time I was hired to write a screenplay I didn't know what they looked like. I had never seen one. So it's serendipity for me that I began to get paid to write these screenplays and, after a few years, to have them made into movies.

JOSYPH: How did the first one find you?

TALLY: The first one that got made was a pretty good television movie, with Lou Gossett Jr., Carroll O'Connor, and Malcolm Jamal Warner, called *The Father Clements Story*, for which I did a rewrite and was given a shared credit. My first feature film was *White Palace*, which was directed by Louis Mandoki and which I adapted from a novel by Glenn Savan. One thing led to another, I began to get offered a lot of books, and I realized I had a skill in the craftsmanship of adaptation, so I focused on that specialty.

JOSYPH: The standard Dramatists Guild contract promises that, at least in theory, if changes are made to a play, the author will be involved. Nothing without your permission. But they can have six or a dozen writers on a film.

TALLY: Right.

JOSYPH: How do you deal with the fact that the performances and, in some cases, the words themselves are out of your control?

TALLY: Well, it depends on your relationship with the director and with the studio. Sometimes the way a film is made is more faithful to a screenplay, sometimes less. In my own experience, the difference between working in the theatre and working in films is largely overstated. Either you're in a collaborative art form or not. In the theatre, you still have to be a diplomat, you still have to give and take. Yes, technically they can't change your words, but they can shut down the production, they can refuse to go on stage because they don't like their speech, they can say the set is too expensive and you'll have to rewrite the scene to make it cheaper. Yes, technically they're your words, but you're collaborating with a lot of different people and you have to keep them all happy. In the movies it's more of the same. You're doing your best to make the script be its own persuasive argument for how it should be done. But I always have to laugh when I read interviews with screenwriters who are complaining about Hollywood, saying: "O, they've distorted my work, they've ruined my script." I always think: "Well, you didn't turn down the *money*. And you're also not pointing out the places where they made you look better."

It's a collaboration, and I've never yet seen a film made from a script of mine where something didn't surprise and delight me that the actor or the director or the cinematographer or the composer did that I didn't see coming. It was *implied* in my work, but I didn't know it was going to come out that way. If you're honest you have to say: "Boy, I didn't know I was that good!" The point being, you're not—until you're in a collaboration. Collaboration gives and it takes, but on balance I think it's the most exciting kind of writing for me. I wish I had the patience and determination to be a novelist, or to go after some purer form of writing. But I like the social interactions. I like the rehearsals, I like the feeling of being on a set, I like seeing something grow in front of my eyes because of other people's contributions. And that has only happened for me in the theatre and in film.

JOSYPH: Did you work closely with the directors on your previous films?

TALLY: I'm always interested in doing that if I can. With *Before and After* I was very much involved for the entire making of that movie. There was a lengthy rehearsal process, which is unusual in movies—for a movie to be rehearsed like a play. But the director, Barbet Schroeder, believes in rehearsing around the table, then with the actors on their feet, if possible in the actual set or location. I was lucky enough to be involved in that, and in all the postproduction, the editing—a lot of choices in that movie. He was secure enough in his ego to involve me in that way. And he comes from a European tradition where the writer is perhaps more respected than in Hollywood. The movie was not successful, but it was a great experience for me to work that closely with Barbet Schroeder and with those actors.

JOSYPH: It's clear that, by the time *Before and After* was shot, everyone knew what they were aiming for. It has a purity that's extraordinary.

TALLY: Most of the time in movies there isn't time to rehearse. It's hard to assemble the actors. They're all over the world doing something else at the last moment. It's expensive and unwieldy. Most movies, if you get one or two runthroughs, that's about it. On *Before and After* we rehearsed all day long for two or three weeks. It was great for me because, coming from the theatre, I was starved for that experience of hearing the script read out loud and getting a chance to hear where the wrong notes were and to change them, and even to have actors say: "Maybe there's a better way to do this. Let's talk about this moment, or this scene."

Silence of the Lambs I was very involved in, from preproduction all the way through the last edit, because Jonathan Demme is very generous as a collaborator. Again, I had the chance to work with the actors on the set, and Jonathan would send me dailies on video sometimes. I'm sure the studio would have had a heart attack if they had known he was doing that! But he would say: "I've shot this scene, take a look at it," and we would talk on the phone. It was an important tool, because he trusted that I knew something else about it besides just the words, that I might have some thought about the look of it or the casting or different production values. And I appreciated the chance to throw in my two cents. I don't think I won very many arguments, but at least they happened. I can remember talking on the phone with him for an hour sometimes when he was on the set of that movie.

JOSYPH: Some directors are scared of writers because they think that all the writer cares about are the words. They don't seem to realize that if it isn't working, you *always* ask yourself: "What'd I do wrong?"

TALLY: I suppose they think the writer will cling to his words in the face of all practical sense, or that the writer is going to screw up everything by giving conflicting notes to the actors—that kind of thing. And I guess if you were impolitic that might happen. But I'm there to be another resource, if they want me there. I can't stay indefinitely because it's too boring. William Goldman said that the most exciting day in a screenwriter's life is his first day on the set of a movie that he wrote, and the most boring day of his life is his second day. But I like to go and stay for a week to ten days when I know key scenes are being shot, and see if I can be helpful. Problems come up every day on the set, and the script has to be adjusted to the realities of the situation. If the rain trucks don't arrive, it can't be a scene about rain anymore and you have to adjust it.

JOSYPH: One of the things an adapter learns is that you need to trust yourself, and your understanding of the material, enough to let yourself *be a writer*, to invent, and to not feel the author is looking over your shoulder.

TALLY: Well, it would be terrifying to think that Cormac McCarthy was perched behind me looking over my shoulder, like Poe's raven! When I choose a book to adapt, it has to be a book that I have genuine affection for, that I really admire and respect; and, generally, that has a lot of humor in it, because I know that I'm going to have to live with that story for the next eight to ten months at least. So the first step is that I have to love it, and the second step is that I have to be so familiar with it that I can step back from it and respect its spirit without being suffocated by it, because you know you're going to have to change that book quite a bit. You know that, at the very least, you're going to have to cut two-thirds of it, even being as faithful as you can. And when you do that kind of cutting you have to invent new scenes and transitions and maybe even a new character here and there. You certainly have to invent dialogue. So, I respect these books, but I'm not doing my best for them unless I'm also willing to put myself into it.

JOSYPH: I was rereading your *Little Footsteps* last week. *(Tally laughs)* There is a vigorous use of the absurd in that and other plays of yours, whereas the humor in *All the Pretty Horses* is very different. You were very well behaved in the way that you handled it.

TALLY: Again, you have to respect the strengths of the story you're working with. The humor in *All the Pretty Horses* is of character and of dialogue rather than of situation. But McCarthy is a brilliantly funny writer, and there are passages in this book that make you laugh out loud every time that you read them. I could listen to those three boys talk all day long, and one of the frustrations of doing a screenplay of this book is that you have to shorten and channel it so that it gets to the point, when in fact I wish they could just ramble on about whatever is on their minds, because it's mesmerizing to read.

JOSYPH: It must have killed you to have to cut Blevins' lightning speech.

TALLY: I think that speech is almost entirely in there. Billy's got Lucas Black talking a mile a minute. You've never heard anybody talk so fast to try to keep that whole speech in there. And it's hilarious. McCarthy has a gift for a kind of vernacular that's very teasing, very jocular, very boisterous and jaunty. It hearkens back to Mark Twain and to Faulkner, but it's really his own voice. It's dry, and a lot of times it's self-mocking in the characters, and it just cracks me up.

JOSYPH: Brad Dourif mentioned McCarthy's pleasure, when they were shooting *The Gardener's Son*, in absorbing the phraseology of the locals around this little town in North Carolina.

TALLY: Well I asked McCarthy about one line that I always love, where Jimmy Blevins is having one of his first conversations with John Grady and Lacy Rawlins—they've just met him—and they're asking him about this unusual gun that has an oversized, rifle-type cartridge. Lacy says to Blevins: "Where'd you get a gun like that?" And Blevins says: "At the gettin place." The ever mysterious Jimmy Blevins! That's the only answer he's going to give. I asked Cormac McCarthy about that, and he said: "Well, I used to hear that expression." I forget whether he had an uncle or someone like that who used that expression, "at the gettin place." Just about everything that comes out of Blevins' mouth is so strange. He reminds me of the character called the city mouse—Harrogate—in *Suttree*.[1] This strange funny waif of a kid who's very eccentric, and the things he says, and the amazed reaction of the other two characters to them, are one of the big pleasures of the book.

JOSYPH: Billy Bob and Matt Damon have told me that Lucas likes to go fishing between takes, and he's some kind of a natural as an actor.

TALLY: He doesn't look as if he's acting at all, and sometimes I'm not sure he is. He's a country boy. Billy said to me one time: "You know, if he never goes to acting school, he could be a very great actor, because he's just so honest and direct and unaffected." Billy also said that as a person, Lucas is more his character than anyone else is. It was interesting to see Lucas and Billy Bob together, because of course they had such a close relationship in *Sling Blade*. To see them several years later on the set, there was a chemistry between them where they only needed a mumble or two to express volumes of what they wanted out of a scene. You couldn't see it happening in front of you between them. It was fascinating.

JOSYPH: How did the project come to you?

TALLY: I have a friend who is a great reader of Cormac McCarthy: Louis Allen, my oldest friend from North Carolina, and he recommended the book. I had never read McCarthy. My friend Louis picks up every McCarthy book the moment it comes out, and he snapped up this one and he read it probably within three days, and he called me up and said: "You've got to read this book. I think it'll make a great movie." I read it and I loved it, but I assumed that by the time it was in hardback the screenwriting job was long since gone, as it normally would be. But I called up my agent and she said: "Mike Nichols has bought the rights to this book, and he does not have a screenwriter yet." I said: "Well ask him if he will meet with me." And the answer came back: "He would love to meet with you. Come into New York and talk to him about it." So I went in and met with Mike Nichols—it was like meeting God—in his office. He was very funny and very charming, and he ended up giving me this job. His respect and his affection for the book were very evident.

I had my doubts about whether Mike would ever actually direct this book, because he's a real city guy and he likes to do movies in New York or Los Angeles, and he likes to do movies with big stars in them. I teased him about it one time. I said: "Mike, I can't see you out there in the desert for six months in one of those trailers." And he said: "Well, those trailers have gotten *very* comfortable these days." But sure enough his attention drifted away to other projects, and it languished for years, to my great frustration. I never really talked to Billy about it, but I guess he struck up a friendship with Mike when he was acting in *Primary Colors*. I don't know who first suggested that Billy read the script. It had floated around Hollywood for years, with different directors saying they wanted to do it, but as I understand it Mike was not satisfied with any of them and didn't want to let it go. My agent told me at one point that over twenty directors had said they wanted to do this movie. So it became one of those famous or infamously unproduced screenplays for years.

Then I got a call one day saying that Mike wants to give this to Billy Bob Thornton to direct. I was pretty excited, because I had seen *Sling Blade* and I knew that although it would be a big challenge for him in terms of scale, he would handle the relationships of the characters wonderfully, and he would get the human drama. The question was, would he also get the David Lean kind of thing, because this is an unusual story. It's an intimate story with a fairly small cast but against this epic background, and that was the only question in my mind. And that question was answered after the first time I saw dailies. He amazed me.

JOSYPH: What was the process of rewriting?

TALLY: I didn't rewrite for him. He shot the draft that I wrote for Mike Nichols, which was basically the first draft. I did a couple of days rewriting for Mike Nichols and we called it a second draft, and Billy tinkered with the draft himself, putting back some things from the book that I had cut that he couldn't bear to part with. But basically he shot very faithfully to the script.

JOSYPH: Screenwriters are held to the rule that every page represents a minute of screen time, and a script should not exceed 120 pages. The script of *All the Pretty Horses* is 150 pages. But there's a lot of story to tell, isn't there?

TALLY: There *is* a lot of story, and that was the hardest thing about adapting this book. It's around 300 pages long, which is mercifully short compared to some of the books I've been seeing—these huge, sprawling, five to six hundred page books. It seems like everybody's writing longer nowadays without writing better. This book is so tightly focused that there is not a wasted scene, not a wasted line, and so before I even started this I was saying to Mike Nichols: "You've got to let me have a long film here. Please don't make me cut this into a two hour movie, because it won't be what it needs to be." I was saying it's got to be two and a half hours at a minimum. Billy's first cut of this movie was probably three and a half hours, and I wish it could stay that long, because it's frustrating to try to cut some of this stuff out.

JOSYPH: When I interviewed Billy it was down to three hours, and he said that if you removed another sentence it wouldn't make sense.

TALLY: Yes, Billy is very proud, justly, of what he put on screen. He shot everything I wrote and a few other odds and ends as well. But as much as I love it, it's just too much of a strain to ask the audience to sit for that long. I don't know what the final length of the film will be, but I would think somewhere between two hours and twenty minutes and two hours and thirty. Which is a long movie, but not excruciatingly long if you watch it emotionally.

JOSYPH: From the start, you knew that John Grady's mother would have to be a suggestion.

TALLY: In the movie as it stands, the mother doesn't have a single line of dialogue, but she's seen a couple of times. A lot of people I know have found it hard to understand the first forty or fifty pages of the book. Characters are identified only by their pronouns. We don't quite understand the relationships among them. We don't understand why some of them are speaking Spanish. We don't understand that this boy's grandfather has died, that he hoped to inherit his grandfather's ranch and live and work there—this was his life's dream—but he's going to lose that chance because his mother's going to sell it. Just that simple plot at the beginning is hard to understand in the book, but it sets the stage for everything else, so it's crucial. In the movie, we have had to tinker again and again with the opening scenes to try to make it clear, so we don't lose the audience. I think we've now reached a point where it will be clear without being overly explicit.[2]

JOSYPH: Have you watched the editing process?

TALLY: Yes, I've seen quite a lot of the dailies and I've seen I guess now four versions of the movie, each a little shorter than the one before. And I've had a chance to talk to Billy about some of the editing, and also to the editor, Sally Menke, who is doing a great job. And they've been open to discussing my questions or concerns.

JOSYPH: Billy Bob likes to put two or more actors into a frame and let them behave.

TALLY: Yes, in a medium shot or a long shot. There are scenes in this movie—not many—that were shot entirely in one take, and that's the version that's in the movie. Other scenes that I was there for he covered just as elaborately as any Hollywood director. I mean, he shot them from everybody's point of view except the horses. If he knew it was going to be a scene where he had to have the tools in the editing room, he would cover himself. But I think he has a certain restraint as a director that goes well with McCarthy as a writer. He doesn't like to push the audience's face into something. He wants them to discover it for themselves. He doesn't talk down to the audience or pander to them as a director. So, he's sometimes reluctant to use closeups, and sometimes reluctant to use reverse shots in conversations, and it creates a style that sometimes feels a little severe, but which seems very appropriate to this harsh landscape and this epic quality.

JOSYPH: Matt told me that Billy Bob was good at getting him out of his own head.

TALLY: Because he's an actor, and a very experienced actor, Billy worked extremely well with his cast and they trusted him in a way that they might not trust a director who is not also an actor. He set them at ease. He created an atmosphere where they could be free.[3] He doesn't give a lot of direction. I've noticed that the best directors give very little direction, because they want the actor to be involved in the creative process. They don't want a puppet, they want a real collaborator, and if they've cast the part correctly they'll get back something interesting without much direction. A lot of times you'll see Billy and the actors rehearsing camera movements, or you'll see them rehearsing the extras so that they don't mess up the shot, but he doesn't have to say too much to the principles. They know what they're doing.

JOSYPH: Directors often say that to focus a film, they constantly ask: "What's it about?" Even if it's a single simplistic sentence, they need that spine to which everything connects. As a screenwriter, do you have that too?

TALLY: I don't always have that in mind. I probably should. A lot of times I'm focused so closely on the trees that I'm letting the forest take care of itself, particularly because I'm doing adaptation. It's a second-generation creativity, and I trust that with a writer as good as Cormac McCarthy those things will express themselves through the actions and the dialogue and not just in the language of the book. The heroism here is contained within the story in a way that is beautifully economical and didn't require embroidery.

JOSYPH: Can you say what the story's about to you, and what's important about it?

TALLY: Well, it's important in ways that I guess I can't articulate very well. It moves me deeply. Mike Nichols said to me one time that this story, to him, is about losing home. It's about losing your sense of your place in the world, and having to go out and try to find a new home for yourself. We've all had the experience of losing friends or loved ones. We've all had the sense of leaving the home we grew up in. And it's that part of the story that touches me most easily. It's a sense that this boy has lost his birthright and doesn't know where he belongs in the world and is looking for his place. He tries to find it through his friendships, he tries to find it in this ranch in Mexico. And, for a time, he does find a sense of belonging again. But Cormac Mc-Carthy's vision is essentially tragic, and he knows that we all eventually lose our home.

JOSYPH: Why does John Grady, smart as he is, have an affair with the boss's daughter under everybody's nose? Does he not realize the trouble he'll get them into? Or is it a dream world he's entered, and he has elected to dream it for as long as it lasts?

TALLY: It's a dream world. I think he's conscious of the danger but he can't help himself. He tells Rawlins there are some things that can't be helped, and it's something that's said to him early in the story, when he's appealing to the lawyer, Franklin, to help keep his grandfather's ranch from being sold. The lawyer says: "It's a sorry thing, son, but there's some things in this world that just can't be helped and I think this is one of them."[4] So it's McCarthy's sense of struggling against fate, and what's important is to never give up, and to struggle in an honorable way. In the end, most of these struggles in McCarthy are tragic, and doomed. His heroes judge themselves by a standard of honor that may be highly eccentric and idiosyncratic, but it is their own standard, and in the end they would rather die than fail that standard. I think that's also what we respond to in these books. That's the heroism of these characters, that their personal code is finally more important than anything else. And, in particular, their loyalty to each other. Their loyalty as men to each other is worth dying for.

JOSYPH: But with the issue of Blevins, the ethics of the story are complicated. These are horse lovers. Blevins is more than likely a horse thief. And yet they pal around with him, protect him, and when the stolen horse falls into Mexican hands, they certainly side with Blevins. Rawlins says: "I'll say one thing for him... The little son of a bitch wouldn't stand still for no-body—"

TALLY: "—highjackin his horse," yes.[5]

JOSYPH: Later, there's a shift back to the stolen horse again, as if the fact that it *was* stolen counts for something more now.

TALLY: Yes, there's a sense that John Grady has come to view what has happened to him as all being about this horse, in a way. "It all begun with that horse." As if it wasn't Blevins' horse, and because we nodded at that, all this tragedy was visited upon us. To set the world right again, I have to return this horse to wherever it belongs. There's something of that in there, yes. How much the audience will understand that or think that's important is another question. But in John Grady's personal code of honor, it's almost as if he blames himself for not having done this sooner, setting straight the ownership of this horse. The movie does still end with him saying: "I'm gonna try to find out who owns this horse," but some of the lines that I had written that make that more explicit have been cut.[6]

JOSYPH: How did you feel about the casting?

TALLY: It's probably, top-to-bottom, the best cast movie made from a screenplay that I wrote. There is not a false note in any of the casting. And Billy Bob, by hook or crook, has been able to get some extraordinary actors to play very small parts. Sam Shepard is in a one-scene part playing Franklin, the lawyer. Rubén Blades plays Rocha, a small part, but he is superb. Bruce Dern, who plays the judge, has a two-scene part, but he is wonderful. When you have that kind of support, it elevates the entire movie. Matt Damon is a wonderful actor. He's very emotionally honest. In any piece of film—in dailies, in rough footage, in rehearsals—I've never seen him give a false moment of performance, or one that wasn't very smart. He's a very shrewd actor. And he's very generous. He understands when a scene is not really about him and he supports the other actors beautifully. He's a great listener on screen, which is a rare quality that, in my mind, only the best actors have. He is just as interesting to watch when he is listening to somebody else as when he is speaking. He is also a very physically skilled actor. For this movie he had to ride a horse convincingly, rope a calf and brand it, break Mustangs without it being terribly obvious when you're switching to his stunt double, and he brings it all off beautifully.

We talked about Lucas Black, who is a natural actor and extremely well cast as Blevins. He never quite does what you think he's going to do, so it's always startling and fresh. And Henry Thomas, who I just love, is the world's sweetest man, very smart, articulate, and the only person in the movie who is a real cowboy. I find things in Henry's performance every time I see this movie that I had never noticed before that are wonderful and touching to me. Penélope is beautiful and very, very talented, and has a kind of fragility and vulnerability that I find very moving in this part. I think she's going to be a *huge* actor when people become aware of her in this country. She's already a huge star in Spain, obviously. Billy fought to have her in this movie, and I'm glad that he never gave up that fight.

JOSYPH: How does Bruce Dern play that wonderful scene with Matt, where they're at the judge's house? Billy was urged to cut it because allegedly *it wasn't necessary*, whereas to him, it's where the film is going.

TALLY: That was always my favorite scene in the book, and I'm sure Billy's too. Bruce is wonderful in that scene, very warm and sympathetic. It was taken almost word-for-word from the book in the screenplay, and it was shot at great length. The only problem is that, by the time you get to that scene you are two and a half hours, or at one point three hours, into this movie already, and it's very hard, that late, to watch a static scene of two people talking for quite a long time. It feels like you're starting another movie. Or, the movie's over, and now you have another scene. It's way past the emotional peaks that happen in Mexico: the death of Blevins, the loss of the girl, the taking of the horses, and the battle with the Captain. All of that is so long past that there is, in the movie, a problem with the storytelling rhythm that you wouldn't have in the book, where you can pick it up and put it down. So the scene with the judge, although it worked wonderfully in various edits, has been forced to get shorter as the movie has evolved, shorter than we would have liked it to be. What you now have is *a glimpse* of that wonderfully memorable scene in the book. That's frustrating, but that's what happens in movies.

JOSYPH: What was McCarthy like on the set?

TALLY: There was a great stir and excitement throughout the whole carnival of the movie to know that he was coming. Word had gotten around. "He's coming! He's coming! Today's going to be the day!" It was like Elvis had entered the building. Billy Bob was nervous and I was very nervous because I had never spoken to this man whose masterpiece I had manhandled through my screenplay. He was very very courtly, and funny, and low-key. He seemed gently amused by the entire goings-on. Because of *The Gardener's Son*, he wasn't a stranger to a movie set. He understood that most of the time you're setting up the shot and then you're watching the same scene being shot twelve times. And he seemed excited to have this story come to a different kind of audience. A lot of novelists nowadays, you get the feeling, as you read their book, that they're writing it with the movie being projected in the back of their head, and the whole point of the book, almost, is to get that movie deal. I don't think that's true of McCarthy at all. I think he's largely indifferent to that. He's a real creature of literature, and the written word is what he's about. But I think there must be some small part of him that's pleased. There's a *little bit* of the moviestruck kid in all of us, and I think he's probably pretty happy about this being done, and hoping it'll turn out well.[7]

JOSYPH: You're extremely articulate about the filmmaking process, and you've learned a lot about how to make movies. Is there an itch, now, to direct?

TALLY: No. No, not when you see those two hundred people out in the middle of the New Mexico desert, and they all stand there looking at you, like: "Now what?" When I see them all looking at Billy Bob, I just think: I don't want that responsibility, I don't want that clock ticking at a hundred thousand dollars a day. I'll probably be drummed out of the Writers Guild for saying this, but if directors get more credit, they also have more responsibility and they also get more blame when things go wrong, so they deserve more credit.

JOSYPH: What about writing a small character piece for you to direct?

TALLY: I could see that, I guess, if it were small-scale and personal. *(Laughing)* If I had to direct something, it would have to be three people in a room, talking.

PART 2

JOSYPH: After shooting *Acting McCarthy*, I could have turned it into a different kind of document by asking the participants how they felt about the project *after* they saw that the version they had discussed with me had never been released. I recall meeting with Barry Markowitz. He was so upset that he could barely speak about it. "It's as if we never made the movie." At the Manhattan premiere, Billy Bob was upbeat on stage, but afterward, when I told him—in attempt to be supportive—that he didn't need the ending that everyone who talked about it had loved—that's the scene with John Grady riding off, alone, in a long take—it was clear that *that* was the ending he had wanted and he *still* wanted it. Now he never discusses the film, and he hasn't directed another movie. There might be other reasons for that, but I cannot imagine that he was pleased with the two-hour version.

Billy had told me that he used to play Daniel Lanois' original score for members of the cast, saying: "This is what the film is about." When Lanois was replaced, he was given back his score, and it's my understanding that unless he will allow that music to be used, there will not be a director's cut DVD. I have, at least, seen some alternate takes on a clip reel, and in one of them Matt is *on fire* when he's dealing with with Miriam Colon—it's more a confrontation than a conversation, compelling in a way that suggests another performance and another kind of film, one in which John Grady's willfulness and drive are more to be reckoned with—more *dangerous*. Then, too, there is the film as described in my documentary, which is *not* this film in which most of the scenes lack the timing, the rhythm, and, frankly, the genius that distinguished *Sling Blade*. On the other hand, I have since seen *Daddy and Them*, in which there is so much wrong that I am *slightly* hesitant to assume that a longer *Horses* would be better, even though I tend to believe it. When I saw the long cut of *Heaven's Gate* that was famously reviled by the critics, I thought: *The film still doesn't work, but there are such astonishing scenes that they, alone, are worth the price of admission.* As Billy Wilder said about one of his own films, *The Private Life of Sherlock Holmes*, which was cut to shreds: "It felt longer when they made it shorter" (266–67). I wonder whether this is true of *All the Pretty Horses*.

TALLY: The editing history of *All the Pretty Horses* is indeed a long, complicated one, and I can't pretend to know all the ins and outs myself. But this is not as simple a story as the one that has sometimes emerged, which is that the noble artist, Billy Bob, is fecklessly tortured by Harvey Weinstein and Columbia Pictures into destroying his dream. The version of the movie that affected me most, personally, was the first one that I saw, alone, in a screening room in Hollywood. But part of that reaction is that it was so fresh to me then, and part of it was that I was partisan, rooting so much for it to be good, even as it was running. But I distinctly remember thinking, as the movie ended, that I had just seen a flawed masterpiece—equal emphasis on both words: *flawed*, and *masterpiece*. The film then was *at least* three hours long. It was slow-paced, deliberate, had its langeurs, was stubborn about what it wanted to achieve, and was certainly not to everyone's taste. An analogy might be to *There Will Be Blood*. It had many odd little quirky moments that were never going to have much meaning except to Billy Bob. But it was visually magnificent, and the performances had real room to breathe. Scenes between Matt Damon and his father, between Matt and Rubén Blades, between Matt and Miriam Colon, and between Matt and Bruce Dern, all had much longer screen time and were more complex and more powerful than those scenes became in the final edit. That is, assuming real patience and openness on the part of the audience. *A lot* of patience. And goodwill.

The problems began to develop when, at every length, in every venue, the movie tested quite poorly. In fairness to us, the test screenings were so problem-plagued that the movie began to feel cursed. At one screening the theatre lost power an hour into the movie and the rest had to be scrubbed. At another screening the film broke and took forever to repair. But even when things went well technically, the audiences weren't buying whatever we were trying to sell. I was at a couple of screenings where many people walked out. After a while Billy Bob stopped going to them, I think. He didn't care what anybody else thought. But this is show *business*. It was only natural for the two studios, Miramax and Columbia, to demand changes. After all, they were on the hook for a lot of money. Billy made some efforts to make changes, the changes didn't make much difference to the tests, and after a while he threw up his hands in a huff and stalked away, leaving the movie to its fate. I can understand how hurt and upset he was, but it seemed to me then, and still does now, that he had a greater responsibility to hang in there and keep battling for his vision, whatever it took. But Billy as a director is not much of a collaborator. He shut me out, he shut out Mike Nichols, he shut out the studio executives—basically everyone but his own closest cronies. The unsung hero of all this, to me, is Sally Menke, his editor, who was left to edit a two hour version. What she came up with was at least coherent and presentable, even though she often lacked sufficient coverage of scenes and the better takes she needed.

Is there a lost masterpiece in *All the Pretty Horses*? I don't know. I, too, would love to see Billy Bob's version released, but I can certainly understand Daniel Lanois' pique. He was treated badly, and whatever the movie's problems, they weren't his fault. His spare, haunting guitar score was exactly what Billy had asked him for. The movie was even shot to those rhythms. Trying to fix a problem movie by changing its score is like trying to fix a broken-down car by buffing its chrome. My personal feeling has always been that the movie would have been best at about two and a half hours. It would have retained its acting complexity without slowing to a complete crawl. But, mind you, it wasn't my money being risked, so it's easy for me to say. It's hard to blame the studios. And it would almost certainly still have flopped at the box office. But it would have been the best it could be, the best tradeoff between richness and pace, which is the battle every movie has to fight. And that time we lost.

JOSYPH: I wonder whether you would agree that the plot of *All the Pretty Horses* is built to work better as a book than as a film. An extraordinarily willful determination is a mark of many McCarthy characters, but in *Horses* the objects of John Grady's will keep shifting, so that the storyline jumps the track repeatedly. At first his desire is to cross over the border and to become a rancher in Mexico... then it is to protect Jimmy Blevins... then it is to be a rancher again... then it is to bed the daughter of his boss... then we are asked to care about Blevins' plight again... then we are back again with the girl and, most strangely, perhaps, for a cinema audience, John Grady then goes after the Captain and Blevins' horse! Is that too much story for a cinema audience? Doesn't the shifting of focus in the hero risk placing it in a position of not knowing what to care about? Is it the ideal of being a rancher? Is it the beautiful girl? Is it the safety of Blevins? Is it his horse? Is it the killer-Captain?

I ask these questions to get at something about the screenwriter's art. If you had, in fact, found this a problem, how would you decide whether it's best to be faithful to the novel as written, or whether to break into its integrity in order to solve a problem in the story—a problem that might only exist in the transition to film? Mike Nichols did, in a sense, *entrust* you with this task, and one would assume that it meant not "tampering" too overtly with McCarthy. Your screenplay, which I have read, is an extraordinarily artful adaptation of the novel. It is also inarguably faithful. Was there ever a point where you grappled with the choice between faithfulness on the one hand, and altering the story to suit the demands of cinema? It seems to me an almost impossible decision—damned if you do, damned if you don't.

TALLY: You pose a shrewd and difficult question. While writing, I really never thought about John Grady's shifting objectives in quite that way, and perhaps I should have. Certainly the plot has an elusiveness that one either enjoys—"Unpredictable"—or finds maddening—"What's this *really* about?" This became of more than just academic interest as the movie moved towards its release date and the marketers, the ad campaigners, struggled to define exactly what they were trying to sell. They settled on "a love story," despite my objections to Harvey Weinstein that the overall narrative—and the footage that we had—simply wasn't set up to support such a pitch. *All the Pretty Horses* is a less straightforward, less film-friendly narrative than either *No Country for Old Men* or *The Road*. But to me the book is a masterpiece, an instant classic—the only such novel I've ever adapted—and so I approached it with what I felt was proper respect and restraint. Everyone who worked on the movie *loved* the book, carried around their tattered copy, and regarded it with something like reverence. Perhaps we were all *too* respectful. Perhaps I should have taken a more critical stance. But really, we all wanted to honor the book, not re-invent it, and that's what we set out to do. In the longer versions of the movie this was especially evident, and perhaps more effective.

To my mind, as I wrote, this was always primarily a "coming of age" story, the only sort of definition that can contain all the sub-genres of the book: adventure, western, romance, revenge tale, etcetera. Think of *Kidnapped*, or *Huckleberry Finn*. Which is why I was alarmed when Miramax tried selling it as a love story. But this coming-of-age view of the story became badly skewed by the casting of Matt Damon, another example of how Hollywood realities alter artistic intentions. Don't get me wrong: I think Matt gives a brilliant performance. And he's one of Hollywood's rare, genuinely nice people. And we might never have gotten the movie made without him. But he was around thirty at the time, and John Grady is written as about 17. So the entire meaning and impact of the story changes. What's more, the budget rises, the studio and public expectations soar, and all of a sudden a smallish story about a Texas teenager trying to find his way in the world be-comes a big, expensive Hollywood star vehicle. In hindsight, the proper way to have made this would have been as an independent film with unknown kids in the leads and a small budget, low on the radar, and let it sneak up on people. In fairness to Billy Bob, that's the way he originally intended to make it. But hindsight is 20/20, and, again, the studios probably never would have made the movie that way. Don't forget, the project languished for six or seven years after I wrote my first and only draft for Mike Nichols.

JOSYPH: At the New York premier, I met Harvey Weinstein. When I told him I was shooting a documentary about the film, his first response was: "What if we don't let you?" I wasn't upset by this—it was more amusing than intimidating—partly because I had shot most of my film, partly because it was such a perfect reaction from a guy who is used to his level of control. In fact, minutes later he agreed to an interview. It never happened, but more because of his schedule than any antagonism. Did you meet with that large, looming, legendary form?

TALLY: I like Harvey Weinstein. I've worked with him on two projects and I spent a good deal of time with or around him during the test screenings and press junkets for *Horses*, both in person and on the phone. I have never been subjected to his legendary temper or bullying, although I can well believe them. With me he was unfailingly polite and generous, and I believe that he genuinely likes and respects writers—and actors and directors. What sets him apart from other movie executives is that he loves *movies*—passionately, with his whole heart. He doesn't just see them as a business, as power, as a way to get laid or anything else. You'd be surprised at how many movie executives dis-dain movies themselves, disdain "the product." Harvey was solicitous enough of my opinion to whisk me out to Hollywood for a press junket—including a three-way interview for the *New York Times* with him, Matt Damon, and myself—and he also asked me to sit for several days in the editing room with Sally Menke. As you know, these are not typical gestures for a studio head to make to a screenwriter. So, yes, Harvey is larger-than-life, a swashbuckler, a pirate—but he's a pirate that I like and respect.

JOSYPH: The theme of the father is big in McCarthy. *The Road* is, perhaps, the most obvious example, and it runs through *No Country* and *Outer Dark*. But one could speak about the Judge and the Kid in *Blood Meridian*; or about Bobby McEvoy and his father in *The Gardener's Son*; or about Suttree and Harrogate, Suttree and his dead son, as well as Suttree and his biologi-cal father, with parallels to McCarthy and *his* father. In your screenplay, it is clear that you are not neglecting this: we have John Grady and his father; we have Rocha as another kind of father; we have Belvins as almost a son to be protected by the older boy; we have the Captain as a kind of anti-father; we have the judge at the end as yet another father, perhaps the one who is most understanding—certainly Bruce Dern felt this way. Did you see the search for a father—*the right father*—as a component for this coming-of-age you've spoken about as central to the story? There is a moment in the film, beautifully played by Julio Mechoso, in which the Captain becomes *almost* fatherly toward John Grady, and one gets the feeling that he honestly believes he is giving him sage advice about how not to "die in this place." I recall discussing this with Billy. He was keenly aware of the father as a motif—one that is clearly lost in the shorter film.

TALLY: The theme of fathers and sons is central to *All the Pretty Horses*, and we were all aware of it. In a sense John Grady's largest search is not for freedom, his lost birthright (a ranch, a way of life), love of the girl, adventure, etcetera. His largest search is to find a new father to somehow replace the one that's already lost to him as the movie begins; to fill that emotional void and give that guidance. In this way he is Hamlet-like. And of course this is impossible, a doomed quest. This theme was far more apparent in longer versions of the movie, especially with a long, heartbreaking scene between Matt and Robert Patrick, who played John Grady's father. But I think a fair sense of it remains.

JOSYPH: Speaking of fathers and sons, when we recorded the first half of this discussion, your son Austin was only nine or ten. Now he's a young man and a writer in his own right. Will Austin Tally establish himself as the next Cormac McCarthy—in other words, is he a novelist—or will he follow his father's path and be a playwright-screenwriter?

TALLY: Austin has written short fiction and essays, but he is also an accomplished musician and he has written hundreds of songs. So, if I had to guess, I would think that he might end up as a professional singer-songwriter. Not an easy gig! But then, what is, in show biz?

NOTES

1. Regarding the relation between Blevins and Harrogate, Henry Thomas told me the following about meeting McCarthy on the set: "The only thing I could talk about were his books, which I was kind of hesitant to bring up because I didn't know whether he wanted to talk about his books, and I didn't know whether I was a good person to be talking to him about his books! We were in New Mexico. It was the scene where Blevins, John Grady and I are riding through town right after the big

thunderstorm, where Blevins lost his horse, when he first spots the guy with his pistol fixing a car. It was actually snowing that day in New Mexico—snow flurries started. I told him that *Suttree* was my favorite novel of his that I've read, and he said: 'O, really?' I was so excited about meeting him, but I didn't want to come across that way because I didn't want to put him off, so I ended up asking him one of the two thousand and one questions I had thought of before meeting him. I said: 'Yeah, I thought there were a lot of similarities between the Blevins character and Harrogate. Did you know someone like that when you were growing up—that type of character?' That's when he said: '*All* of those characters in *Suttree* were based on people that I knew in Knoxville.'"

"It's so strange," Henry continued. "When you meet someone that you admire, there's some onus to come away with a good story or to have an in-depth conversation with this person. It doesn't always happen, and I think sometimes it's better that way, because everything I know about him is exactly what he's presented to me as a reader, and that's enough. I like his books, and I told him as much, and that is all the interaction I need with the man. But he was a very charming, very nice guy. You wouldn't really notice him in a crowd if you didn't know."

2. The first part of the story, which is presented in brief sequences during the opening credits, advances with the aid of a sparse narration which is quietly delivered by Matt Damon. The narration briefly resumes at the film's conclusion.

3. All of the actors that I interviewed verified and amplified this positive view of working under Billy Bob's direction. About the prospect of working with him again, the response was typified by Julio Mechoso, who said: "What's wrong with you? My bags are packed."

4. Tally is paraphrasing Franklin, who says roughly the same thing in the novel, the screenplay, and the film.

5. These lines, which are in Tally's script, do not appear in the finished film.

6. Although the filmmakers described it with pride and affection (Thornton called it the most beautiful scene he had ever shot), the sequence for which these lines (or versions of them) were written—the farewell between John Grady and Rawlins—did not make the final cut.

7. Henry Thomas's perception of McCarthy on the set was similar. "Basically, he told a few jokes," Henry told me. "That seemed to be his basic interaction with strangers. The prop guy was very proud that he had managed to get hold of all the bizarre calibers and rare brands of guns that he had written into *All the Pretty Horses*—Blevins' pistol, for instance—and he was showing those to McCarthy, who was very pleased by that. But really he was just kind of quiet. He seemed a bit out of place on a film set—but interested. I think he stayed there most of the day and had lunch, and he seemed to have a certain sense of excitement/trepidation about the film. He wanted it to be something that he would like watching. I got that sense from him, that he was excited but he was a little bit worried. But I think that he was happy with what he saw there that day. He seemed very... almost... almost excited that: 'O wow, I *wrote* this—here it is.'"

How to Flunk the Final Exam
on Cormac McCarthy

Answer all questions. Keep to the subject. You have 45 minutes to complete the test.

1. Question. How high do you rank McCarthy above the American verse poets of his century?

1. Answer. I was driving a rented truck full of my paintings down to a house in South Miami that first belonged to the novelist Harold Robbins, then to pharmaceutical outlaws who shot it out with G-Men and lost, then to my old McCarthy bud Rick Wallach, who one day dug a machinegun out of his garden but, alas, no drafts of *The Carpetbaggers* or *A Stone for Danny Fisher*. I had traversed an indecent amount of road and I was stealing a moment in one of the stalls of a reststop, listening, with the punch-and-blow of airtowels, the latching of doors, the plunging of soap and the spinning of Rollmasters, to the deep slow voices of Southern men. *Not like us*, I thought, *they are not like us at all*. But it was a young man initiating his son—"Go on in there... take some paper off the roll... wipe the seat"—that made me sad for the South, sad for myself, sad for the world, sad for that stinkhole of a family truckstop men's room, and that triggered, unaccountably, the image, in *All the Pretty Horses*, sad too, of John Grady Cole using his jeans cuff as an ashtray and jacking his boot behind him against the wall of the gilded lobby in the San Antonio theatre where he goes to see his mother, his mother who has abandoned him to treat with a pack of strangers, painted strangers who mean nothing, who aren't real: theatrical fictions. Like Suttree's shave at a brass spigot behind a warehouse with his small shavingmirror on a nail, as if that were all of himself he cared to see, this image typifies the kind of writer McCarthy is, able to show something big in something small; small, like the heel of a boot against a wall; big, like a young man's soul. It choked me up and I cried a little there in the Southern stall with my pants down. I was writing, at the time, about *Blood Meridian*, that jaunty little American Book of the Dead on which I was trying, with pretzel logic, to suggest a bit of the praise and the hard time it deserved. My emotion in the stall was good for the project. *Remember this*, I thought. *That scene in the lobby—this is why you're on McCarthy's side, because McCarthy is on yours.*

2. Question. Examine McCarthy's French forbear, Émile Zola, with an eye to either a) the varieties of hereditary determinism working in both writers, or b) their respective reputations as Writers Who Research; e.g. McCarthy touring the Southwest in a pickup, Zola in the Paris dawn with marketeers converging on Les Halles, etc.

2. Answer. At the outset of *All the Pretty Horses* we learn that John Grady's house was built in 1872 and that "seventy-seven years later his grandfather was still the first man to die in it" (6). This places the start of the book in 1949, which is verified by one of the more oddly resonating lines in McCarthy, when John Grady's father looks at a headline and says: "How can Shirley Temple be getting divorced?" (13) How indeed. To divorce you need to have married unhappily, and for any marriage at all you need to have grown up; but there floated the California wreckage, indisputable, when the Los Angeles County Courthouse granted Temple her divorce from Jack Agar Jr. on December 5, 1949. And if *that* impette could get a divorce, who couldn't? "After Christmas she was gone all the time" (18) we are told of John Grady's mother, which takes us into the following year. Or ought to. In fact, 1949 starts all over again on page 18 of the novel, for the record storm in which John Grady enters San Antonio occurred at the end of January and the beginning of February of that year. Nothing wrong with placing the snowstorm of 1949 in 1950, but it's not characteristic of McCarthy and it could be a jolt to Texas readers who lived through it, especially as it did not snow once in San Antonio in 1950. So I am proceeding on the assumption that in *All the Pretty Horses* the year 1949 occurs on both sides of January. McCarthy's publisher, Knopf, either came to the same conclusion or read the novel carelessly. The fifteen months of the story span three consecutive years, but the dustjacket reads: "Set in 1949... " Critics who turn tales into texts about text could have a field day with this, for if it is every character's fate to repeat, forever, the years to which they are sentenced, what does it matter when they start?

3. Question. Consider the influence of the following on *All the Pretty Horses*: William Faulkner's "Spotted Horses," Ted Hughes' "A Dream of Horses," Larry McMurtry's *Horseman, Pass By*, Vardis Fisher's "The Scarecrow," Charles Neider's *The Authentic Death of Hendry Jones*, Stevie Smith's "The

Galloping Cat," B. Traven's *The Treasure of the Sierra Madre*, the Navajo "War God's Horse Song," Shakespeare's "Venus and Adonis," Kajiro Yamamoto and Akira Kurosawa's *Uma (Horse)*, and Robert Lowell's "A Mad Negro Soldier Confined at Munich."

3. Answer. In casting about for a Texas Oil Company roadmap for 1949, I discover the 80th edition of the *Rand McNally Commercial Atlas and Marketing Guide*, a green monasterial tome with beautifully colored maps and pages of interesting statistics. Once owned by the U.S. Department of Justice, this grand musty volume is such a load that I pack a bathroom scale into an attaché case and bring it into the library to weigh it (20 pounds). It is part of the fine map collection at Stony Brook University where, along the high brick walls of the galleria one flight below me, I had taken my first ride in a cherrypicker to hang an exhibition of large canvases, including one of the batch that I later drove to Miami and others you never would recognize because, unless you want to collect yourself, you often take a perfectly fine work, say, a rendering of Thomas Jefferson's chair, and treat it as a surface for painting Cormac McCarthy's desk. Walking one day with a director of the library, noticing it was really too dark in the corridor, I asked him about it. "We're on austerity," he said. *Austerity* meant removing some of the bulbs. It taught me a few things about state education and none of them were good, but the map room is great and there the lighting understands you.

"You'll probably find out some things you didn't know about Texas," the Map librarian, David Allen, tells me, obviously a fan of Commercial Atlas and Marketing Guides. Easy to see why. On page 26 of this gargantua that cannot be carried without torquing the lower vertebrae—in fact it can't be carried at all, it has to hauled like a slab of concrete—there are lists of Principal U.S. cities showing their growth since 1910 with populations for each decade. San Angelo being alphabetized above San Antonio makes it very easy to guess at what John Grady feels when he travels from one to the other. At that time the population of San Angelo was 25,802; of San Antonio, 253,854. Between 1910 and 1920, San Antonio rose from 96,614 citizens to 161,379, whereas San Angelo *lost* people, falling from 10,321 to 10,050.[1] How many of these West Texans were, like John Grady's ancestors, "dead by rumor" (6)? When McCarthy says of Grandfather Cole's seven brothers, all of whom died on the young side of 25: "They seemed to fear only dying in bed" (7), is he not describing most of the men in his novels? Even in *Blood Meridian*, a meaner story in which it is said that there is no good place to die, the chief gangster—or gangster chief—John Glanton is hatcheted *on* his bed, not *in* it, in opposition to the way that he dies in Chamberlain's *My Confession* where, at the time of the Yuma attack on Fort Defiance, he is last seen "tied hand and foot, as usual when on a spree to prevent him from doing mischief" (329).

In 1948–49 San Antonio was the third largest city in Texas, boasting 104 hotels compared to eight in San Angelo. It is thus not only the farthest point to which John Grady has traveled, it is the busiest. No wonder he asks a waitress whether the time zone is different. Of course it is, years different, and the man at the end of the counter who says: "Same time... Same time" (20) is incorrect, and the waitress who warns John Grady not to believe him is right. In traveling up in population, he travels up in time. This is as modern as John Grady has ever been, as modern as he will be for as long as we know him. For an adolescent who much prefers a saddle to an Oldsmobile, to be modern and truly Texan is no more possible than to be urban and truly Indian. John Grady has also come down in the world literally, for the San Antonio altitude is one third lower. Homeless, frostbit, wounded by women, downed by law and geography, insulted by oil, unfathered by war, John Grady is bound to cross another temporal border, this one into the past, where a self-respecting cowboy can, at least, get himself killed after living, however briefly, horse to horse, barrel to barrel, blade to blade, blood to blood, and is not likely to die in bed. With the prospect before him of yet another 1949, John Grady can be admired for riding off in the other direction.

4. Question. How is McCarthy's vision of Texas formed, misinformed, or *de*formed by his birth in Providence? Find passages in the novel to support your opinion.

4. Answer. My librarian's prediction about the *Rand McNally Commercial Atlas and Marketing Guide*—"You'll probably find out some things you didn't know about Texas"—resonated further as I consulted a page of economic maps. These maps revealed that in Texas there is oil, there is gas, there is hay, oats, corn and wheat and there is cotton and sugar and there is even some tobacco, flax, and rice. With each black dot representing 5,000 head of cattle, Texas is fairly dense with dairy cattle, even more so with beef. Shocking, though, is a map showing such a mass of dots that it is solid black. This is the map for sheep.

Texas—a nation of sheepherders.

This was more than I could encompass in one day. I left the *Guide* and I left the building with renewed respect for librarians and thinking about sheep. Why not? The American cowboy originated at the tip of Long Island, for the first mounted herdsmen in the country appeared at Montauk Point. If the cowboy is a New York phenomenon, it oughtn't to be a surprise that a herd of sheep was enough of a Texas thing to blacken a map.

Musty old books, as much as musty old men, can teach you a thing or two if you give them a chance to have their say.

5. Question. Compare the title character of Kleist's *Michael Kolhaus* to John Grady Cole; compare Consuelo Saltello in Bret Harte's "Chu Chu" to John Grady's impossible love, Alejandra; and compare Felipe Rivera in Jack London's "The Mexican" to Alejandra's aunt, the Dueña Alfonsa, answering the charge that her lecture on Mexican history is a mistake and, as McCarthy's one chance to flapdoodle about fate and to report back from his latest history binge, anticipates the stylistic quagmire of *The Crossing*.

5. Answer. A special report from Dallas to the *New York Times* dated January 30, 1949, stated that "all of Texas except the Rio Grande Valley was covered tonight by snow that in parts of the state broke all records" (1). The storm, which a Texas paper called "a king-sized cold snap" (1), was part of a larger pattern that punished much of the country, including Omaha, South Dakota, Baton Rouge, and New York City. The man who built the China-Burma Road during the war, Major-General Lewis A. Pick, led an emergency operation of the Missouri River Division of the Army Corps of Engineers, using snowplows, weasels, and bulldozers to open up snowpiled roads. Dumping up to nine inches of snow on some states, the storm froze orchards of Georgia peaches, wrecked a million dollars worth of Louisiana strawberries, starved a hundred thousand stranded Nebraska cattle, threatened floods in the Mississippi Valley, shrunk sales and shipments of Texas livestock (sheep included), and was *not* providing a warm Texas welcome to either the annual Wool Growers Association—which met, with slashed attendance, at the Gunter Hotel in San Antonio, corner of Houston and North St. Mary's—or to a San Angelo shitkicker in search of his lost mother at the Majestic Theater a few blocks away. **SNOW TIME, ALWAYS FUN, FROLIC TIME UNDER COVER OF WHITE** read a San Antonio headline, while at least eight storm-related deaths were being mourned (39). The storm, like John Grady's life, like all of McCarthy's fiction, was playing out nature's cruel contrasts.

6. Question. How do Dr. Gulliver's horses differ from John Grady's, and how do they differently represent the truth?

6. Answer. The Majestic Theater of San Antonio has produced legitimate theatre since it reopened for business in 1974; but prior to that, all the way back to its origins in 1929, it had shown only films. When John Grady came to town, the Majestic Theater was not giving a play, it was showing a John Wayne flick called *The Wake of the Red Witch*. In this South Seas adventure—adapted from a bestselling novel by Garland Roarks, directed by Edward Ludwig, a second feature specialist from Russia who later worked in television—Wayne is terrific as Captain Ralls, a pearl-thirsty, steel-fisted, hard-drinking rogue and the skipper of a three-masted schooner that he scuttles for its gold. For a B-movie, *The Wake* is overplotted and murky, but it's your only chance to see John Wayne wrestle an octopus, and at times the adaptation is almost literate, as in this Ralls monologue to his beloved, Angelique:

> A ship? It's more than a ship. It's a home. A world. A breathing thing. Nothing holds it back. The wind takes it and carries it for 10,000 miles. Every one of those miles, you're free. Like being a bird, only instead of the sky it's the sea. You have a whole empire of freedom—sea freedom. You're alive the same way the ship is alive. You run before the wind and you never want to stop. You—aw, I'm talkin foolish.

I do not know how the film did in New York City but in San Antonio it was a hit. Nevertheless as soon as I learn the title of the play that Mrs. Cole— or, more properly, Mrs. No Cole—was starring in at the time, I will carry the information to the Ministry of Truth, where a grandson of Winston Smith will correct the theatre listings in all old copies of the *San Antonio Express*, for this is how it has to be when a writer is more interesting than God—or John Wayne. Meanwhile, I can't hear the Majestic dialogue that John Grady hears without hearing behind it—from backstage, so to speak—the odd admixture of the demure, the profane, and the ridiculous scripted for the *The Wake of the Red Witch*.

One can assume that this is John Grady's first encounter with theatre, where he expects to learn something about life. Whatever the play is, it isn't surprising that John Grady saw "nothing in it at all" (21). "She's in a play or somethin over there" (12) he says to his father, unable even to say the word *play* without a meaningless qualifier: "a play or somethin." With the demeaning exception of the disillusioned White in *The Sunset Limited*, and perhaps Judge Holden, who would be lying anyway, it is hard to imagine any of McCarthy's characters saying anything nice about a work of literature, about the profession of acting, about writing, about any of the arts. We never hear from John Grady's mother—we wouldn't expect to. Suttree reads Tom Swift without regard, and he thinks: "From all old seamy throats of elders, musty books, I've salvaged not a word" (14), clearly betraying the fact—or pretending to the fact—that he's never seen a *Rand McNally Commercial Atlas and Marketing Guide*. Even the Kid keeping a Bible toward the end of *Blood Meridian* is less about interpretation than mystification (or, possibly, a ruse for getting along a little better), for he can't read a word of it. Ben in *The Stonemason* speaks about the Bible as if God spat printer's ink directly onto the page in the English of King James, overlooking the centuries of wordsmen who made it, and one gets the feeling that Black, in *The Sunset Limited*, might be of a similar view. But one book spoken of, and well of, in the novels is *The Horse of America* by John Hankins Wallace, a seventy-five year-old publisher whose literary legacy is *The U.S. Trotting Association Yearbook*, a Chinese wall of racing statistics descended from *The Wallace Trotting Register*, the first of which was published by Wallace in 1871, and *Wallace's Monthly*, founded by Wallace in 1875.

Whether John Grady's father, who once made a little less than twelve hundred an hour in a twenty-two hour card game, consulted *The Horse of America* for gambling or for breeding we aren't told; nor, for that matter, are we told why Don Héctor and John Grady Cole—who has read it "front to back" (116)—so admire it. My own father, who received two horses in payment for a gambling debt, was an unschooled bookmaker from Mulberry Street who had once, as a boy, killed a bad New York bully with the handle of half a revolver and so, of course, he wanted to be a judge and read mostly about law, not horses (his favorite book was *To Kill a Mockingbird*), and he would doubtless not have known *The Horse of America*. When one of those horses, a beautiful chestnut mare, threw me and dragged me around a corral by one still stirruped boot, my own riding career terminated and Wallace waited for me for thirty-five years until I rode again in McCarthy.

Born in Allegheny, Pennsylvania, in 1822, Wallace began to study the horse after he married and moved to a farm in Muscatine, Iowa, in 1845. Completed at number 40 West 93rd Street in Manhattan and published, by himself, in 1897, *The Horse of America* derived from more than fifty years of research. It was not reprinted until 1973. *Wallace's American Stud Book*, published in 1867, devoted most of its 1,017 pages to thoroughbred pedigrees with only a supplementary hundred pages devoted to trotters, but for the rest of his life Wallace was wholly absorbed in what an appendix to *The Horse of America* charmingly calls "the literature of the trotter" (550). Nevertheless, although the horse of the book's title is the trotting horse, and the point of the book is to trace its particular history, Wallace believed that "before reaching that point we must consider the beginnings of, practically, nearly all the varieties of horses in the world" (1). This is why, when John Grady tells Don Héctor that he has read every page, he is talking about five hundred seventy-five of them, and why the book's full title is *The Horse of America in His Derivation, History, and Development. Tracing His Ancestors, By the Aid of Much Newly Discovered Data, Through All the Ages from the First Dawnings of History to the Present Day. Including the Horses of the Colonial Period, Hitherto Unexplored, Giving Their History, Size, Gaits and Characteristics in Each of the American Colonies. Showing How the Trotting Horse Is Bred, Together with a History of the Publications Through Which the Breed of Trotters Was Established.*

To someone hearing about Wallace without reading his book, he could sound like one of that breed of obsessive cranks who write oddball tracts in very bad popular prose. Far from being the work of *a character*, Wallace's book is surprisingly erudite, responsibly reasoned, bravely argued, and written in a

prose that is personal, polished, opinionated, and, in occasional passages—
such as "and thus the wild horse became conglomerate in the elements of his
blood" (204)—beautiful in a way that reminds one of McCarthy and would
have to be appreciated by any horse who knows how to decode. As with all
high caliber non-fiction, among the book's pleasures are the ways in which
the author's love for his subject becomes apparent without his having to state
it. And the book is an education in more than horses. If John Grady read only
one book of the horse he could have chosen far worse.[2]

Chapter XVI, which looks at "The Wild Horse of America" through
history, paleontology, anthropology, and linguistics, has the cheek to chide
T. H. Huxley on the deficiencies of that great man's comparative anatomy
and then, after visits to the Museum of Natural History in Manhattan,
the pampas of South America, and the Las Animas Valley in Colorado,
it skips along, with Wallace's characteristic easy confidence, to summarize
the conquest of Mexico and de Soto's expedition to Florida. Chapter XIII,
"Antiquity and History of the Pacing Horse," includes among its sources
the Elgin Marbles, the Piazza San Marco, the Great Seals of British royalty
from Richard to Elizabeth, Fitz Stephen the Monk (12th century), Polydore
Virgil (16th century), Gervaise Markham (17th century), *The Art of Riding*
by Thomas Blundeville (1558), the South American and West Indian journals of the Earl of Cumberland's chaplain (1596), the Duke of Newcastle's
A New Method and Extraordinary Invention to Dress Horses, and Work Them
According to Nature and Also to Perfect Nature by the Subtilty of Art Which Was
Never Found Out, but by the Thrice Noble, High, and Puissant Prince, William
Cavendish, Duke, Marquess, and Earl of Newcastle (1667), as well as the more
recent writings of H. F. Euren, John Lawrence, and William Youatt.

Wallace is most engaging when, at the end of Chapter V, "The English
Race Horse," he chronicles his personal search to find and verify the painting, made from life by D. Murrier, of a horse called the Godolphin Arabian
(which, Wallace argues, is *not* Arabian), allegedly the founder of the English
race horse and regarded as the greatest horse of the 18th century. Wallace
convinces the reader that an engraving by a well-respected painter named
Stubbs, purported to be a portrait of the selfsame horse and widely publicized
as such, was in fact a distorted copy of a copy of the Murrier oil by a man who
had never seen the actual horse and who "followed his copy just as closely as
he could while converting a big-boned, stout saddle horse into a long-necked,
spindle-shanked race horse" (77). Wallace reproduces both pictures, and we
can probably use the Stubbs as an aid in visualizing the pack of impossible
horses, with their mismatched anatomies, in the painting above the sideboard
of the Grady diningroom, of which McCarthy tells us: "They'd been copied
out of a book" (15–16).

Chapter XV, "The American Saddle Horse," contains a passage by a Tennessee publisher, Major Hord, who, in his newspaper *Spirit of the Farm*, provides an answer to a pivotal question for Wallace: "Has any family or sub-family of saddle horses come from pure running ancestry and without any admixture of pacing blood?" (191). In the process he answers our own question as to whether *The Horse of America*, which I have assumed was passed down from John Grady's father, possibly his grandfather, was useful either for betting or for breeding. "It matters not," says the worthy Major Hord, "how good or bad the other blood may be, a strong dash of pacing blood will almost invariably improve the animal for saddle purposes, and never, under any circumstances, does a pacing cross detract from an animal's qualities for the saddle" (191). In other words, the book contains the sort of information that would be useful to know for either or both purposes, especially in the days before periosteal elevations, transphysial bridges, anabolic steroids, and electronic stimulants warped and discredited the act of perceiving a fine horse. By reading *The Horse of America*, we see that Don Héctor and John Grady admire the book because McCarthy admires the book, and the reason Don Héctor names the book to begin with is not because he is testing the boy or sounding the boy's character, it is because McCarthy is eager to put in a plug for *The Horse of America*, which is as good as any reason to introduce it into a novel.

When I spoke to Matt Damon about playing John Grady, I saw that John Grady was indeed well served by the profession in which he seemed so disappointed at the Majestic. Matt knew the novel as well as John Grady knew *The Horse of America*. On the day of the conversation, I brought that gracious and dedicated actor a couple of gifts. One was a copy of René Clément's *Plein Soleil*, the 1960 adaptation of Patricia Highsmith's *The Talented Mr. Ripley*, featuring Alain Delon in the part that Matt played, in the version directed by Anthony Mingella, just before he starred in *All the Pretty Horses*. I was so sure that Matt and half the cast of Mingella's film had all watched it some night when they were shooting the movie in Rome that I left the tape in my case until Matt saw it there. "O, look at this, you've got it," he said, taking it out with pleasure. "Anthony wouldn't let us watch it." As *Plein Soleil*'s highlight, for me, was an uninvited roach crawling across one of the props, I assured Matt that he had not been missing anything special. My second surprise for Matt was *The Horse of America*. "Henry and I wanted to read it," he said, "but we couldn't find it." Both actors did, however, take a long trip together on horseback. "All the extra baggage I had for Ripley," Matt said, referring to the fact that Ripley, as a character, was highly self-conscious and manipulative, "that was really bad for John Grady. A few months before the movie started we got into Henry's truck and we went to San Antonio together. Henry has the way you need to have around a horse—never loud, no sudden movements, and it comes naturally—so we both kind of felt, well, let's spend a month riding horses all day." When I met him in Los Angeles, Henry Thomas told me: "Most of what we did, as far as rehearsal, was when we were riding every day, so we commiserated a lot on the various sore muscles and the pains that we had, and that was most of our bonding." They might not have gotten to read *The Horse of America*, but they did, at least, ride it.

John Grady's vacuous experience at the play, while effective for the story, has less to do with the fact that he went to the theatre than that he went to the wrong theatre. Had he hitchhiked in another direction, to New York City, he would have frozen under an equally bad blizzard but he would have seen better theatre, including Lee J. Cobb in *Death of a Salesman* at the Morosco, Laurence Olivier in *Hamlet* at the Park Avenue Theater, Henry Fonda in *Mister Roberts* at the Alvin, and Marlon Brando in *A Streetcar Named Desire* at the Barrymore. Because Olivier, with Olivian bravura, was doing a Saturday late show at 11:30 p.m., it would have been possible for John Grady, who had the stamina if not quite the will, to see, in a single day, Cobb in the afternoon, Brando in the evening, Olivier at night. If that were not enough, uptown, on East 70th Street, John Grady could have gone to the Lenox Hill Playhouse where he might have been intrigued by *Uniform of the Flesh*, a mistitled adaptation of *Billy Budd, Sailor*, performed by the Experimental Theater, which included, as one of the sailors, a young Lee Marvin. Even if this too had left him cold, the events of the coming year would have given him cause to ponder it in retrospect. In reviewing the play for the *New York Times*, Brooks Atkinson considered it in terms that are strikingly suited to John Grady's future and to McCarthy's approach to the novel that contains him. "Melville was a seer with a terrible suspicion that life is infinitely complex," Atkinson wrote. "To him Budd represented pure good and Claggart pure evil. He believed that neither one could live in this world in a pure state, but that they would destroy each other" (33). Watching Billy Budd, John Grady would at least have gotten closer to his mother, his legitimate mother, the mother who cared for him, for McCarthy, who gave birth to and raised him into the fine fictional character he became and even compromised his well-publicized privacy by doing a *Times* interview to guide John Grady into the world of readership, is, by his own admission, an avid reader of Melville. What the late Elizabethan John Dryden said of Shakespeare is also true of McCarthy, that "he needed not the spectacles of books to read Nature; he looked inwards, and found her there" (149); but McCarthy is not at all like Suttree, or any of his heroes, for if ever there were an author who has drawn upon men and what they have written for information and inspiration, it is McCarthy.

7. Question. What is McCarthy saying to non-Spanish speaking readers by representing passages of dialogue in Spanish?

7. Answer. When John Grady sits in the lobby of the Menger Hotel, waiting to see his mother, who strolls out on the arm of a fancy man at nine in the morning, it is never so stated but she has become, in her son's mind, a prostitute. Of course unmarried mothers who are taken by other men are often viewed as whores, especially by their sons, and there is an equally long history of women on the stage being seen in the same light. As an actor I ought to say, in his mother's defense, that given the chore of managing a ranch for a burntout, shellshocked, chainsmoking gambler who, if he won as much as twelve hundred an hour certainly loses more than that and is sure to piss both my money and my dear life away, I'd be glad to have a part at the Majestic, and that play doesn't exist that has a line John Grady would want to hear from me.

Despite differences, this trip to San Antonio reminds me of the chapters in *East of Eden* where the young boy Cal stalks his mother, Kate, in and around the Monterey brothel where she is the madam. In the 1955 film directed by Elia Kazan, James Dean, who would have played John Grady had the novel existed then, gives an interesting performance. "Would she talk to me?" he says to the bouncer at the brothel. "I just want to talk to her." As he is dragged out of the building, he shouts: "Talk to me! Talk to me please, mother!" John Grady is less demonstrative—partly because he doesn't need his mother to talk to him, he needs her to leave him the Cole ranch—but the scene in the Menger lobby is McCarthy at his best.

Once John Grady has watched his mother leave, McCarthy does a curious thing. "He sat there for a long time" (22) he says of his hero, who is sitting in one of the lounge chairs with a copy of the paper from which I have quoted the storm reports and which has carried no sign of his mother's achievement, unless it be the notice of her divorce. The next sentence is: "After a while he got up and folded the paper and went to the desk" (22). The phrase "after a while" is redundant: it would have to be after a while if he sat for a long time. Strictly speaking, it ought to read: "He sat there for a long time. Then he got up and folded the paper and went to the desk." But this redundancy of *long time* and *after a while*, although it could be a stylistic lapse, is effectively justified: it's precisely that time in which John Grady is halfway orphaned of father and mother. When he inquires at the desk whether a Mrs. Cole is registered, the clerk's answer, "No. No Cole" (22), is only a confirmation of what he has already divined: mother is now a kept woman, not his, not his father's—not herself anymore. Last night, a star in a dumb show; this morning, a kind of whore. If no Cole is there, no mother is there. Skipping a month, McCarthy moves briskly to subtract the boy's father, for here is the

following phrase: "They rode together a last time on a day in early March..."
(22) And after the first father can there ever be another? Not in this family,
not in this procession of candidates. The lawyer Franklin, Don Héctor, the
Mexican Captain, the Ozona judge—they all have a chance and they all fail
to father him. By the end of the tale John Grady, a lover of the horse who
protects a horse thief, has not even a friend to travel beside him, only a horse
with no rider, a horse that, like the world, refuses all claimants and would
seem to belong to no one, least of all the trinity who swear out papers in a
case of what the judge calls "bad mistook" (289) identity.

In the film *East of Eden*, Cal's father, played by Raymond Massey, who
hated James Dean (Steinbeck thought him a snotty kid who was perfect
for the part), wants to know why, when Cal first heard the truth about his
mother, Cal was sure it must be so. "Cause she ain't no good and I ain't no
good," Cal says. "I... I knew there was a reason why I wasn't." In the novel,
Cal is talking to the family cook, Lee, an educated Chinese immigrant who
bawls Cal out for using his mother as a scapegoat. "Whatever you do, it will
be you who do it—not your mother" (449), Lee says. Later, Cal has this
exchange with Kate:
"What Lee said was true."
"What did Lee say?"
Cal said, "I was afraid I had you in me."
"You have," said Kate.
"No, I haven't. I'm my own. I don't have to be you."
"How do you know that?" she demanded.
"I just know. It just came to me whole..." (466).
Does John Grady wrestle with any of this? As, for instance, when he is
so determined (a little unbelievably) not to aggrandize himself that the Ozona
judge, kindly understating the case, views him as a kid that "maybe tends to
be a little hard on theirselves" (291)? Suttree certainly wrestles with it. When
he talks to Uncle John about his father's attitude toward his mother, he says:
"Cant you guess that he sees in her traces of the same sorriness he sees in
you?... He probably believes that only his own benevolent guidance kept her
out of the whorehouse" (20); and when Uncle John says: "You know, you and
me are a lot alike," Suttree says: "But I'm not like you. I'm not like him... I'm
like me. Dont tell me who I'm like" (18). Leaving aside the situation in Mc-
Carthy's own family—his father being a lawyer for the TVA, which was, to
say the least, ungenerous to some of the worlds McCarthy has written about
with such compassion—one can word-search *Faulkner* in McCarthy criticism
for a clue as to why he might identify with people who say: *Don't tell me who
I'm like*. Robert McEvoy, in *The Gardener's Son*, is so hypersensitive about his
identity that he doesn't even want his beloved sister presuming upon it. When

she tells him: "Dont be that way Bobby," he answers with an anger that achieves a kind of cruelty: "What way am I? You dont know how I am. You dont know me" (39). In *Blood Meridian*, Elrod tells the Kid: "I knowed you for what you was when I seen ye" (322), and is paid for his presumption with a bullet before dawn. When the Kid, like St. Peter, denies his savior three times—"I aint studyin no dance"—"I aint with you"—"I never come here huntin you" (327–328)—it is a last vain attempt to remain opaque, inviolate, unfathomable. To be possessed is to be sat upon, which is what the Griffen whore does to the Kid, symbolically, before Judge Holden quite properly, and literally, shows how graspable, embraceable, devourable he is after all.

When I first began reflecting on this scene in the Menger, I thought: *Are you going to stand there, McCarthy, and tell me that a young Texas boy of sixteen, who has hitchhiked to ole San Antone, beats it out of town without going to see the Alamo? Or that he did go see it and you didn't bother to tell me?* Then I looked up the address of the Menger Hotel: 203 Alamo Plaza. When John Grady walks out of the Menger, the Alamo is just around the corner. When I stayed in the Menger, I saw that you are practically *in* the Alamo. McCarthy teases us with a nondescriptive passage: "He walked around town in the snow" (20), leaving me yet to wonder: *Did he, before he left, walk around to see the Alamo, or did he head back to the Y, fetch that 19th century suitcase that belonged to his grandfather, and hitchhike home?*

Much has been said about John Grady's innocence, or naiveté, in contrast to what he learns in Mexico; but I can see him as already oppressed under the weight of mature concerns—if not his own, at least McCarthy's. I don't care *how* upset he is, that would have to be an awfully damn strange serious boy to pass up the Alamo in the heart of Alamo City. That's downright unhealthy. Even the Rand McNally Road Atlas, thoughtfully inserted into a pocket of the *Atlas and Marketing Guide*, shows the Alamo beckoning you in small red print beside the grey blotch of San Antonio. I, who idolized Walt Disney's Davy Crockett and will never forgive the Alamo for killing Fess Parker, made a point of going to see it and sent a postcard to Mom. Even Oscar Wilde, in his knee britches, scarlet stockings, and silver-buckled slippers went to see the Alamo. Rawlins would have said: "Meet you over the Y. I'm... goin to have a look't the Alamo." Suttree at least would have gone and pissed on it or gotten his crown cracked against it. Judge Holden would have blown it up by remote control. One definition of John Grady, old before his time, is: *He doesn't give a shit about the Alamo.*

When I was staying at the Menger, I tried to rectify this lapse; or, at least, I tried tipping my hat toward it. Filming an interview with the Chinese translator of *All the Pretty Horses*, Yu-Ming Shang, I posed him against a wall of the Alamo and I urged him to answer me in English and Chinese. It was charming to see Shang, dressed in a blue and white checkered cowboy shirt, blue trousers and a wide brown belt, holding up a Chinese copy of the book and making a bilingual pitch for the privilege and honor of translating McCarthy, which he pronounced as *McCarcy*. What a distance from that great stone wall to this one; distance, too, in reverse, for because of Shang's efforts, John Grady *did* visit the Alamo—in Chinese, and John Grady journeyed to China too.

With the sounds of the Burlington Northern-Santa Fe in the distance, long soothing sounds that signaled the transport of cars, coal, grain, wood, and eternity from as far away as Vermont, sounds that seemed to last the length of the conversation, as if the train were miles long, Shang held proudly his Chinese translation, seeming to reassure himself that it was done, really done, and that it would not slip away. As if he were filming a public service spot, he spoke in measured, scripted tones. With its statuary niches emptied of their sandstone saints and its beautiful white limestone, quarried nearby and ornamented by a San Antonio carver (Dionico de Jesus Gonzales), the wall held its own behind Shang and it had as much to say as he and his book.

"I was first given the chance to read this magic book in 1995," Shang said. "That was in English, one of the few copies in China. I was immediately attracted by the touching plot of the novel, and by the vigorous, magnificent portrayal of the American-Mexican border. Especially, too, by the uneven destiny of the young American horsemen in mid-20th century. I was carried away by the book, and I attribute that to Cormac McCarthy's magic writing technique. And so I decided to translate it into Chinese to introduce this great book by a contemporary American novelist to numerous Chinese readers. I could only use my spare time for the job, in the night and on weekends, as I was heavy burdened with my teaching and administrative work. In my family I did not have a computer, so I did it the primitive way, all by hand. It took me five months to finish the job since it was not an easy thing for me to do. In the city where I lived we had some English teachers from abroad, but few of them knew about Southern American slang. My wife and my daughter helped me in copying the manuscript. But I enjoyed that time, although it was very hard, since I was doing a meaningful job for Chinese readers."

"At that time," Shang said, "Cormac McCarthy was unknown to Chinese readers. Even up to now this is the only translation. So the first printing was very moderate, 5,000 copies, for such a big country. The publishers would not put out more. When I came to the U.S. I had the chance to publish articles about Cormac McCarthy's novels in Chinese magazines and newspapers. With more interest in Cormac McCarthy and in America's westward expansion, there was a growing demand; hence, the publisher will put out a second printing of 50,000 copies of *All the Pretty Horses*. That is *ten times* as many as the first printing! And now they plan to publish the entire Border Trilogy, which it is still my honor to do."

The book is a paperback with an improbable stagecoach on the front, more horses in a small square on the back, the title printed in bright red calligraphy. As Shang pronounced the four red characters for me, they sounded like this: *Chu-eeem Ma Chang Sssszih!* "The first printing is not that luxurious," Shang said, paging the book at the perfect height for a medium shot, as if he had done this before. "It is not that exquisite, with hardcovers... but, after all, it is in Chinese... it is in China... and it is the first one! So I can still be proud of it."

8. Question. Discuss *Moravagine* by Blaise Cendrars in relation to *Blood Meridian* and apply your conclusions to *All the Pretty Horses*.
8. Answer. Shang also said: "For some Spanish sentences that appear in the book, I have no one to help me! So I searched all the big libraries in my province to translate these tough paragraphs."

In my room at the Menger, a place where O. Henry liked to stay, I talked about translating McCarthy with the French critic and translator Béatrice Trotignon. Béatrice has translated McCarthy for her own criticism, but as a professional translator she has had to favor pulp the way that Paulo Faria has had to support his family by translating thrillers. "McCarthy was translated in France almost as soon as he started publishing in America," Béatrice said, "but the readership in France developed with *All the Pretty Horses*. People started buying previous translations, and *The Orchard Keeper* was translated again. When *Blood Meridian* was translated in 1986 by François Hirsch, it received the Maurice-Edgar Coindreau award, and Hirsch, working with Patricia Schaeffer, translated the Border Trilogy. On a TV broadcast, Hirsch discussed the difficulty of rendering Cormac McCarthy's language, its extravagant floridity—and also its extravagant simplicity. French is grammatically very rational, so the sentences have to be simple and clear, whereas McCarthy's language can be *so* dense that you have to make difficult choices in French to render it."

Béatrice paused.

"I think I have to say this again," she said. "That's not very clear! I tend to read McCarthy the way I read poetry. Because of my focus on the meaning that comes through the rich sonorities, the syntax, and the rhythm of the text, my analyses of McCarthy have to be grounded in the original. When I do look to see how an incredibly dense sentence has been translated, I sometimes discover that the translator could not retain the ambiguity: French syntax doesn't allow it. But McCarthy's range is so wide. I'm always surprised at how he can go from the most incantatory writing to the sparest sentences, and

I'm fascinated to discover simplicity in complexity, complexity in simplicity. One tends to focus too much on the extravagant side of his style. The effects of the conjunction *and* that is so much used in the Trilogy occupied a lot of my work. François Hirsch discussed this as well, the difficulty of translating *and* in McCarthy. *Blood Meridian* is one of my favorites because of the sheer power of language, even though there are times when we would throw the book away because of the violence that seems to be directly on the page. I tend to see other things, things that are happening with the words. With the tree of dead babies, I couldn't help hearing *broken sobs* behind the *broken stubs* from which the babies were hanging. One has to take one's time with Mc-Carthy. It's the kind of writing that slows down reading and contemplation."

One has to take one's time with McCarthy... This is what Ted Tally told Mike Nichols about adapting *All the Pretty Horses*. And clearly it's what Billy Bob Thornton told himself about the film. It's what he told *me* when I spoke to him in his favorite hotel in Los Angeles, the Sunset Marquis.

"What the studio was not going to stand for," Billy said, "was a movie that's not **MATT DAMON *IS* ALL THE PRETTY HORSES**, with his face on a poster with a horse superimposed over it—like they always do, and have a lot of loud stuff, *excitement*, and it's an hour and twenty minutes. But that is *not* what they were going to get. They were also going to get my crew that I made *Sling Blade* and *Daddy and Them* with. The people that I work with don't do what they do to have it *noticed*, they only want to do enough to make it real, because they know it's what *I* do, they know exactly what I like— we don't even have to talk about it, and they haven't boned anything yet. And they were going to get a movie that was made the way I made *those* movies. Watching my little crew from *Sling Blade* make this big movie for the studio, and all along the line saying: 'No, we'll do it our way—see you guys later,' it made me feel great. And this is the movie that gave me confidence as a direc-tor. The other two movies are *exactly* what I wanted them to be, but I knew I could do what I wanted with *my* movies. With this one it was: 'What if I can't do it? This is a big deal—I have forty some-odd million dollars!' We had just barely enough to eat on the others. So we came in early and under budget, but for some reason they don't like that. Is that some *accounting* thing?"

"Now they've had their two previews," Billy said. "They bring in an audience and they trick the filmmaker and they trick the audience into changing the movie however they want. They were doing it in New Jersey and they said: 'Where else would you like to do it?' I said: 'Austin.' If you let an audience in Austin just come in and watch this movie, they'll get it. But the first trick was that it wasn't *in* Austin. The night that I went there for the preview—which I didn't want to go to, because it means nothing to me—I screwed around and got ready in my own good time, I went down with Bruce

Heller, my producer-partner, and we got into the car and he was freaked out and nervous and driving really fast. I said: 'What's the problem?' He said: 'It's forty-five minutes away!' I said: "*What?* Why aren't we staying *here*, in the middle of town?' We got to some place like Beehive Texas or something, it's a strip mall, it's like: 'Wait a minute—this is *not* Austin—I said *Austin!*' I took one look and I said: 'These are *not* the kind of people who are going to come and see this movie.'"

"So it's a setup," I said.

"It's a *total* setup," Billy said.

"So they can say: 'You see, there *are* problems with it—it's not working.'"

"Absolutely. There were a lot of older ladies, over seventy. I said: 'This is a three hour movie, it's always going to be a three hour movie, if you didn't want a three hour movie you shouldn't have bought the book because you can't do it in less than three hours.' The original cut was four. I managed to take an hour out. But I've cut it to a point now where, *if you take one sentence out*, the story won't make sense. You won't know *who* the Captain is, you won't know why he's afraid of the aunt, you won't know *anything* if *anything's* taken out now.

"I *begged* them to not let me make this movie. I've never been keen on making movies from novels, and I knew that I wasn't going to do it the way they wanted me to do it. In the movie business, even when they tell you that they want *you* to do something, they don't really mean that. And everything I've directed has been out of my own head. But the essence of this book is something that's very close to me, so I thought that if I could get the essence across, and keep the spirit of the book, put that on the screen—that's the hard part. Dialogue's easy. How do you get the narrative on screen? That's the tough thing and that's what's really important in this book, and what's going on in the boy's head, which is more than *O my God there's another Mexican guy—do you think he wants to kill me?*

"I said: 'I'm the wrong guy. You're going to have a three hour movie that's shot like *Sling Blade*. It'll look *big*. If you want John Ford, you got it'—where we shot in Texas and New Mexico, you flip a switch, which a Chimpanzee could do, and there's going to be a gorgeous sky and mountains and it's going to look great—'but when they're talking to each other it's not going to be *three* sentences, it's going to be *forty*, like you have in the book.'

"So they got these people in there at the preview. Of the ones who weren't ladies over seventy—and a few gentlemen over that—there was also an audience of young people whose main concern was like, Dad wouldn't let them borrow the car, and a few people who run backhoes, or who work for the Sanitation Department, who by God wanna see Bruce Willis blow somethin up! *That ain't what this is.* Then they hand out cards to people and they say: 'Listen, your opinion doesn't matter in the world, but we've come in from Hollywood and you read all the magazines about us and you read the *Inquirer* and see what alien landed on Mel Gibson's front lawn, and we think so much of you people that we're going to let you tell us how to make our movie, and afterward we're going to take twenty of you for a focus group and we're going to ask you: "Is the movie *too long*, don't you think?"'

"So what I told them was this: 'The way movies should be directed in this day and time is, take a hundred Neilson families and let *them* direct the movie. Cut out the middleman. You don't need directors. If you want *me* you get a very specific thing. Hire some guy who wants the money and will do whatever you say, don't hire me.' But they insisted."

"It's as if they hired you for the rough draft," I said.

"Right," Billy said.

"It's the same in publishing," I said. "You write a novel, they might take it, but they take it because they know what *they* want to do with it. Frank Lloyd Wright, in a letter to one of his clients who suggested all these changes, said: 'All of the details are mine.' *All* of the details, that's what makes a work of art. You don't hire someone as an artist and then say, well, it's only a couple of cuts, or only a couple of scenes. There's no *only a couple of sentences*—not if you're a writer! There *is* no *only*."

"Right," Billy said. "They don't understand *why* people like something. It's something very subtle in a painting, a record, a movie or a book. There may be one sentence, or one moment, one note that affects you. You may not be conscious of that, but if you take that out, you could show it to them again and they wouldn't like it. But you can't tell these people that. 'Art and business don't mix.' You hear that every day from everybody, we all say the same things: 'You've got to fight the studios, do what you believe in,' blah blah blah—we've all heard it so much—commerce versus art—that we're immune to it. Do you know how you want to say something to someone and you want them to know how important it is and they *agree* with you, but they're agreeing to the cliché? You say: 'Listen, we can't go to your Grandma's for Thanksgiving because there's a *tornado* outside,' and they say: 'Yeah, I know—we may have to pull over,' and you say: 'You don't understand—*there's a tornado coming over the house*, we're going to be *killed* unless we get down into the basement—*don't get in the car*,' and they say: 'Yeah, I know, it's gonna be rainy out there—better get your galoshes on.' Well that's what this is like. 'I'm telling you, art and business *don't mix*—we've got to *stop* this madness,' and everybody *agrees*, even the studio people. 'I know you're right, only we've got a job to do and we have a bottom line—' 'No, you don't understand. Nathan Hale is *not here anymore* and we need him *really bad* in this business. We need somebody to say *No*.' And in my own small way right now that's all

I'm doing. My contract, from now on, for the rest of my life, only says three words: **KISS MY ASS**."

But Billy's contract with Harvey Weinstein told Billy to kiss Harvey's ass unless the film were cut to under two hours… and so *All the Pretty Horses* was chopped into a two-hour cineplex earner that disappointed more people than went to see it. One scene in particular, the last, I was only able to see through the remembrances—reenactments, really—of Henry Thomas, Matt Damon, Billy Bob, Barry Markowitz, and Bruce Dern, who knew the entire project by heart and even acted out several parts for me, including the old guy dancing and all of Julio's performance! This was wonderful to witness, but what does it say of the movie business when you need to watch a film *about* a film in order to see the ending acted out in L.A. and New York hotels and apartments?

9. Question. Using Derrida, deconstruct Jimmy Blevins' dark devotion to lightning, demonstrating why, in the end, he was right about it.

9. Answer. Why *does* John Grady, a horse lover, want to help Jimmy Blevins, a horse thief, to steal a stolen horse that is allegedly stolen again by Mexican men who find it roaming in the road?

Is it because the assassin Blevins stole the horse first, from a man John Grady has decided to dismiss?

Is it because an American, even a horse thief, is on a higher plain than an anonymous Mexican?

Does the prematurely mature John Grady feel fatherly toward the kid?

It doesn't square with me. Blevins is John Grady's enemy, or should be: *the kid has stolen a horse.*

That day with Billy Bob in the Sunset Marquis, I quoted him a remark from a Cormac McCarthy conference. "There are two things Texas men take seriously: their women and their horses." To which Billy Bob said, in effect: well, *some* do. Perhaps he was onto something, a reasonable assumption when you are speaking with Billy Bob. Is it possible the plotline of *All the Pretty Horses* allows or requires John Grady to not care *quite as much* about horses *or* women as McCarthy implies that he does? Let me repeat myself: it is odd that in the struggle to remain in the life of his mistress, John Grady displays none of the monster willpower with which McCarthy is so adept. It doesn't matter that the affair can never work, and that between father and daughter the emotion, if not the act, of incest is too strong a force for competition. Most of McCarthy's adventurers are shipwrecked before they climb aboard. All that settling of score with the Captain seems a little bizarre to me, pre- cisely because at this point in the story this is *not* the score that cries out to be settled, it's a transference of it: it's the boy who mistook his mistress for a horse. One could even argue that McCarthy, at least subconsciously, knew that if his hero was fated to point a revolver at someone, it ought to have been Don Héctor, or even, perhaps, Alfonsa or himself; or, to put it differently, he knew that over the course of his career he had managed to write himself into a corner by expectation of what his characters need to do, and there was only one way to extricate John Grady: sleight-of-hand, a technique we have seen in McCarthy previously, one that he has mastered and has earned the right to employ.

If, at a critical point in the story, we are standing in Zacatecas on page 251, saying to Alejandra: "I'll make it right," and if she is wrapped in a towel on page 254, and if by 258 John Grady is saying: "I come to get my horse," we might well wonder whether we dozed off a little. If we see that it's up to us to get with the program and finish this other novel that seems to have started— or started again—on page 255, surely you can get over the prestidigitation, even if I have not. But has McCarthy gotten over it? One could speculate that in the fine rain that falls on page 255 there is an adroit authorial trick, a little Mississippi shuffle to which McCarthy might say: "Yes I know all about it, it was the only way out, take it or leave it," or: "I thought I gave you sufficient clues that I wasn't going to do a *Child of God* with John Grady—after all, what does he do when he loses the ranch? *He goes to see a lawyer*, and then what does he do? *He goes to see a play*, so I thought you could figure this was not *Blood Meridian*." But one could also posit that in the fine rain that falls on page 255 there is the point of the pointless sacrifice of John Grady's life over a girl who doesn't exist—not really—as a character in *Cities of the Plain*, and that it's one book paying for the sins of another.

If, with Anna Karenina, I was never so glad to see a body diving under a train, I have no such emotion about the departure of Alejandra. As a woman in McCarthy she is, by default, an inferior creation and she is certainly annoying, but she can stay or she can go. I have never loved her. I cannot even say that I have wanted to meet her, for to bed Alejandra is to make room enough for Don Héctor, and I would prefer curling up with *The Horse of America*. But I am at least partially human, and when I met Penélope Cruz I could see where Matt was going—and why—in an outtake of the film supplied to me by Miramax in which he says to Alfonsa: "Then you should've left me there," and: "Then I'd've died," as if to rip Alfonsa's head off, a level of intensity that is missing from the truncated semblance of Billy's film that carries his name without his vision. I was especially disappointed to have my own Don Héctor, my own controlling Alfonsa—at Penélope's PR agency, PMK—making it impossible for us to have a real conversation about the film. She certainly has a pair of eyes and a hand for a handshake. And by the logic of the novel, I *do* want to be with Alejandra—I want to die for her—and I refuse to let her leave, as if a train could carry love away—*a train!*—and McCarthy, after the now notorious 255, makes me angry that I don't, in fact, prove what I say ("I'll make it right"), prove that even starcrossed love doesn't alter when it alteration finds. And McCarthy makes me wonder why I don't tell Blevins what a piece of shit he is for taking a horse from a man who might love horses as much as I do.

When I drove to Alabama to interview Lucas Black, I asked him about this issue. Lucas is a rare natural talent with a catalyzing imagination, reliable instincts, a preference for one or two takes, and an uninflated regard for film-making. During the shooting of *Sling Blade* he caught fish between setups. At that time he didn't see all that many films—he preferred hunting, or golf—although we discovered a shared affection for the Disney Davy Crockett (we both had the coonskin cap), and so we know whether Lucas would have seen the Alamo, and we know whether Lucas would have seen *The Alamo*, for his favorite director, Billy Bob, played Davy Crockett in the latest incarnation of the story. Unlike the other superb actors who have worked on McCarthy, Lucas was not an in-depth analyst of character. If, for Lucas, the Great Blevins Issue didn't exist, that's because *no* Blevins issues existed. Lucas played the scenes as directed, using his intuition to put two and two together, allowing himself to believe without cerebral interference or support. He did not read the book. About the script, Lucas said: "When I read it, I would just put my-self in the situation, and the first thing that comes to my mind is what I do." Ted Tally said: "He doesn't look as if he's acting at all, and sometimes I'm not sure he is." In his own way, though, Lucas does naturally what a trained actor does, only it sounds like a few seconds' thought. "I would think about what *I* would do," Lucas told me, "but then you have to look in Blevins' mind and see what *he* would do, and so you kinda put those two together. If *my* daddy was mean to me, or beat me up, I would probably run away from home too. I would probably do the same thing Blevins done."

About the issue of the horse, Lucas's answer was not complicated, and I recalled what Matt had said to me about Lucas: "Why would he complicate anything? It's a total waste of his time."

"Nobody really knows the story," Lucas said. "I guess the movie wants you to think he just ran away from home, stole this horse, and he just kinda runs up with John Grady and Rawlins and causes a lot of trouble between them two and… that's *it*."

When I spoke about Blevins and the horse with Henry Thomas—a Texan *and* a horseman—he understood my concern. "For me it's always been this stolen horse," Henry said, "this beautiful horse that this kid is riding, the source of all this trouble. You can blame the horse. But after Blevins is killed, the horse becomes a kind of metaphor. It's the only thing John Grady under-stands: horses, and the only way he can justify Blevins' death is by giving the horse back, even though it didn't belong to him. It's that part of the novel that really struck me, because it's that elusive nature of right and wrong in Texas versus Mexico, a weird sense of justice in both places. Somehow they miss each other. Just barely, but they never connect. It's the whole idea of: 'Well we *found* it—it's ours.' 'Well, no, it's not—it's *his*, he *lost* it.' 'Yes, but it wasn't really his, because he *stole* it.' 'Well is it really yours because you found it?' 'Yes.' 'Well I don't think so.' Who's right? Who's wrong? In a sense, that's the whole issue here: there isn't a right or wrong, there are just two worlds and you can't walk between them, you're stuck in one, and if you choose to walk between them you've got to pay the price."

About the Blevins Issue, Ted Tally said: "Yes, there's a sense that John Grady has come to view what has happened to him as all being about this horse, in a way. As if it wasn't Blevins' horse, and because we nodded at that, all this tragedy was visited upon us." Matt Damon, however, did not appear all that concerned about the theft; or, at least, he didn't seem to feel any great contradiction in John Grady's connection to Jimmy Blevins. "Well, it *could've* been his horse," Matt said. "As John Grady says to the Captain: 'He had it in Texas. I know because I rode it across the river with him.' It certainly is *not those people's horse*, you know? And what's the kid going to do with no clothes, and on foot, in the middle of the desert in Mexico? He's completely screwed. It's more a matter of: 'We can't *leave* him here. It's just not right. We've got to do something to help this kid.' And then Blevins kind of goes off and does it on his own. He's incorrigible, basically, but his stubbornness—they respect it to a degree because he's willing to go a really long way to protect what's his. And he *was* in the right in that situation. It wasn't their horse. It wasn't their gun."

"While Blevins is with the horse," I said to Matt, "John Grady protects Blevins, and when Blevins isn't around any more, he tries to protect the horse, to get it back to where it belongs."

Matt said: "Yes, it's become like an albatross, or something around his neck."

"What was in my head," Billy said, "and Matt's too—because we discussed this—is that the horse becomes John Grady chasing his own redemption over his guilt about Blevins being killed. It doesn't matter if the horse was his or not any more. He probably doesn't even want to think about that, or whether he'll find the owner. What matters is that he's going to *do* something. It's not a righteous thing—it's partly a selfish thing. He wants to stay a little bit in denial by trying to make things right somehow. He's chasing something that will absolve him—find the owner of the horse. You're just a kid, I'm going to give the horse back, and now you're going to be okay. It's one of those things that we do. On a bad day on the set I have a coloring book and I'll color Skooby-doo or whatever—you have no idea how back to childhood I get. There's always something that you do in your life to keep you from thinking how screwed up something is. What you said about Texans before—well, maybe some Texans are that way, maybe some Texans don't give a damn at all! In terms of what's true to what they think about ownership of horses or anything else—it wasn't important to me. It was the psychology of this character. Everybody wants me to cut the scene at the end with the judge. *Everybody.* I won't do it. I'll *never* do it. You know why they want me to cut it out? 'Well, you've had the scene in the courtroom, the judge lets him off the hook, so why do you have to have him come to the judge's house—it steals the thunder from the final scene with him and Rawlins when they part.' *I* say, you know what? *There's no thunder in the movie like that scene.* That scene is *the scene that the movie hinges on.* This is what it's about. If he doesn't *ever, ever* tell somebody what he feels—if he *never* says to somebody: 'You know what? I fucked up. *I* went, screwed the girl, did this, killed somebody in prison—and here you let me go, *just like that*! I just simply told you a story—you have *no* way to know whether you can trust me or not! And I want you to know that I'm feelin bad because I let that fucking guy take that kid out there and kill him. *I didn't say a word!* And it ain't right!' 'Well, would it have done any good?' 'No, but you know what? I literally just sat here, didn't even try. I'm talkin about *for myself,* I don't even have the satisfaction of knowing that *I piped in!*' Without that scene, you've got no movie."

"Without that scene," I said to Billy, "he'd be a dangerous guy, wouldn't he?"

"Yes," Billy said. "That's his therapy session right there. He needed more from the judge than being let off the hook in an official capacity. He needed someone to say: 'You're just a kid. You're all right. You've done what you've done, now you're headed for the future.'"

I wondered whether John Grady was acting more or less on a fatherly instinct.

"Yes," Matt said, "Blevins is still a kid. He's out in the middle of the desert riding around, he doesn't have anything, he's lonely and he wants to hang out with them because they're older and more mature and they might know what to do. It's also that they're Americans, so he understands them. We were all supposed to be from West Texas, but Blevins you never really know *where* he's from, and Lucas has a serious Alabama accent that gives a sense of otherness. The guy's like a Martian, you don't know *what* the hell, you don't know *where* he's from, he just shows up and he's on this huge horse and it's like: 'Where did this guy *come* from?' He's got something going on and there's a sense of foreboding. There's a radio guy named Jimmy Blevins, so clearly that's not his name. You never know anything about him. He's a total mystery."

It was up to Julio Mechoso, who plays the Captain, to clear things up for me completely; or, better to say, to represent someone with whom I completely empathized. I should have expected it from the Captain. In an animated talk at his home in Los Angeles, Julio exemplified the manner in which a great actor blurs the distinction between his own personality and that of his character. Sometimes it was Julio talking to me, not the Captain; but whenever the Captain spoke, it was Julio as well.

"In the scene where I take Matt to prison and I'm telling him what's happening," Julio said, "and Matt says: 'You didn't have to go out there and kill that kid,' it wasn't in the script where I say: *When a man goes to do something, he finishes. What, he changes his mind in the middle? No. When a man goes out to do something, he completes it.* I was the one who brought that to Billy and Matt's attention."

"In the book," Julio said, "there is a beautiful long story I would *love* to have used. It's where the Captain says: Listen, when I was a kid, there were all these kids playing at this big party, and we went to do a prostitute on top of a hill. When I went there with my friends—I was the smallest of the group—the prostitute laughed at me, like: 'You're a little kid—what're *you* going to do?' And I thought, well, I can go back down the hill and say I've had her, but no, people will know the truth in your face. And you know what? When I walked down that hill, nobody laughed at me, okay? I told Matt and Billy this is central to his character. I know this guy. I grew up in poor neighborhoods. When I come down that hill, nobody laughs, all right? And you know what? They *can* tell the truth in your face, so the whole neighborhood will know. That's what I think is essential to this scene. If I don't kill that kid, everybody in that town is going to know—and I'm not the Captain anymore. Especially in that era. 'What, a gringo got the better part of you? You let him go? What are you, afraid of the United States?' And so then I tell somebody: 'Hey, you can't keep your sheep there anymore,' and they say: 'What, a gringo came here, killed *two* of us, you didn't do shit about it?' Because he [Blevins] killed two, and he wounded another. It's got to be paid with blood."

"I've had some tough times," Julio said. "I had to come down that hill and nobody was going to laugh at me. My neighborhood—Little Havana, around the Orange Bowl—and the people I hung around with, they were not easy people. This guy was well-written. And in that prison, brother— you know how many prisons I've been in? I worked for the Criminal Justice Department. I used to travel, going from prison to prison. Prisons are not populated by our best human beings, in Mexico *or* the United States. History is full of characters like this. I don't see the Captain as particularly evil, although you know that saying: 'Power tends to corrupt; absolute power tends to corrupt absolutely.' I think this guy has a lot of power in this town. He isn't sadistic about it. I *know* he didn't enjoy killing that kid—not on a conscious level, but on a subconscious level he felt good that he did it, because his tribe respects that, and *expects* that of him. We've only been living in cities for the last five thousand years. We used to belong to a tribe of from fifty to a hundred people. He's the chief of his tribe, and that's his responsibility, to take care of his tribe and enforce the laws of his tribe."

"And you know what?" Julio said, reaching the closest point of agreement between me and the Captain. "Blevins, I'm telling you, if you look at him really, he's one of those kids that I grew up with that was *just trouble*, okay? When I was a kid we had this little group, and there were kids in our group that would cause *me* trouble, because when I went to a place I was looking to have fun, but there were one or two guys that were just *looking* for trouble, so when the trouble starts, now *you're* obligated, like Matt's character, to do something for that member of your tribe. We always said: 'Hey, our guy's always right, okay?' That type of mentality. *Afterwards* you counsel him. 'Hey, don't try that again—that's stupid.' Which I'm sure they wanted to do: 'What the hell did you do!' But they stick with him because they have that tribal bond. That, I think, Cormac understands. That's human nature, brother. That's not Mexican and American—that's almost anywhere in the world. If we're in an argument, we're going to defend our tribe against the others. And I see that Cormac is in contact with human nature.

"Was it correct politically? Humans don't think about political correctness unless they are intellectual and are living in this time. At that time there was no such concept. Did this guy finish high school? He went to maybe first or second grade. All his life, his father he never knew. His mother helped him. He has killed before. He drinks himself to sleep every night. He's got a couple of girls he does in the neighborhood and anybody who wants to get onto his good side. He has about four or five kids by I don't know how many different women. His teeth are rotten, and a couple of them are black because he's gotten into a lot of fights. My teeth had to be darkened. I go to the dentist every six months, I've never had a cavity in my life, I brush my teeth I don't know how many times a day!"

I asked Julio whether his Captain was jealous of John Grady.

"I think the Captain was satisfied in that little town," Julio said. "And these guys come in and they're making his job *a lot harder*. The whole matter complicates itself because they are Americans. Big difference between that and three, four, five Mexicans who come to that town and they kill a couple of people. Three Americans, this can bring more trouble. But he's gotta do what he's gotta do. The way I play him, he did not enjoy that consciously. Deep inside, in an animal sense, he'd say: 'Okay, got rid of him—good.' Our ancestors didn't take people to courts! It was pretty much decided right there. He's not a sociopath, but he's a tough guy, brother, and you don't want to mess with him. He's not looking out for trouble, but this Captain's the type of guy who, when he comes down from that hill, nobody's laughing at him. And if somebody laughs at him, they're making a mistake. *Big* mistake laughing at this guy.

"You ride into my town and you kill three people just because you want your horse back? No. You come to see me, maybe I can do something about it. You killed just one or two? One is too much. Just *wounding* someone in my town—I don't like that. You kill someone in my town, something bad is going to happen to you. From my point of view, *they* were the ones who were wrong. And this kid Blevins, he was no choir boy, okay? That's what that scene is about. I say: What, he's a good boy, then he comes here and he does bad? No. He was always a bad boy. What're you telling me? He's an angel when he came down here? Did you see how he shoots? The way he killed those people—he's a good shot—don't you think I know that? What, you think just because I'm a Mexican Captain I don't know who knows how to kill and who doesn't? He knew what he was doing. That kid was a badass. Yes, his father beat him up when he was a kid—usually badasses *are* that way, they get abused when they're kids—they have a story too. Poor kid, who knows what they did to him—he might have been beaten with a switch I don't know how many times. That doesn't give you an excuse to come into my town and do any deeds. And I *know* those people that he killed—don't you think I know them? Horse shows up: 'Hey, what the fuck—that's mine.' The gun also. 'Hey, I found it in the road.' They didn't rob him or insult him or anything like that, okay?"

"One thing about the book," Julio said. "It's not black and white. If you read the book carefully, it's not that the Captain is really that bad and everybody else is good. I like that ambiguity. That's what makes great writers. It's all these shades. The Captain likes John Grady. He respects this kid a lot. But if the Captain had to kill him he would kill him too, you know? It's like *The Old Man and the Sea*. Fish—I love you, but I have to kill you! Or *The Last of the Mohicans*, when they kill that deer. Deer—I'm sorry I killed you but we're going to eat tonight!"

Henry Thomas—as Rawlins (or is it Rawlins as Henry)—had an interesting response to the Captain's perspective. "I go: 'Whoah! What are you *talking* about!' But that's how it is with the Captain *'That's* how I am. *That's* what I have to do. Just because you can't understand it doesn't mean that I'm wrong, it just means that you're different, you don't belong here, so we're sending you to jail.' If you look into it, at least in the forties, that's a part of the Mexican culture, that whole ideal: 'I do it this way because *this is how a man does it*. You're an outsider. How can you even *hope* to understand?' In the Border Trilogy there's that wandering prophet character, an old Mexican guy or someone who's lived in Mexico, who goes off on this tangent, this preaching, of how the world is and what to look out for. In *All the Pretty Horses* it's halfway between the Great Aunt and the Captain. It's an interesting theme that recurs in those novels."

10. Question. Discuss the foreshadowing, in *All the Pretty Horses*, of John Grady's fate as it is played out in *Cities of the Plain*.

10. Answer. Can't be done, because they aren't the same characters. John Grady is finished with *the darkening land, the world to come* on page 302 of *All the Pretty Horses*. If there is any more of him, it is on page 3: *The candleflame...*

11. Question. As some readers sense something neo-fascistic in McCarthy, especially the anti-intellectualism, the blood worship, and the idealization of physical prowess and pistol justice in *All the Pretty Horses* and other works, how do you think these readers ought to be dealt with, and at what time of night?

11. Answer. What *I've* been wondering is, does it matter how John Grady hitched back and forth to San Antonio?

Boy does it matter, for he could have been picked up by Neal Cassady and Jack Kerouac in Neal's new sleek n' low '49 Hudson.

"It was one of the worst winters in Texas and Western history," Kerouac, alias Sal Paradise, says in *On the Road*, "when cattle perished like flies in great blizzards and snow fell on San Francisco and L.A." (133). If they *could* have persuaded John G to enter the now world of wheels, the blue world of the white line in that sparked Texaco Texas and dig that cool gone Chicken Jazz n' Gumbo DJ show beamed out of N'Orleans, and Neal's mad sweaty angel rampage rants about hicks, kicks, chicks, God, life, Mississippi mud, Mexican mambo, molasses, bebop and goofballs, bennies, booze, tea, M, coke, H, Marylou and old Bull Burroughs in a Panama hat and his drunken father—"Getting down into the hot country now, boys, the desert rats and the tequila... Gawd-damn! this is where my old man comes in the wintertime, sly old bum!" (222)—and dig Jack's improvised rengasized Mexico City haiku blues and then spin out some sweatfilled allnight whuppers of his own about the time he and Rawlins were scaling the wall of the Alamo and... but this is fruitless speculation, for those beats would have thrown John Grady out of the car because no McCarthy character would last for three minutes in a Kerouac car *or* novel, and no Kerouac character would last for three minutes in *All the Pretty Horses*, not even on Route 87. In fact, a way to define the geography of *All the Pretty Horses* is this: *a place in which Kerouac is impossible.* Unless, perhaps, you read it in Chinese.

In Texas again the following year, Sal/Jack says: "We were already almost out of America, and yet definitely in it and in the middle of where it's maddest. Hotrods blew by. San Antonio, ah-haa!" (222), and Neal says: "... you and I, Sal, will cut around and get these streets dug—look at those houses across the street, you can see right into the front room and all the purty daughters layin around with *True Love* magazines, whee! Come, let's go!" (222), and later: "I never knew this mad San Antonio! Think what Mexico'll be like! Lessgo! Lessgo!" (223)

Well: all the purty daughters is not *All the Pretty Horses*. Could Sal Paradise make it in *Suttree*? I would like to discuss this... along with Joseph Delteil's "I have never seen San Antonio but I am going to describe it to you just the same," which sounds like a line from *Black Spring* or one of the *Tropics*... and the fact that "I can take a whirl in San Antone for a few days... and have some fun" (186) is not another quote from Dean Moriarty but from John Platt, of Navarro & Platt's Dry Goods Emporium, in O. Henry's "The Buyer from Cactus City," 1906... but I see that my time for the examination is up... so, yes, McCarthy compares to T. S. Eliot because the scene in the Texas lobby, where John Grady, as I was saying, uses his jeans cuff for an ashtray, confirms the practicality (the horse sense, if you will) behind J. Alfred Prufrock's decision to wear his trousers rolled. The answer, J, is sure you should wear them rolled because there ain't no cure for the summerschool blues and that warden likes to step on my blue suede shoes and a man should never gamble more than he can stand to lose but you can't live like that, so Viva John Grady! Viva James Dean! Viva *The Horse of America*! Viva Laurence Olivier's 11:30 performance! Viva Julio, Henry, Lucas, Matt and everyone else in Billy Bob's movie that no one has seen! Viva Bruce Dern for understanding the judge and for being the greatest guy who ever lived in Malibu—or anywhere—and for saying to me: "Anybody pisses on you, call me"! Shouts out to Oscar Wilde, who said that on examinations the wise ask questions fools can't answer! Raise a bumper, boys, to the Stony Brook map room—and pass round the hat for a few lightbulbs! Here's to drives across America with cars full of crazies, trucks full of art, old Penélope'd souls with thumbs in the road, heels in the stirrup, crude in the nostrils—and death to the death of the salesmen—bring *them* along too! Let it snow like mad and close it *all* down! Viva Rand *and* McNally! Viva old John Steinbeck! Viva John Dryden! To hell with John Wayne for hating *High Noon* and for running its author, Carl Foreman, out of town—and screw Elia Kazan, who named names for that other McCarthy and was never sorry for it, the bastard—but we don't *need* no stinkin badges—Viva Zapata! Viva Marlon Brando! Viva Lee Marvin! Viva

Visions of Cody! Viva the Great Wall of China! Viva the Sunset Marquis! Viva Zola! Free Dreyfus! Good-bye to you, old *Rights of Man*! God bless Captain Vere! Nostrovia to those who prefer *not* to! Twelve kisses to the waitress who has your all's orders! Remember the Alamo! Bring back Radio Row! Viva Rhode Island! Viva Prufrock! And Viva McCarthy.

NOTES

1. The West Texas town of Ozona, where John Grady goes to court, currently has a population of 3,802, which is over 150 *fewer* people than at the time in the novel. A flood in 1954 wiped out half the town.

2. An obvious descendant of *The Horse of America* is *The American Saddle Horse* by Earl R. Frashler. Published out of Louisville in 1933, this interesting work contains copious quotations from previous horse authors, including a 30-page chapter from *The Horse of America*. Its supply of horse lore, horse argument, and horse instruction is a combination that I—who have no interest in *the horse* as a subject—find surprisingly entertaining, to a degree that makes it easy to imagine how it might have appealed to John Grady. Frashler is no Wallace, but his prose, though clumsy at times, is serious, down to earth—never overwrought—and, as with Wallace, the author's affection for his subject and the information gleaned from experience make it a distinctively American document that's as much a memoir as a treatise on *the horse*. On practically every page are examples of what I call *horse music*: prose that, to an ear that hasn't been bred to horse literature, sounds wonderfully peculiar and strangely resonant, leading one to suspect that it's impossible to write about *the horse* without tapping into a code for the revelation of human absurdity. There are pages that might have been the envy of Kafka or Beckett. If William Burroughs had picked it up, as I did, waterstained, broken, sunned and stinking of must, he would have cut it up for one of his novels, and some bits, such as Frashler's cure for horse masturbation in a chapter called "Vices," could have worked their way into one of his routines.

Bibliography

Allen, Tom. "Film: *The Gardener's Son.*" *Village Voice*, 1978.

Andrew, Dudley. "André Bazin: The Godfather." *Film Comment* 44, no. 6 (2008): 38–42.

Arnold, Edwin T. "Cormac McCarthy's *The Stonemason*: The Unmaking of a Play." *Southern Quarterly* 33, Nos. 2–3 (1995).

———. "A *Stonemason* Evening." *Cormac McCarthy Journal* 2, no. 1 (2002): 7–11.

Arnold, Edwin T., and Dianne C. Luce, eds. *Perspectives on Cormac McCarthy*. Revised. Jackson: University of Mississippi, 1999.

Balfour, Graham. *The Life of Robert Louis Stevenson*. Vol. 2. New York: Scribner's, 1901.

Beaton, Cecil. *Beaton in the Sixties: The Cecil Beaton Diaries as He Wrote Them, 1965–1969*. New York: Alfred A. Knopf, 2004.

Bloom, Harold. *How to Read and Why*. New York: Scribner's, 2000.

———. *Novelists and Novels*. New York: Readers' Subscription / Chelsea House, 2005.

———. *Shakespeare: The Invention of the Human*. New York: Riverhead, 1998.

———. *Shakespeare: The Seven Major Tragedies*. Prince Frederick, MD: Modern Scholar / Recorded Books, 2005.

Boehme, Jacob. *Six Theosophic Points and Other Writings*. Translated by John Rolleston Earle. London: Constable, 1916.

Bresson, Robert. *Notes on the Cinematographer*. Copenhagen: Green Integer, 1997.

Burgess, Anthony. *Joysprick: An Introduction to the Language of James Joyce*. London: Andre Deutsche, 1973.

Campbell, Joseph. *Joseph Campbell on James Joyce: Wings of Art*. St. Paul, MN: HighBridge, 1995.

Cassavetes, John. *Cassavetes on Cassavetes*. Edited by Ray Carney. London: Faber and Faber, 2001.

Chamberlain, Samuel E. *My Confession: The Recollections of a Rogue*. Edited by William Goetzmann. Austin: Texas State Historical Association, 1996.

The Clockmaker. Film directed by Bertrand Tavernier, 1973. Kino Video: 2002.

Cohen, Patricia. "No Country for Old Typewriters: A Well-Used One Heads to Auction." *New York Times*, December 1, 2009.

Cornford, Tom, and Peter Josyph. "Believing in *The Sunset Limited*: A Talk with Tom Cornford on Directing McCarthy." In *The Road Ahead: Interdisciplinary and Intertextual Approaches to Cormac McCarthy*, edited by Nick Monk and Rick Wallach. Forthcoming.

Cramb, Ian. *The Art of the Stonemason.* White Hall: Betterway Publications, 1992.

Crowe, Cameron. *Conversations with Wilder.* New York: Alfred K. Knopf, 1999.

Daugherty, Leo. "Gravers False and True: *Blood Meridian* as Gnostic Tragedy." *Southern Quarterly* 30, no. 4, 1992.

de Goncourt, Edmund, and Jules de Goncourt. *Pages from the Goncourt Journal.* Edited and translated by Robert Baldick. New York: Penguin Books, 1984.

Dickens, Charles. "Night Walks." In *The Uncommercial Traveller.* New York: Books, n.d.

———. *The Posthumus Papers of the Pickwick Club.* Philadelphia: n.p., 1837.

Documentary Filmmaker Richard Pearce, Who Never Worked on Fictional Drama Before, Conceived, Produced, and Directed "The Gardener's Son" for "Visions." Press release for the film *The Gardener's Son.* 1978.

Dryden, John. "An Essay of Dramatic Poesy." In *Criticism: The Major Texts*, edited by Walter Jackson Bate. New York: Harcourt, Brace, 1952.

Ellis, Jay. *No Place for Home: Spatial Constraint and Character Flight in the Novels of Cormac McCarthy.* New York: Routledge, 2006.

Ellmann, Richard. *Ulysses on the Liffey.* Lyndhurst, NJ: Barnes & Noble, 2009.

Emerson, Ralph Waldo. *From Journals and Letters: The Norton Anthology of American Literature.* Vol. 1. New York: W. W. Norton, 1989.

Faulkner, William. *Absalom, Absalom!* Narrated by Grover Gardner. Newport Beach, CA: Books on Tape, 1993.

———. Unattributed quotation from *A Sound Portrait of William Faulkner.* A Question of Place series, Part 8. National Public Radio: 1980.

Fields, Curtis P. *The Forgotten Art of Building a Stone Wall.* Dublin, NH: Yankee, 1971.

Frashler, Earl R. *The American Saddle Horse: Tracing the Evolution, Origin, History, Derivation and Development of the Saddle-Bred Horse, with a Treatise on Breeding Principles and a Section Devoted to the Training of Gaited Animals.* Louisville, KY: Standard Printing Company, 1933.

The Gardener's Son. Film directed by Richard Pearce, written by Cormac McCarthy. Shown on PBS Visions series, 1976.

Ginsberg, Allen. *Journals: Early Fifties, Early Sixties.* Edited by Gordon Ball. New York: Grove Press, 1977.

Hall, Wade. "The Continuing Vitality of Southern Literature: Six Books by Cormac McCarthy and Heather Ross Miller." *Twigs* 5 (1970): 273–292.

Hall, Wade, and Rick Wallach, eds. *Sacred Violence: A Reader's Companion to Cormac McCarthy.* Rev. 2 vols. El Paso: Texas Western Press, 2002.

Harris, George Washington. "Sut Lovingood's Sermon: Teaching Ye Cat-Fishe Tavern." In *Sut Lovingood. Yarns Spun by a "Nat'ral Born Durn'd Fool." Warped and Wove for Public Wear.* docsouth.unc.edu/southlit/harrisg/gharris.

Hemingway, Ernest. *Selected Letters: 1917–1961.* Edited by Carlos Baker. New York: Scribner's, 1981.

Henry, O. "The Buyer from Cactus City." In *The Pocket Book of O. Henry Stories*, edited by Barry Hansen. New York: Washington Square Press, 1948.

Hesse, Herman. *Siddhartha.* Translated by Hilda Rosner. New York: New Directions, 1951.

Hooper, Edward. *Images of America: Knoxville.* Charleston, SC: Arcadia, 2003.

Hughes, John Taylor. *Doniphan's Expedition: Containing an Account of the Conquest of New Mexico.* 1847. Reprint. College Station: Texas A&M University Press, 1997.

James, Caryn. "'Blood Meridian,' by Cormac McCarthy." *New York Times*, April 28, 1985. http://www.nytimes.com/1985/04/28/books/mccarthy-meridian.

Johnson, Samuel. *Johnson's Dictionary: A Modern Selection.* Edited by E. L. McAdam Jr. and George Milne. New York: Putnam, 1963.

Josyph, Peter. *Liberty Street: Alive at Ground Zero.* Film. Lost Medallion Productions, 2005.

———. *Liberty Street: Encounters at Ground Zero.* London: University Press of New England, 2006.

Joyce, James. "Chamber Music." In *The Portable James Joyce*, edited by Harry Levin. New York: Penguin Books, 1976.

———. *A Portrait of the Artist as a Young Man.* New York: Viking, 1964.

———. *Ulysses.* New York: Modern Library, 1961.

Jurgensen. John. "Hollywood's Favorite Cowboy." *Wall Street Journal.* November 13, 2009.

Kazan, Elia. *Kazan: A Life.* New York: Knopf, 1988.

Keats, John. *Letters of John Keats to His Family and Friends.* Edited by Sidney Colvin. London: n.p., 1891.

Kennedy, Randy. "McCarthy's Typewriter Sells for $254,500." *New York Times*, December 5, 2009: C2.

Kennedy, Stephen M. *Practical Stonemasonry Made Easy.* Blue Ridge Summit, PA: TAB Books, 1988.

Kerouac, Jack. *Lonesome Traveler.* New York: Evergreen, 1970.

———. *Mexico City Blues.* New York: Grove Press, 1959.

———. *On the Road.* New York: Viking Press, 1957.

———. *Visions of Cody.* New York: McGraw-Hill, 1972.

Kriegsman, Alan M. "Public TV's 'Visions' of Expanded Dramatic and Creative Horizon." *Washington Post*, January 1977.

Luce, Dianne C. "Cormac McCarthy's First Screenplay: *The Gardener's Son.*" *Southern Quarterly* 30, no. 4 (1992): 51–71.

———. "Cormac McCarthy's *The Sunset Limited:* Dialogue of Life and Death: A Review of the Chicago Production." *Cormac McCarthy Journal* 6 (2008): 13–21.

Luce, Dianne C., and Edwin T. Arnold, eds. *Perspectives on Cormac McCarthy*. Revised. Jackson: University of Mississippi, 1999.

McCarthy, Cormac. *All the Pretty Horses*. New York: Knopf, 1992.

———. *Blood Meridian or The Evening Redness in the West*. New York: Random House, 1985.

———. *Child of God*. New York: Vintage, 1973.

———. *The Gardener's Son*. Hopewell, VA: Ecco Press, 1996.

———. *Meridiao de Sangue ou O Crepúsculo Vermelho No Oeste*. Portuguese translation of *Blood Meridian*, by Paulo Faria. Lisbon, Portugal: Relógio D'Água Editores, 2004.

———. *The Stonemason: A Play in Five Acts*. Hopewell, VA: Ecco Press, 1994.

———. *The Sunset Limited: A Novel in Dramatic Form*. New York: Dramatists Play Service, 2006.

———. *Suttree*. New York: Random House, 1979.

McMurtry, Larry. *Lonesome Dove*. New York: Simon & Schuster, 1985.

Melville, Herman. *Moby-Dick; or, The Whale*. New York: Penguin Books, 1986.

Miller, Arthur. *Death of a Salesman. The Portable Arthur Miller*. Edited by Harold Clurman. New York: Viking Press, 1971.

Miller, Henry. *Aller Retour New York*. New York: New Directions, 1991.

———. *Tropic of Cancer*. New York: Grove Press, 1961.

———. *Tropic of Cancer*. Narrated by Campbell Scott. New York: Caedmon, 2008.

Milton, John. *Lycidas: The Riverside Milton*. Edited by Roy Flannagan. New York: Houghton Mifflin, 1998.

Morgan, Robert. "Cormac McCarthy: The Novel Raised from the Dead." In *Sacred Violence: A Reader's Companion to Cormac McCarthy*. Rev. 2 vols. El Paso: Texas Western Press, 2002.

Morgan, Wesley. *Searching for Sut: A Reader's Guide to Cormac McCarthy's* Suttree. Forthcoming.

———. *Searching for Suttree*. http://web.utk.edu/~wmorgan/Suttree/suttree.htm.

Morrow, Mark. *Images of the Southern Writer*. Athens: University of Georgia Press, 1985.

O'Connor, John. "TV: WNET Showing Haunting 'Gardener's Son.'" *New York Times*, January 6, 1977.

Ogg, Oscar. *The 26 Letters*. New York: Thomas Y. Crowell, 1948.

Owen, Mark. "McCarthy Is One of Nation's Most Remarked Young Authors." *Maryville-Alcoa Times*, February 26, 1971: 4B.

Paré, Ambroise. *On Monsters and Marvels*. Translated by Janis L. Pallister. Chicago: University of Chicago Press, 1982.

Pearce, Richard. Foreword to Cormac McCarthy's *The Gardener's Son*. Hopewell, VA: Ecco Press, 1996.

Peters, Edward. *Torture*. New York: Blackwell, 1985.

Plimpton, George, ed. *Writers at Work: The Paris Review Interview*. New York: Penguin Books, 1977.

———, ed. *Writers at Work: The Paris Review Interviews*, 3rd series. New York: Penguin Books, 1986.

Proust, Marcel. *On Reading*. Translated by Jean Autret and William Burford. New York: Macmillan, 1971.

Rabelais, François. *The Portable Rabelais*. Edited by Samuel Putnam. New York: Viking, 1946.

Rand McNally Commercial Atlas and Marketing Guide. 80th ed. Chicago: Rand Mc-Nally, 1949.

Sacks, David. *Letter Perfect: The Marvelous History of Our Alphabet from A to Z*. New York: Broadway Books, 2004.

Schimpf, Shane. *A Reader's Guide to* Blood Meridian. Gainesboro, TN: BonMot, 2008.

Selzer, Richard. *Letters to a Best Friend*. Edited by Peter Josyph. New York: State University of New York Press, 2009.

Sepich, John. *Notes on* Blood Meridian. Louisville, KY: Bellarmine College Press, 1993.

———. *Notes on* Blood Meridian. Revised. Austin: University of Texas Press, 2008.

Shakespeare, William. *The Life of King Henry the Fifth. The Complete Works of Shakespeare*. Edited by David Bevington. Glenview, IL: Scott, 1980.

———. *Henry IV Part 2. The Complete Works of Shakespeare*. Edited by David Bevington. Glenview, IL: Scott, 1980.

———. *The Tragedy of Hamlet. The Complete Works of Shakespeare*. Edited by David Bevington. Glenview, IL: Scott, 1980.

Shapiro, James. *Shakespeare and the Jews*. New York: Columbia University Press, 1996.

Simenon, Georges. *The Clockmaker*. Translated by Norman Denny. New York: Harcourt Brace Jovanovich, 1977.

Simon, Paul. "Diamonds on the Soles of Her Shoes." *Graceland*, 1986. Song.

Sontag, Susan. *At the Same Time: Essays and Speeches*. New York: Farrar, Straus and Giroux, 2007.

Southern Quarterly 30, no. 4 (1992). Special issue: Cormac McCarthy. Edited by Edwin T. Arnold and Dianne C. Luce.

Stallone, Sylvester. *Rocky*. Unpublished script of the film directed by John Avildson, 1976.

Steinbeck, John. *East of Eden*. New York: Viking Press, 1952.

Stevenson, Robert Louis. *Edinburgh: Picturesque Notes*. London: Seeley, 1896.

Thoreau, Henry David. "From Journals and Letters." *Norton Anthology of American Literature*. Vol. 1. New York: W. W. Norton, 1989.

———. *Journal of Henry David Thoreau*. 1906. Salt Lake City, UT: Peregrine Smith, 1984.

———. *Journal of Henry David Thoreau: Volume 1: 1837–1846*. Edited by Bradford Torrey and Francis H. Allen. Salt Lake City, UT: Smith, 1984.

———. *Walden*. Columbus, OH: Charles E. Merrill, 1969.

———. "Walking." *The Portable Thoreau*. Edited by Carl Bode. New York: Viking Press, 1980.

———. *A Week on the Concord and Merrimack Rivers*. 1849. Boston: Houghton, n.d.

Thurber, James. *Selected Letters of James Thurber*. Edited by Helen Thurber and Edward Weeks. New York: Little, Brown, 1981.

Tierney, John. "A World of Eloquence in an Upturned Palm." *New York Times*, August 28, 2007: F1, F4.

Trollope, Anthony. *Dr. Thorne.* London: Zodiac Press, 1951.

Truffaut, François. *Correspondence 1945–1984.* Edited and translated by Gilles Jacob and Claude de Givray. New York: Cooper Square Press, 2000.

Vidal, Gore. *Views from a Window: Conversations with Gore Vidal.* Edited by Robert J. Stanton and Gore Vidal. Secaucus, NJ: Lyle Stuart, 1980.

Virgil. *The Aeneid.* Translated by Robert Fitzgerald. New York: Random House, 1983.

Voltaire. *Candide. The Portable Voltaire.* Edited by Ben Ray Redman. New York: Viking Press, 1968.

Wallace, John H. *The Horse of America in His Derivation, History, and Development.* New York: Author, 1897.

Wallach, Rick, ed. *Myth, Legend, Dust: Critical Responses to Cormac McCarthy.* Manchester, UK: Manchester University Press, 2000.

Wallach, Rick, and Wade Hall. *Sacred Violence: A Reader's Companion to Cormac McCarthy.* Revised. 2 vols. El Paso: Texas Western Press, 2002.

Walter, Jacob. *The Diary of a Napoleonic Foot Soldier.* New York: Penguin Books, 1993.

Warhol, Andy. *I'll Be Your Mirror: The Selected Andy Warhol Interviews, 1962–1987.* Edited by Kenneth Goldsmith. New York: Carroll & Graf, 2003.

Weil, Simone. *The Iliad, or the Poem of Force.* Translated by Mary McCarthy. Wallingford, PA: Pendle Hill, n.d.

Whitman, Walt. *Democratic Vistas.* Facsimile of 1871 edition.

———. *Leaves of Grass.* 1855 edition. Nashville, TN: American Reniassance, 2009.

———. "Old Actors, Singers, Shows, &c." In *The Complete Poetry and Prose of Walt Whitman*, vol. 2, 526–530. New York: Pellegrini & Cudahy, 1948.

———. *Walt Whitman's Camden Conversations.* Edited by Walter Teller. New Brunswick, NJ: Rutgers University Press, 1973.

Williams, James G. "The Anthropology of the Cross: A Conversation with René Girard." In *The Girard Reader*, edited by James G. Williams. New York: Crossroad, 1996.

Wister, Owen. *The Virginian: A Horseman of the Plains.* 1902. New York: Penguin, 1988.

Young, Thomas D., Jr. *Cormac McCarthy and the Geology of Being.* Ph.D. dissertation, University of Miami, 1990.

———. "The Imprisonment of Sensibility: *Suttree.*" *Southern Quarterly* 30, no. 4 (1992): 72–92.

Index

About the Author

Peter Josyph works concurrently an an author, a painter, a photographer, and in theatre and film as an actor-director. His books are *Liberty Street: Encounters at Ground Zero*; *What One Man Said to Another: Talks with Richard Selzer*; and, as editor, Richard Selzer's *Letters to a Best Friend*, which he also illustrated, and *The Wounded River*, which was a *New York Times* Notable Book of 1993. Josyph's fiction, personal essays, criticism, and conversations have appeared in *Lapham's Quarterly*, *Chelsea*, *Newsday*, *Southern Quarterly*, *Salmagundi*, *The Bloomsbury Review*, *Library Journal*, *Twentieth Century Literature*, *Studies in Short Fiction*, *Medical Humanities Review*, *Journal of Medical Humanities*, *The Arden*, *MD*, *Year One*, *Paragraph*, *Antipodes*, *Southwest American Literature*, the *Four-Way Reader # 1*, the *Cormac McCarthy Journal*, and *New York Stories*.

Josyph directed the award-winning documentary *Liberty Street: Alive at Ground Zero*, and he co-directed *Acting McCarthy: The Making of Billy Bob Thornton's* All the Pretty Horses. His work as a painter has made him a *New Yorker* Talk of the Town and a Fellow of the Pollock-Krasner Foundation; his art has been used for the Portuguese edition of *Suttree*, for John Sepich's *Notes on* Blood Meridian, and for posters of the Cormac McCarthy Society; and his exhibition *Cormac McCarthy's House* has shown at the Centennial Museum in El Paso, Texas; the CAPITAL Centre in Coventry, England; and the Kulturens Hus in Luleå, Sweden. For twelve years Josyph was Artistic Director of Victory Rep in New York, where he acted, directed, and wrote fifty plays; and for seven years he was artist-in-residence at the Smithtown Township Arts Council on Long Island. He has been a speaker in the Program for Humanities in Medicine at Yale University; for the Department of American Studies at the University of Miami; for the New York Council for the Humanities; and as a keynote for the Cormac McCarthy Society.